Housing Options and Services for Older Adults

Ann E. Gillespie
and
Katrinka Smith Sloan

Choices and Challenges: An Older Adult Reference Series
Elizabeth Vierck, Series Editor

ABC-CLIO

Santa Barbara, California
Oxford, England

Library of Congress Cataloging-in-Publication Data
Gillespie, Ann E., 1958–
    Housing options and services for older adults / Ann E. Gillespie
and Katrinka Smith Sloan.
        p.   cm. — (Choices and challenges)
    Includes bibliographical references.
    1. Aged—Services for—United States. 2. Aged—Housing—United
States. I. Sloan, Katrinka Smith, 1955–   . II. Title.
III. Series.
    HV1461.G54   1990   363.5'946'0973—dc20   89-48191

ISBN 0-87436-144-3 (alk. paper)

97 96 95 94 93 92 91 90   10 9 8 7 6 5 4 3 2 1

ABC-CLIO, Inc.
130 Cremona Drive, P.O. Box 1911
Santa Barbara, California 93116-1911

Clio Press Ltd.
55 St. Thomas' Street
Oxford, OX1 1JG, England

This book is Smyth-sewn and printed on acid-free paper ∞.
Manufactured in the United States of America

Housing Options
and Services
for Older Adults

This material purchased with a
PRIME TIME HEALTH INFORMATION GRANT
administered by the
INDIANA STATE LIBRARY
and sponsored by the
LIBRARY SERVICES AND CONSTRUCTION ACT

Choices and Challenges:
An Older Adult Reference Series
Elizabeth Vierck, Series Editor

Housing Options and Services for Older Adults, Ann E. Gillespie and Katrinka Smith Sloan

Mental Health Problems and Older Adults, Gregory A. Hinrichsen

Paying for Health Care after Age 65, Elizabeth Vierck

Forthcoming

Legal Issues and Older Adults, Linda Josephson Millman and Sallie Birket Chafer

Older Workers, Sara E. Rix

Travel and Older Adults, Allison St. Claire

Volunteerism and Older Adults, Mary K. Kouri

To
Eliza and Robert Smith
and
in memory of
Joan and John Gillespie

Contents

PART TWO   **Resources**

Preface

Our society is aging. The population age 65 and over is growing at a faster rate than the rest of the population. In 1900, there were almost 4 million older persons, and, by the year 2000, there will be about 34.9 million older persons. All segments of our society are affected by this change in demographics, but in particular it has spurred the development of an array of service and shelter options to meet the needs and desires of older adults. The development of these and other options should be encouraged to help us meet the dramatic growth in America's older population. Housing older people must mean more than just satisfying a simple need for shelter. As a nation, we need to look at better ways to provide supportive environments where social, physical, and emotional needs are met without jeopardizing one's independence.

As people age, they are likely to face a number of changes in their lives. Physical changes, such as chronic illness or vision or hearing impairments, are not uncommon. Lifestyle changes such as retirement, freeing up more time for oneself and family, occur at some point in one's later years, and personal changes, such as children leaving home or loss of a spouse, are common occurrences. They need not be debilitating, if it is acknowledged that there are ways to cope with or compensate for these changes.

The availability of affordable, appropriate housing continues to be a major concern for many older people. Frequently, traditional forms of housing will not, in and of themselves, meet the needs of older persons. They may lack services, accessibility, affordability, or companionship, depending on an individual's needs and preferences. In response, an assortment of community-based services and housing options has emerged. These options and services are designed to meet various needs, including nutrition, health care, housekeeping, personal security, financial security, shelter, and companionship. They acknowledge the heterogeneity of the older population, in that they provide services to persons in their homes or their communities or in residences to which they may move. But, of greater significance, they acknowledge that, for the older population, housing and services are inextricably linked. To enable older persons to maximize their independence, particularly in their later years, services must be available to them.

Housing Options and Services for Older Adults presents this range of housing and service options. It addresses a number of alternatives that can be of direct benefit to an older person who either wishes to remain in his or her home, or who chooses to move to another type of housing. It has been written as a guide for older people, their families, and their advisors to assist them in choosing options and services that suit their needs and resources.

The book is divided into two parts. Part One covers types of housing or service options, with information organized for ready access. For each option, key data are given, followed by information that answers the following questions: What is it? When is it appropriate? How does one find it? and How much does it cost? The section on that option concludes with a list of things to remember and a consumer checklist, which will help guide the reader through the process of selecting a given service or living arrangement.

The first three chapters present a host of services for persons who wish to remain in their own homes and consider the circumstances in which these may be appropriate. Chapter 1 focuses on home health care and community services. Chapter 2 looks at home repair and maintenance programs, as well as possibilities for adapting the home of a person who has become frail or disabled. Chapter 3 presents finance-related alternatives—reducing regular expenses such as utility bills or converting equity in a home into a cash resource—and includes a state-by-state chart of available programs.

Chapter 4, Options for Relocating, presents a range of possibilities for persons wishing to change homes, ranging from those offering minimal supportive services but perhaps a secure environment to those offering both security and long-term care.

Part Two includes resource listings for assistance or further information. Organizations, associations, and government agencies concerned with housing options for older adults are listed and described in Chapter 5. Chapter 6, Reference Materials, is an annotated bibliography of printed resources, grouped by the topics considered in the first four chapters. Chapter 7 presents annotated listings of audiovisual materials and computer-based information sources.

Terms one is likely to encounter are defined in the Glossary, and the Index provides additional access to both the discussions in Part One and the resources in Part Two.

It is the authors' hope that this reference book will help those researching housing options and services for older people to find alternatives that will enrich lives.

Acknowledgments

The authors wish to express their appreciation for the time and efforts of Dottie Ruppert and Rick Sloan, whose patience and understanding helped to produce this book. We are also grateful to Elizabeth Vierck, Lee Norrgard, Susan Weiss, Evelyn Fieman Munley, Mary Reilly, Robin Talbert, Suzanne Rathburn, and Elaine Ostroff for their technical input.

Our thanks, as well, to our families and friends, whose encouragement made our task a little easier.

How To Use This Book

Each book in the Choices and Challenges series provides a convenient, easy-access reference tool on a specific topic of interest to older adults and those involved with them, including caregivers, spouses, adult children, and gerontology professionals. The books are designed for ease of use, with a generous typeface, ample use of headings and subheadings, and a detailed index.

Each book consists of two parts, which may be used together or independently:

A narrative section providing an informative and comprehensive overview of the topic, written for a lay audience. The narrative can be read straight through or consulted on an as-needed basis by using the headings and subheadings and/or the index.

An annotated resource section that includes a directory of relevant organizations; recommended books, pamphlets, and articles; and software and videos. Where appropriate, the resource section may include additional information relevant to the topic. This section can be used in conjunction with or separately from the narrative to locate sources of additional information, assistance, or support.

A glossary defines important terms and concepts, and the index provides additional access to the material. For easy reference, entries in the resource section are indexed by both topic and title or name.

Housing Options
and Services
for Older Adults

Introduction

The rate of growth in the number of people age 65 or over in the United States has been dramatic. According to the Census Bureau, the number of Americans in this age group will increase from 25.7 million in 1980, to 34.9 million in 2000, to 65.6 million in the year 2030. Not only are more people getting older but they are also living longer. Life spans have been extended as a result of medical advances and life style changes. Older people can no longer be lumped together into one homogeneous group. According to one survey, only 12.6 percent of the 65–74 age group required assistance with daily activities. Such help was needed by 25 percent of those between the ages of 75 and 83 and by nearly 46 percent of those 84 or over.[1] Although age is not always an indicator of functional ability, it does provide a benchmark for looking at potential service needs. The old are getting older and staying healthier longer. These data about the *way* people are growing older has a significant impact on the kinds of shelter and services that should be developed now and in the future.

Today, shelter and services for older people can be thought of as a continuum of housing, programs, and services. These range from programs geared toward enhancing one's ability to live independently (retirement communities, home equity conversion, home repair and maintenance programs, property tax relief) to semi-independent arrangements (adult day care, congregate housing, assisted living facilities, home health care, home adaptations) to more comprehensive approaches for dependent older persons (continuing care retirement communities and nursing facilities). Some of these options require public sector involvement; others rely solely on the efforts of volunteers. Some have eligibility requirements; others do not. Costs vary dramatically.

3

The variety of shelter and service options available are numerous, as they should be. One type of housing option cannot serve and satisfy all kinds of needs. Living arrangements for some need only enhance one's independence, while for others it may provide supportive services that allow an individual to better manage the daily activities of life. A relatively small but growing segment requires a more protected environment in which health care and personal needs can be met as required.

Where do older people live? As with the population in general, nearly half of all Americans 65 or older live in California, New York, Florida, Illinois, Ohio, Michigan, Pennsylvania, and Texas.[2] However, states with the highest concentration are in the Midwest, where older people have stayed after younger people have left. More older people live in suburbs than major cities.[3]

Although there are many older people in sunbelt states like Florida, Arizona, and California, there has been a trend toward countermigration in recent years from the sunbelt states back to states of origin. In general, assumptions about migration are misleading. Less than one in ten of all retired persons moves more than 200 miles from the area where she or he lived prior to retirement.

For those older persons who do relocate, there are arrangements ranging from condominiums to continuing care retirement communities that may offer a variety of shelter and services to suit different needs. Books such as *Sunbelt Retirement* and *Retirement Places Rated* (see Chapter 6, Reference Materials) rank and discuss hundreds of favorite retirement areas nationwide. These guides look at everything from climate to taxes and caution readers considering a move to take their time making a decision, make several visits, compare costs, and seek the help of a trusted advisor.

The predominant housing choice among older persons is remaining in their own homes for as long as they live. A survey conducted by the American Association of Retired Persons in 1989 revealed that 84 percent of respondents age 55 or over said what they'd really like to do is stay in their own homes and never move. Home, whether it be a single-family residence, an apartment, or a duplex, represents far more than a roof and four walls. It represents stability, security, and independence and it connects people with friends, family, and neighbors. It is familiar and comfortable.

As many people age, however, their homes may be incongruent with their needs. They may be less able to negotiate steps or keep up with yard work or may simply feel more vulnerable in their residences. This does not happen overnight, nor do these changes happen to all persons as they age. But such changes can be addressed through a myriad of community-based programs and services discussed in this book.

Although the housing and services continuum does exist, it is not an uninterrupted, ordered sequence. What exists today is more like a broken radio that only picks up certain stations. A person who wants to enter a nursing facility can "tune-in" to comprehensive care yet still face inconsistencies in terms of quality, size, and sponsorship. The older person who wants to remain at home, yet needs services, may, in some communities, only get static or a sampling of the music they wish to hear. The challenge for older people and their families is becoming familiar with what *is* available in the community and planning, as best as possible, for future needs.

Notes

1. *Aging in America: Trends and Projections,* 1985–1986 ed. U.S. Senate Special Committee on Aging. Pg. 15.

2. Ibid.

3. Ibid.

PART ONE

Housing and Service Options

Chapter 1

Home Health Care and Community Services

Many older persons can maximize their independence in their homes by taking advantage of services that may be available in their communities. These services can range from health-related services, such as home health care, to security-related services, such as personal emergency response systems. Often, an individual's needs are very specific and can be readily addressed by tapping a community service. In other situations, needs are broader, and it is necessary to utilize a variety of services, which, together, make it possible to continue to live independently.

This chapter addresses formal services, such as home health care, meal programs, and adult day care, as well as more informal services, like telephone reassurance and friendly visiting. The formality of a service is a function of how and by whom it is delivered. Home health care is delivered by licensed or certified personnel under a formal plan of care. Telephone reassurance, on the other hand, is usually done by volunteers on a mutually acceptable basis. More often than not, these services are provided, not by an agency, but by family members. For those older persons who received help in 1984, about 80 percent came from family members.

Nonetheless, agencies and organizations do exist that can supplement or substitute for the services provided by family members. Availability of these services is likely to vary from community to community. Although the presence of services is generally increasing, some services are subject to cutbacks as a result of reductions from funding sources. Programs also vary in terms of their eligibility requirements. These issues should be explored well in advance of the need for a service, if at all possible.

Most of the services described have been around for some time. In particular, homemaker services and home health care may have strong roots in your community. Others, such as care management and adult day care have evolved more recently. The amount of time a service has been present in a community does not correlate directly with quality of care, but it may be an indicator of how easy or hard it will be to locate the service. Each section includes suggestions for locating the service in the community.

Community services make an important contribution to enhancing people's ability to live as independently as possible. Their importance should not be underestimated. They offer a number of possibilities for helping older persons and family members.

Home Health Care

Home health care is a relatively new term for a time-worn method of caring for those who are frail or sick. It simply refers to the provision of health care services in one's home rather than in an institutional setting. Home health care of today, however, includes skilled nursing care, acute care, and care that requires technologically advanced equipment and procedures.

Key Data

- For the disabled older population living in the community, relatives represent 84 percent of caregivers for males and provide 89 percent of days of care. For older disabled females, relatives represent 79 percent of caregivers and provide 84 percent of days of care.

- More than four out of five persons 65 or over have at least one chronic condition, and multiple conditions are commonplace among older persons.

- The leading chronic conditions for the elderly in 1987 were arthritis, hypertensive disease, heart disease, and hearing impairments.

- Approximately 1.1 million disabled older people receive formal home health care and 600,000 of them pay for some part of their care. They spend an average of $164 a month out of pocket.

- In 1987, Medicare beneficiaries received 35 million home health visits with an average of 1,068 visits per 1,000 enrollees.

What is home health care?

Home health care is diagnosis, treatment, rehabilitation, monitoring, and/or supportive care provided in one's home. It is growing in availability and capability and becoming a highly competitive business. Its growth has been fueled by the aging of the population, shorter hospital stays, and an increasing preference for home care over nursing facilities and hospitals. Current estimates place total spending for home health care in 1985 at $9 billion. At the same time, it is not highly regulated in many states.

What kinds of services are available?

Most home health care agencies or organizations provide a range of services from skilled nursing care to therapy to nutrition services.

Skilled nursing refers to services provided by a skilled nursing professional. Included are changing dressings, administering drugs, and monitoring for changes in a patient's condition.

Personal care is assistance with the activities of daily living. These activities are bathing, grooming, dressing, getting into and out of bed, and preparing and eating meals.

Therapy in various forms may be provided by home health care agencies. Included might be physical therapy, occupational therapy, speech therapy, and respiratory therapy.

Nutrition services including meal preparation and serving are often included among the services of a home health care agency.

Medical equipment and supplies such as hospital beds, wheelchairs, walkers, and oxygen equipment are provided or can be made available.

Diagnostic aids and high-technology treatments may be available. This is a relatively new level of home health care and is changing all the time. Included are electrocardiogram (EKG) equipment, portable x-ray units, and intravenous therapy.

When is home health care appropriate?

Home health care may be appropriate when one is discharged from a hospital or nursing facility and not fully recovered from the illness that required that high level of care. Or it may be appropriate in the case of a chronic condition that requires frequent or ongoing monitoring, such as a heart condition or kidney disease. For persons who are terminally ill, home health care may be an alternative to nursing facility care. Persons who need care because of either emotional or physical problems that would otherwise require them to leave home may be able to remain in their homes with the assistance of home health care services. Because the kinds and levels of care that are provided by a home health agency are diverse, the situations in which home health care may be appropriate are varied. Of course, home health care may not be the best or only solution for every situation.

How does one find home health care?

Who provides these services?

Most home health care is provided by family and friends. This requires a high level of commitment and time and can be very stressful for those in the caregiving role. Increasingly, there is a preponderance of public, private, for-profit, and nonprofit agencies that provide home health care services for a fee. The organization purported to be the original home health care agency is known today as the Visiting Nurses Association. It was created in the 1800s in several East Coast cities. In the early 1900s, welfare agencies provided home health care for children whose mothers were sick. Gradually, but hastened by the availability of reimbursement, home health care has moved toward serving primarily the elderly. Now, more than 11,000 agencies provide home health care services. Of these, about 500 are independently run Visiting Nurse Associations.

Other organizations that provide home health care are community service organizations, agencies based in hospitals or nursing facilities, commercial firms including small private agencies and large national chains, Veterans Administration (VA) hospitals, city or county health departments, hospice organizations, and homemaker/home health aide services. About 2,000 of the nation's hospitals also offer home health care services. Among this wide range of possible providers, for-profit agencies are the fastest growing segment today.

Often, friends and colleagues of consumers can provide recommendations of agencies. Home health agencies will vary greatly in the quality of services provided and in the fees charged; it is always useful to have a recommendation from someone with direct experience with the agency.

Persistence pays off. Resources vary greatly from community to community. If the search for home health care services follows a hospital stay and assistance is needed in achieving full recovery or rehabilitation, the medical social worker or discharge planner at the hospital can help. Because of the limitations on the days for which a hospital can receive reimbursement following any particular illness, hospitals have a particular interest in discharging patients expeditiously. They have staff to help patients determine a post-hospital method of receiving care, which very often involves home health care. However, one may need to request assistance from the hospital discharge planning staff, which should be done early enough to avoid a crisis the day of discharge. These staff are likely to be familiar with home health care providers in the community.

If the need for home health care is not hospital related, the local library may be able to provide a list of appropriate agencies or organizations. Another resource is the telephone book. Often, it has a "Guide to Human Services," listing agencies according to the problems or issues they handle. The county office on aging will be listed with government agencies in the yellow pages, under "Aging," "Senior Citizens," "Elder" or "Elderly." An additional resource is the National HomeCaring Council, a national nonprofit organization that operates as a division of the Foundation for Hospice and Home Care (see Chapter 5). The council accredits homemaker/home health aide services and operates a toll-free number to answer consumer inquiries.

If the illness or disability is the result of a disease, consumers may contact the appropriate voluntary agency, including the American Cancer Society, the Arthritis Foundation, the National Parkinson Foundation, the National Kidney Foundation, or the American Diabetes Association. Local chapters may have a list of local agencies or organizations familiar with providing care for a patient's particular needs.

How To Select an Agency

Before selecting an agency, a consumer should determine, with the assistance of a physician or caregiver, what is needed. Not all agencies provide all of the services listed above. (Some agencies may be willing to secure needed services that they don't provide, but not all will do so.)

It is also important to discern what kind of agency one is considering. Is it a home health care agency or is it a nurses' registry or employment agency for health care professionals? This may make a difference in the comprehensiveness of the services provided.

Structure and Staffing

Related to this, consumers should learn how agencies are set up and what they do. Generally, agencies employ registered nurses, licensed practical nurses, nurses' aides, nutritionists, social workers, and therapists. Some also employ homemakers, companions, and live-in personnel. In most cases, the nurse works under the supervision of a physician, who is in charge of the team. However, there is a growing trend to permit nurses to diagnose and treat illnesses and prescribe medications without a physician's supervision.

There are various types of licensed nursing personnel. Registered nurses (RNs) complete between two and four years of education and training before being permitted to take a state's licensing examination. A registered nurse is required to perform patient assessment, establish a plan of care, and carry out skilled nursing functions. A licensed practical nurse (LPN) attends a one-year program, must pass a state examination to be licensed, and then must work under the direct supervision of an RN. An LPN can carry out skilled nursing procedures established by a registered nurse. A nurse practitioner is first licensed as an RN and then completes additional advanced coursework in order to become a nurse practitioner. Some nurse practitioners seek certification, which requires successful completion of a nationally administered examination. (At this time, certification is voluntary.) Nurse practitioners are highly trained. Some work independently, while others work as part of the team with a group of physicians.

Home health aides, or nurses' aids, are the most widely used home care providers. They are trained by voluntary and proprietary agencies and generally have up to 60 hours of classroom work and supervised practice. They provide personal care and help with grooming, mobility, eating, shopping, and cooking. In home heath care situations it is often the home health aide who has day-to-day contact with the care recipient and plays a critical role in implementing the care plan developed by the professional staff of the agency.

Social workers often serve as intake coordinators, responding to inquiries from potential patients or their families over the phone. In addition to a screening function, they are sensitive to the total needs of the client. These go well beyond the medical needs with which health professionals are primarily concerned. The social worker can determine needs, identify support systems, and arrange for their use.

When asking questions of a potential agency, a consumer should find out not only how the agency carries out its care arrangements, but also how the agency itself is structured. What is its source of funds? Can it provide professional references? Does it operate under the auspices of a larger entity, such as a local government, a hospital, or a health care corporation?

Licensure and Certification

Other questions are: Is the agency accredited? Is it Medicare/Medicaid certified? Is it bonded and licensed?

Licensure refers to a system operative in about two dozen states in which the state provides a standard occupational license for some home care agencies. A license is generally issued by the state's health department if the agency has met the established requirements for supervision of its employees. In states that have specific licensure requirements, the strength of those requirements varies.

Effective January 1, 1990, home health aides, homemakers, and personal care attendants in Medicare/Medicaid certified agencies must show they are both trained and competent to provide such services. They must have completed or be enrolled in a training program that meets minimum standards. Home health agencies will have to provide regular review and inservice education to assure competence.

Certification is an authorization to receive payment for Medicare home health care services. In some states, certification applies to receipt of Medicaid (or, in California, MediCal) payments as well. To be certified, agencies must meet minimal federal and state standards for patient care and financial management. Specific standards and their enforcement vary by state.

A bonded agency simply means that the agency has paid a preset fee to obtain a bond, which protects the agency against financial claims involving its employees. A security check of bonded employees is rare; therefore, a bond has little practical value to the consumer. If, for example, a bonded employee steals from a client, the client can collect his or her losses only if the employee is actually convicted of theft or if the client sues in court and wins. Bonding does not indicate good services and, in fact, few agencies bond their employees.

Accreditation is a voluntary process established by an independent standard-setting body. It indicates that the agency has met certain standards of conduct and training. Generally, the standards are tougher than those required for licensure. But, it is important to remember that the process is voluntary, unlike licensure, which is mandatory. Accreditation generally means that management, operations, planning, and delivery of services have been evaluated and that the quality of services is continually checked. The national organizations that accredit aspects of home care are:

Joint Commission on the Accreditation of Healthcare Organizations. When hospitals apply to the commission for accreditation, the commission reviews any hospital-operated services including home health care services.

Foundation for Hospice and Home Care. The foundation, through its National HomeCaring Council division, accredits programs that provide homemaker/home health aide services. Its review process pays close attention to screening, training, and supervision of aides.

National League for Nursing. Jointly with the American Public Health Association, the league accredits community nursing services such as Visiting Nurse Associations and home health agencies.

Development of Care Plans

Other questions a consumer should pursue with an agency relate to the development of a care plan. A care plan is a detailed description of the services the client will receive, the treatment goals, and the equipment and supplies that will be necessary. Prior to developing a care plan, the agency must conduct a thorough assessment of the individual's situation, which includes an examination of the current care being received, the home environment, the client's mental and physical state, and the client's family/friend support system, as well as the client's financial status. If the client is under a physician's supervision the care plan should be approved by the doctor. Consumers should find out who conducts the assessment and develops the care plan, how thorough the assessment is, and whether he or she will receive a copy of the written care plan. The consumer should also ask how often the care plan is reviewed and revised.

Because the person developing the care plan is often not the person who will implement it, the consumer should find out how the delivery of care will be supervised and by whom. Does the supervisor visit frequently to make sure everything is as it should be? The agency should be asked about staff turnover. In particular, do they anticipate personnel changes and can they accommodate special personnel requests? The rapport with and trust in the staff assigned to a client is critical to his or her recovery or rehabilitation progress.

How much do home health care services cost?

Home health agencies charge for services on either a visit basis or an hourly basis. A visit is a session or treatment. Home health care services generally cost less than the same services provided in a hospital or nursing facility because the consumer only pays for what he or she receives. In institutions, the consumer pays for 24-hour care; home health care is generally for shorter periods.

Fees vary dramatically from agency to agency and can also vary regionally across the country. They also tend to change frequently over time. Generally, the more highly skilled the service that is needed, the higher the fees. Sometimes, agencies will offer services on a sliding fee scale, according to one's ability to pay. One should inquire about this possibility when asking questions about an agency's payment arrangements.

Some agencies may charge for a minimum number of hours, rather than for the services required. Others often charge a higher rate for evenings, weekends, and holidays or may charge for assessment and supervision in addition to direct service. The policy on charging for medical equipment and for transportation and meals of agency employees should also be checked.

Usually, the agency bills insurance companies directly on a regular basis for services rendered. The agency is then responsible for paying personnel and covering the insurance and social security costs of employees. It is important to realize at the outset that not every service provided by a home health care agency is reimbursable and that not every insurance carrier covers home health care. This is an area of tremendous confusion and it is wise for consumers to explore at the outset what is covered and what is not.

Medicare

Medicare is a federal health insurance program for persons age 65 or over who are eligible for Social Security or Railroad Retirement benefits. Individuals under age 65 who are eligible for Social Security disability benefits or who have kidney disease that requires dialysis are also eligible for Medicare. Under Part A of Medicare, which is the Hospital Insurance, some home health services are covered as long as those services and supplies are provided by Medicare-approved agencies or personnel. About 6,000 home health agencies are certified by Medicare. In 1987, Medicare paid $1.7 billion for home health care services.

Services covered under Medicare include:

Part-time skilled nursing care

Physical therapy

Speech therapy

If any of the above services are required and are regularly reviewed by a physician, Medicare will also cover:

Part-time or intermittent services of a home health aide

Medical social services

Medical supplies and equipment provided by an agency

Occupational therapy

Part-time care refers to less than 24 hours a day. Intermittent care is no more than six days per week. Beneficiaries who need care for up to six days per week are entitled to coverage without any time limitations for as long as needed.

A beneficiary must be enrolled in Medicare Part A, confined to home, and under the care of a physician who certifies the need for care. There must be a need for intermittent skilled nursing care, physical therapy, or speech therapy. The intermittent requirement applies only to skilled services. Once a beneficiary meets these requirements, he or she may receive skilled services as well as home health aide services, medical social services, and occupational therapy. The nonskilled services may be received any number of days a week, subject to a 28-hour per week limitation. There are no out-of-pocket costs to the beneficiary.

Under Part B, Medicare helps pay for doctors' services and outpatient hospital, therapy, and mental health services. All services covered must be delivered by Medicare-approved personnel or agencies. This includes therapists, home health aides, chiropractors, ambulances, etc. In order to be approved, a facility must meet all licensing requirements of state or local health authorities. Services covered include:

Diagnostic tests and procedures

Services of doctor's nurses

Drugs and biologicals that cannot be self-administered

Medical supplies and equipment

Physical and speech therapy

Home health aide services specified by a doctor as necessary

Transfusion of blood and blood components furnished on an outpatient basis

Almost as important as what is covered is what is not covered. Medicare does not cover personal care, nor does it cover prescription drugs or home health care if there is no need for skilled nursing care or if the patient is not homebound.

Under Medicare Part B, payment for covered services or supplies is made on the basis of an established reasonable charge for that service. Actual charges are often higher than Medicare allows as reasonable, and consumers may have to pay the full amount of charges in excess of Medicare's reasonable standard. A doctor who accepts assignment is willing to accept Medicare's reasonable charges as full payment for services rendered.

Medicare coverage is subject to change by the U.S. Congress.

To find out about Medicare coverage, one should contact the local Social Security office.

Medicaid

Medicaid is a government health insurance program for the aged, blind, and disabled poor. Applicants must be residents of the United States and meet income and resource eligibility requirements. Generally, the eligibility standards for an individual applicant in 1989 are no more than $368 to $497 a month in countable income, depending on the state, and $2,000 in assets, excluding the home. However, 14 states use eligibility standards that are more restrictive than these.

Medicaid is administered by the individual states. Some states have established their own eligibility requirements and schedules of assistance. In 1987, 3,260,328 persons age 65 or over received $16.1 billion in Medicaid vendor payments.

Federal law requires states to cover medically related home health care services requiring part-time skilled nursing, a home health aide, or medical supplies and equipment. Specifically, coverage is provided to individuals who are entitled to skilled nursing facility care. Home health services under Medicaid also include one optional service (physical therapy, occupational therapy, speech pathology, drugs, and personal care). These services generally must be medically related and prescribed by a physician. Some states require participants to pay a small fee for services.

To find out about Medicaid eligibility, one should contact the local Social Security or Public Assistance office.

Private Health Insurance

The language on most health insurance policies is unclear as to its coverage of home health care services. Qualifications and restrictions may be hard to discern. Often, coverage under private health insurance plans depends on whether the care has been ordered by a physician and whether it includes specific tasks that must be performed by various health professionals. In some cases, an insurance company will cover up to a certain number of days per year, but only if the home health agency has a specific agreement with the insurance company and the patient has been hospitalized for a specific number of days prior to the home health care visits.

Consumers should carefully research what is and is not covered. And, because coverage is often specified in terms of "visits," a thorough record of the visits of health care professionals should be kept.

Health Maintenance Organizations (HMOs)

HMOs provide prepaid health and medical services from physicians and suppliers affiliated with the HMO. Some HMOs may include home health care in their coverage.

Veterans Administration (VA) Benefits

The VA provides home health care benefits for military service-related illness or injury. Contact the Veterans Administration for more information about coverage and eligibility requirements.

Tax Deductions

If home health care expenses qualify as a medical expense and medical expenses exceed 7.5 percent of a consumer's adjusted gross income, they may be deducted from taxable income. If an individual pays for home health care for a disabled spouse so he or she can work or look for work, the couple may be eligible for a dependent care tax credit. For specific information on these tax provisions, contact the Internal Revenue Service (IRS). Information on deductions can be found in IRS Publication 502, *Medical and Dental Expenses.*

THINGS TO REMEMBER

Home health care services can be arranged through a number of sources, including private agencies, hospitals, and public health departments.

Not all agencies offer the same services.

Fees and accepted sources of payment vary from agency to agency.

Request a written care plan and check regularly to be sure that the care received is what is prescribed by the physician.

To initiate home care, a recipient must sign a consent agreement, release of medical information, a service contract, a form outlining cost and payment obligations, and financial or insurance disclosure authorizations.

Keep records of all care provided and check bills carefully.

CONSUMER CHECKLIST

About an Agency

____ Is it currently accredited, certified, and/or licensed for home care? For what services? By what organization?

____ Does it have written statements outlining its services, eligibility, cost and payment procedures, employee job descriptions, and malpractice or liability insurance?

____ If only limited services are available, what assistance can be provided to obtain other home care services as needed, such as home-delivered meals?

____ Can it provide you with references from professionals, such as hospital or community agency social workers, who have used this agency?

About an Agency's Plan of Care (Treatment or Services)

____ Is the plan carefully and professionally developed with you and your family? Or is it based solely on your own view of the home situation and request for services?

____ Once developed, is the plan written out? Are copies given to the workers in the home?

About the Personnel

____ If you are dealing with an agency, are references required by the agency and on file?

____ Are homemaker/home health aides who are not required to be licensed or certified adequately trained?

____ Are homemaker/home health aides who are not required to be licensed or certified adequately supervised? Is supervision provided in the home? How often? How soon?

____ How available is the supervisor? What arrangements are made for emergency situations?

About Costs

____ What are the hourly fees? Are there minimum hours or days per week required?

____ Who pays for the employee's social security or other insurance? Are there any additional costs, such as for travel, supervision, or home evaluation? (Most quality agencies include supervision and evaluation in their fees.)

____ How does the agency handle payment and billing?

SOURCE: *All about Home Care: A Consumer's Guide.* Reprinted with the permission of the National HomeCaring Council, a division of the Foundation for Hospice and Homecare.

Homemaker Services

Homemaker services assist with day-to-day household chores, differing from home health care in that the services are not health-related. They perform a critical function for persons who need a modest amount of assistance to continue to live independently.

Key Data

- 23 percent of the population 65 or over living in the community have difficulty with one or more of the seven personal care activities (see the glossary under "activities of daily living"). Only 10 percent reported receiving help with one or more such activities.

- 27 percent of the population 65 or over living in the community have difficulty with at least one home management activity (see the glossary under "instrumental activities of daily living"). Only 22 percent reported receiving help with these activities.

- The proportion of people reporting difficulty with one or more personal care activities rose from 15 percent for people 65–69 years of age to 49 percent for people 85 years or older.

What are homemaker services?

Homemaker services involve:

Light housekeeping

Laundry

Food shopping

Planning and preparing meals, including special diets

Paying bills

Care of clothing

Planning expenditures

Rearranging work areas

Certain personal care

The first homemaker service was established in Philadelphia in 1923 by a Jewish social service organization. During the 1930s the Works Progress Administration established a housekeeper project, which gave homemaking services a temporary boost. Poor, unemployed women were hired to conduct these services. After the depression, homemaking services went back to the domain of the private sector. Since that time, they have grown in scope and availability. Still, however, homemaker services are not available in all communities.

When are homemaker services appropriate?

Homemaker services are designed for individuals or couples who, because of a frailty or incapacity, are unable to manage day-to-day household chores. They may be appropriate for persons who cannot, because of crippling arthritis, prepare their own meals. They may be suitable for an individual whose vision is impaired and, therefore, cannot write checks or manage household expenses. Or, they may be appropriate for a person who must rely on a walker and cannot negotiate light housekeeping chores.

Prior to contracting for homemaker services, it is important to do a needs assessment to determine what kinds of homemaking assistance are needed. For example, is help needed with laundry, housecleaning, meal preparation, or grocery shopping?

Are there other needs that might be met with assistance from a homemaker? Is personal care, such as bathing, dressing, grooming, eating, or toileting, needed? Not all homemaker services provide personal care services. If personal care is also a need, it is important to determine whether this service is available. Social, financial, and transportation needs should also be considered.

How does one find a homemaker service?

There are several good ways to locate homemaker services. The local office on aging (county or city) has information and referral experts who may be able to refer consumers to one or several agencies. Check the yellow pages, under "Homemaker," "Home Health Services," or "Aging." Often, homemaker services are a component of the services offered by a home health care agency.

Another good source may be the local library. Reference librarians often have a lot of good information on local services at their finger tips, or at least can point consumers in the right direction.

Finally, friends and neighbors can provide valuable references. It is always reassuring to contract with an agency that has been used and deemed reputable by someone else.

Selecting a Homemaker Service

As with most services, there is great variation in the quality of care one will receive from homemaker services; it is important to shop around. It is also important to know who may be providing these services. The agencies offering homemaking services are a variety of public, private, for-profit, nonprofit, religiously affiliated, and corporate entities. The services themselves are performed by homemaker aides, often called housekeepers or home managers. This is unlike home health care, in which services are performed by nursing assistants or home health aides under the supervision of licensed personnel.

Homemakers are generally trained by their agencies or other voluntary or private organizations. It is important when selecting an agency to find out what kind of experience or training it requires of its aides. One should check the references, which agencies should readily provide. One of the key questions to ask when considering homemaker services relates to supervision: Does the agency directly supervise the aides it employs or does it operate more like an employment agency? How does the supervision take place? Is it through regular, unscheduled visits to the workplace or is it more indirect or informal? Who is the supervisor and what is his or her training? Is he or she a caseworker, a home economist, or a nutritionist?

It is important to realize that homemakers are not extensively trained. Yet, because of their jobs, they are often called upon to react quickly or make judgment calls. An aide must be able to make quick decisions, if necessary, and must be trained that this is part of his or her responsibility. One should inquire whether the agency under consideration is licensed, bonded, or accredited.

Homemaker services that are affiliated with home health care services may be accredited by a voluntary national nonprofit organization, the National HomeCaring Council (see Chapter 5, under the Foundation for Hospice and Home Care). One can contact the council to find out if an agency under consideration has been accredited or to receive a directory of accredited agencies. The council emphasizes staff training, screening, and supervision in its standards of accreditation.

Licensure refers to a system operative in a number of states in which the state provides a standard occupational license for homemaker services. Other states have criteria by which they specifically license homemaker services. However, in those that do have specific licensure requirements, the strength of those requirements varies.

A bonded agency simply means that the agency has paid a preset fee to obtain a bond, which protects the agency against financial claims involving its employees. A security check of bonded employees is rare; therefore, a bond has little practical value to the consumer. If, for example, a bonded employee steals from a client, the client can collect his or her losses only if the employee is actually convicted of theft or if the client sues in court and wins. Bonding does not indicate good services and, in fact, few agencies bond their employees.

Contracting with an Agency

When hiring or contracting with a homemaker agency, the needs for service will be a primary consideration. Generally, the intake worker, often a caseworker, interviews all potential clients to be sure that homemaker services are appropriate. A potential client must define and describe the duties and tasks to be performed. The caseworker then sets up a plan, identifying the responsibilities and the hours of the homemaker. If services are required that are not provided by the homemaker service, the plan should include other agencies to be called upon.

Some homemaker services employ case managers in addition to caseworkers. Case managers help individuals negotiate the array of available services and pull together a comprehensive, personalized plan to meet an individual's needs (see the section titled "Care Management"). The plan developed by the caseworker may not be as comprehensive as that of a case manager. But, if there are any services not provided that would be beneficial, such as modifications to make a home more suitable for a disability, a caseworker could help locate other service providers.

Most homemaker services do not provide chore services, which go beyond homemaking. Chore services refer to help with heavy housekeeping, floor and window washing, yard work, and minor home maintenance and repair. Homemaker services may, however, make referrals to agencies or organizations that do provide chore services.

The homemaker agency is likely to set up, in addition to the plan for care or service, a referral procedure. Because of the close and regular contact with a client, homemakers are often the first to recognize a change in condition or the need for additional services. They generally have a mechanism for reporting such changes.

Hiring a Homemaker on One's Own

It is not necessary to go through a homemaker/home health agency to find a homemaker. Many people undertake this search on their own. The risks may be greater, as one cannot screen as easily for third party benchmarks such as licensure or accreditation, but it is likely to be less expensive, as agency fees and overhead will not be incurred. One should keep in mind, however, that for those fees the agency maintains responsibility for all paperwork, such as record keeping and tax withholding.

In looking for a homemaker, a good first step is to ask friends or neighbors for names and check with organizations with which one has some affiliation, such as a fraternal organization, a church, or a synagogue. If these word-of-mouth vehicles are unsuccessful, placing an advertisement in the local newspaper may prove helpful.

One must screen callers well when they respond to an ad, relying heavily on instincts. It is not uncommon to receive some unacceptable responses to an ad. For those persons deemed worthy of a face-to-face interview, one should try to set up an initial interview in the applicant's home, if feasible. This is likely to provide a better feel for the applicant.

If the first interview goes well, the employer should set up a second interview in his or her home or, if it is another person for whom the homemaker services are being secured, in that person's home. This should give a good assessment of the potential homemaker's comfort level in the home and with the client.

During this interview, the expectations of all should be discussed. Specifically, the tasks to be performed, the daily routine, and the physical condition of the client must be outlined. It doesn't pay to hide information that is difficult to talk about or that it is felt the homemaker might not wish to hear. Only by being honest will one be able to assess the possible satisfaction or dissatisfaction of the potential employee.

It is important to discuss salary in this interview. But, before doing so, one should become familiar with the ongoing rates charged by public and private agencies and with the wages paid by others who may have homemakers. Also, by learning in advance the typical benefit packages—vacation and sick leave and weekend rates—a full discussion of salary and related issues can follow in the interview. Finding out what the employee requires, such as transportation or the option to bring a child with him or her during school vacations or holidays, is important. All of these issues should be put on the table at the outset. While the employer must clearly set limitations, he or she must also be sensitive to the applicant's needs. All applicants should be asked for at least two references, which should be thoroughly checked.

Once a homemaker has been hired, his or her routine and tasks should be put in writing, making sure all instructions are clear and all questions answered. This will not only establish a healthy pattern of communication at the outset, but also will avoid mistakes and misunderstandings.

As an employer, there are certain paperwork responsibilities. If the pay is over $50 a quarter, the employer is responsible for withholding Social Security from the employee's pay and for making a matching contribution. An employer can negotiate in the salary discussion whether or not to pay the employee's share.

The employer must obtain a copy of the IRS Form 942, *Employer's Quarterly Tax Return for Household Employees.* The employer does not have to withhold federal or state income taxes, but must make sure such a decision has been discussed with the employee. If taxes are not withheld, the employee must sign a statement that he or she agrees with this arrangement.

Work hours should be recorded and the employer should apply for an employer identification number. The IRS has employer identification request forms.

Filing information on Social Security is likely to trigger a response from the unemployment division of the state Department of Human Services regarding payment of a state unemployment tax. If the employee is paid $1,000 or more in a calendar year, there is a federal unemployment tax that must be paid. Form 940 will be sent to the employer as a reminder of the contribution made by the employer and the state to the federal unemployment fund.

About half the states and the District of Columbia have laws known as workman's compensation holding employers liable for domestic workers' on-the-job injuries. Generally, homeowner's insurance policies do not cover this, but some policies do, so it is wise to check. Household workers are increasingly being included under workman's compensation laws. It may be possible to attach a rider to a homeowner's insurance policy to cover this liability. More likely, however, a separate policy will be needed. In most states, it is necessary to take the initiative to add the coverage oneself.

In summary, if a homemaker is hired independently, responsibility is assumed for:

Social Security withholding and matching Social Security payments to the federal government (IRS Form 942)

Federal and state unemployment taxes (IRS Form 940, plus the state form)

Withholding federal income tax, if it is agreed to by both parties

Workman's compensation coverage, if required in the state in which the homemaker will work

How much does a homemaker service cost?

Homemaker services are generally billed on an hourly or a per visit basis. If the services provided are primarily housekeeping or homemaking, they are unlikely to be reimbursable by public or private insurance carriers; they must be paid out-of-pocket. Fees will vary greatly, both regionally and within communities. Some agencies may have sliding fee scales that vary depending on one's ability to pay.

One should keep track of the hours or visits provided by the homemaker service aide and check them carefully against each bill. Also, one should inquire about the agency's policies regarding coverage for employees' meals and transportation and fee differentials for weekends, evenings, or holidays.

Most agencies will treat their homemakers as employees and, therefore, cover the costs of Social Security and fringe benefits .

and withhold taxes. Check on this at the outset to avoid, unknowingly, being charged for a share of these costs. As a general rule of thumb, approximately half the fee charged by the agency is to cover these kinds of expenses and agency overhead; the rest goes to the homemaker.

There are very few instances of insurance for homemaker services. States have the option of choosing to cover personal care services under Medicaid, or they can get waivers from the federal government restrictions on covered Medicaid services. In a few states, homemaker services have been covered for persons who are at risk of entering an institution.

THINGS TO REMEMBER

Homemaker services are not the same as home health care services. Do not expect medical care or the services of a nurse.

Determine the extent to which the homemaker will be supervised by a trained caseworker or home economist. This may be critical in securing the quality of services expected.

Homemaker services are generally not reimbursable by public or private insurance. Fees must be paid out-of-pocket.

CONSUMER CHECKLIST

____ Is the aide carefully screened and trained by the agency?

____ Has the aide received at least 40 hours of training and does he or she receive ongoing inservice education?

____ Have the duties and any special plan of care been clearly spelled out? Has the aide received any special instructions?

____ Who assumes responsibility for the care given? Is that person available in an emergency?

____ Will a responsible person from the agency visit at regular intervals to make sure all is going as it should?

____ Is personal care being provided as part of the care plan? If so, is nursing supervision provided to the aide?

___ What are the qualifications of the professional staff at the agency? Do they have at least a bachelor's degree in social work, home economics, or a related profession, plus a year or more of related experience?

___ Is there a written statement available from the agency that tells whom the agency will serve? If an agency will not serve an individual, will they make any effort to help find an appropriate service?

___ Does the agency have legal authorization to operate? Has it been certified or licensed, if required?

___ Will the agency readily answer questions about itself, its source of funds, and cost of service? Does it issue an annual report and make it available upon request?

___ Does the agency have a board of directors?

___ Has the agency been approved or accredited by an independent, national standard-setting body?

___ Does the agency protect its workers with written personnel policies, basic benefits, and a wage scale for each position?

Meals on Wheels and Nutrition Services

For many older persons, particularly those who live alone, getting the proper nutrition is a challenge. Shopping for food may be more and more difficult and cooking may become less and less interesting. While older people need fewer calories, they do need the same amount of each essential nutrient. Proper nutrition is, therefore, important.

Key Data

- Older people need less calories but the same amount of each essential nutrient.

- 2.1 million people a year eat congregate meals at group sites.

- In FY 1987, almost 85.9 million home-delivered meals, serving 729,301 older persons, were provided to home-bound elderly as a result of federal and other funding. Over 146 million meals were served in congregate settings in the same year.

- 82 percent of home-delivered meal recipients receive a meal in their homes five times each week.

What are meal and nutrition services?

At a minimum, meal programs and nutrition services provide one nutritionally balanced meal per day to older persons either in a congregate dining setting or through the provision of home-delivered meals. Meal programs were established in the middle of this century. The first home-delivered meal program in the United States was started in Philadelphia in 1954, although the idea originated in England in 1939. Meal programs take many forms and serve a variety of needs other than simply nutrition. They now exist in many communities around the country, either as home-delivered meal programs (referred to more familiarly as meals on wheels) or as group or congregate meals at nutrition sites, for those who are more mobile. In 1982, approximately 800,000 meals were served each day by these programs combined.

Meal services and nutrition programs have been successful in improving dietary intake, particularly calcium intake. However, these programs also address a number of problems faced by many older persons, including social isolation, loneliness, and limited access to social and health services. Nutrition and meal programs have prospered because of an initial infusion of federal support and endorsement beginning in the 1960s. In the 1980s, there was a decline of federal support, but state and local governments and private agencies, organizations, and businesses have been able to sustain some of the services. In 1987, over 2.7 million elderly received meals at congregate sites.

Home-delivered meal programs deliver a hot noon-time meal and, often, an evening meal that is cold and needs only simple heating. Generally, meals are delivered five days a week, although there are programs that deliver meals on weekends and holidays as well. Menus rotate on a six-week cycle, to promote variety, and meals tend to be low in sodium and low in fat, with no concentrated sweets. Spouses may also receive meals if it is considered to be in the best interest of the housebound person.

Group meal programs also tend to serve the noon meal. Often, this is provided in an adult day care center, church, school, senior center, community center, or some other place that is accessible by older persons. There is clearly an effort to establish them in close proximity to where a majority of eligible or potential recipients reside, preferably within walking distance. The majority of organizations that administer meal sites prepare meals in central kitchens or at the meal sites themselves.

Transportation is a key to the ability of the group meal program to meet the needs of the older persons in the community. Eight out of ten sites offer transportation to those who are going to the site to enjoy the meal. Sometimes reservations for a meal must be made at least a day in advance. Menus often appear weekly in the local newspaper.

More takes place at the meal program than simply eating a meal among friends and peers. Through federal efforts, nutrition sites are encouraged to provide certain supportive services if needed. They will often have exercise programs, games, field trips, chamber music, or other activities that will promote interaction and socialization among the participants. Others may have counseling, information and referral (see Glossary), shopping assistance, or escort services. Sometimes there is an effort to link nutrition and general well-being, through health screening, fitness programs, and educational programs about health or nutrition.

Participants in both congregate and home-delivered meal programs tend to participate with some regularity. Two-thirds of congregate participants attend meal sites three or more times each week. Over 80 percent of home-delivered meal recipients receive a meal five times each week.

There has also been an effort at a number of meal programs to diversify the meals to include religious or ethnic foods. Meal programs have emerged that serve, for example, Portuguese meals, Hispanic meals, or Chinese meals.

There are several other types of meal programs that are not so widely available but deserve mention. Luncheon clubs, for example, are comprised of a group of older persons who get together one or more days a week to share a meal, generally at the home of the club leader, although it could also be at a housing facility for seniors. Generally, the clubs try to bring together people with similar interests, such as playing bridge or listening to a particular type of music. These activities can then be incorporated into the meal.

Escort services may also be available. Because group meal programs and home-delivered meals provide only some of the meals a consumer will need to eat in a week, escort services have emerged to assist older persons in grocery shopping. Escorts may either accompany an individual to the store or deliver an order of groceries.

When are meal and nutrition services appropriate?

Meal programs enhance dietary intake. They are appropriate if a consumer has trouble grocery shopping, whether because of frailty, lack of transportation, or some other reason. It is also for those who may have trouble preparing meals or for those who cannot meet the costs of food or of having someone prepare meals for them. Meal programs provided in a group setting are particularly suited for those who suffer from loneliness or isolation. The social benefits may be equally as important as the nutrition itself. Meals delivered to the home may provide a real service if one is homebound as he or she recovers from an illness or temporary disability.

Some meal programs may have eligibility requirements. For example, it is not uncommon to see an age restriction of 55 or 60, a requirement that a consumer be suffering from an incapacity that prevents him or her from preparing meals, or an income restriction. Often, these programs target as priority clients those who are of advanced age, low income, minority, isolated, mobility impaired, or who have limited ability to speak English. However, these kinds of restrictions will vary from service to service. Consumers should not be dissuaded if they are ineligible for a given service, as there may be other sponsors in their community.

How does one find meal and nutrition services?

The first place to check about the availability of home-delivered meal programs or group meal programs is the local office on aging. Very often this office contracts with local providers to offer these services. Local libraries may also be able to help find a meal program, and these services are also likely to be listed in the yellow pages.

How much do meal and nutrition services cost?

Meal programs are low-cost or, in some situations, no-cost services. Very often, much of the food is donated or the program is supported by local, state, or federal funds and the cost to an older individual is minimal. Volunteers, most of whom are also participants, provide much of the labor that makes these programs possible. Typically, contributions are requested. Sometimes fees are charged on a sliding scale ranging from 50¢ to $3 a meal; food stamps are sometimes accepted in lieu of a cash contribution. Contributions are used to increase the number of meals served and to facilitate access to meals, rather than to recover costs.

THINGS TO REMEMBER

Eligibility requirements may vary from program to program.

Inability to pay for a meal should not be a deterrent. These programs are designed to serve those who need them.

Nutrition is a key to maintaining your health in later years.

The social benefits of participating in congregate meal programs are ranked higher by participants than the meal itself.

CONSUMER CHECKLIST

If you are interested in a nutrition site or group meal program, the following questions may provide guidance in selecting a specific program.

____ Is the site within walking distance or is transportation readily available?

____ Do participants have to wait long in line?

____ Are staffers/volunteers courteous and friendly to participants?

___ Do participants seem to be enjoying the meal?

___ What other services are available at the site?

___ What do meals cost? Are meal charges voluntary? Is there a sliding scale?

___ Are menus posted in advance?

___ Can special dietary needs be met?

If home-delivered meals are being considered, the following may help in identifying a suitable program.

___ How frequently are meals provided?

___ Are meals served on weekends or holidays?

___ What do meals cost? Are charges voluntary or is there a sliding scale?

___ Can special dietary needs be met?

___ Will they provide a menu in advance?

___ Is an evening meal delivered along with the hot noon meal?

___ Is there a waiting list for this service?

Adult Day Care

There is a strong sentiment among some gerontologists and service providers, including family caregivers, that individuals who are in need of medical, health, and/or health-related social services should be served in the community rather than in an institution. Adult day care is an alternative that has emerged from this philosophy. It can help to alleviate isolation, prevent or delay unnecessary institutionalization, and provide relief from full- or part-time caretaking responsibility for family members.

Key Data

- There are more than 1,400 adult day care centers across the country that serve approximately 66,000 older persons.

What is adult day care?

Adult day care is a community-based service designed to meet the needs of functionally impaired adults through an individual plan for care. It provides a variety of health, social, and related support services in a protective setting to which participants are transported for all or part of the day. It does not provide 24-hour care. Adult day care is also referred to as adult or geriatric care, therapeutic day care, day treatment services, day health care, senior improvement services, or day hospital care.

Day care for adults has its origins in Britain, where, during the 1940s, outpatient centers for psychiatric hospitals were established. In 1947, the first geriatric day hospital opened in the United States in conjunction with the Menninger Clinic. Since that time, availability has increased and adult day care centers can be found in most states.

A range of services and programs are offered in adult day care settings, including health monitoring; skilled nursing services; physical, occupational, and speech therapy; personal care; nutritional services; counseling; transportation; recreational services; and assessment of client needs. Usually, a hot noon meal and snacks are provided. The purpose, organization, kinds of participants, setting, services, and structure differ from center to center. More often than not, the care and services provided depend on the needs of participants. The services are conducted in accordance with the individual plan for care that is developed by the center. It can range from active rehabilitation for patients recently released from a hospital to provision of one or more health-related social services for chronically disabled persons.

Unlike senior centers, which operate on a drop-in basis, adult day care is scheduled, often with a minimum requirement of two days per week. Again, depending on the clients' needs as well as on the center's resources, clients may spend up to a full eight hours in the day care center for a period of one to seven days a week. Most day care centers are small, serving 15–25 persons a day, with a client to staff ratio of about eight to one.

Adult day care can be broken down into two models of service delivery. One is a health-care model, in which health and rehabilitative services are emphasized. These services include nursing and physical, occupational, and speech therapies to individuals with significant functional impairments or to those who have chronic health problems and are in need of maintenance health care. These programs are most often operated under the sponsorship of a nursing home or hospital.

The other model is a social-service model. This model emphasizes recreation, socialization, assistance with daily activities such as walking and grooming, as well as nutritional counseling. Participants generally have relatively limited functional impairments and simply need maintenance care and supervision. This model is most often in a senior center or in conjunction with a family service agency. Staff tend to be social workers, social service, and recreational professionals.

There are a limited number of adult day care centers (about 5 percent) that serve only adults with dementia (Alzheimer's disease). Most serve mixed populations. Those that serve only adults with dementia have a lower client-staff ratio and a more skilled staff. They do different activities, such as reality orientation, sing-alongs, and physical exercise to improve or retain memory and physical functioning.

When is adult day care appropriate?

Adult day care is designed for persons who need assistance in retaining or attaining maximum physical and mental well-being. Specifically, this may include physical rehabilitation, alleviation of depression, or enhanced social involvement. It is also designed to serve family caregivers, providing them with temporary respite or a more permanent custodial service for working caregivers.

Adult day care generally serves chronically ill or disabled elderly individuals, although in most cases adults of any age may participate. However, some additional eligibility criteria may apply because of the institution or organization offering the day care or because of funding sources. For example, a Veterans Administration hospital and a family service agency may serve very different clientele.

There are individuals who are difficult to serve in adult day care settings. Among these are individuals who are seriously disoriented, who are dangerous to themselves or others, or whose behavior is extremely disruptive. Often individuals who are incontinent are difficult for an adult day care program to manage.

How does one find an adult day care center?

Adult day care centers are located in hospitals, nursing homes, community centers, churches, and other community buildings. They are listed in the telephone book under "Community Services" or can be found by contacting the local office on aging. Another resource for locating adult day care centers is the National Institute on Adult Daycare (see National Council on the Aging in Chapter 5). There is a small but increasing number of adult day care centers.

There are no federal standards for adult day care. However, as of 1989, 42 states and Puerto Rico had adopted their own standards for regulating adult day care centers. Standards vary considerably among states, usually reflecting the availability of reimbursement sources. For example, states that allow Medicaid reimbursement have adopted a health care model, with standards providing for health care professionals at adult day care centers. Other states have adopted a social service approach to standard-setting. Voluntary standards have been developed by the National Institute on Adult Daycare.

How much do adult day care services cost?

In 1989, the cost of adult day care was $30–$40 a day, depending on the location and the services offered. Often transportation to or from the center may be an additional $3–$7. These costs are considerably less than home health care or nursing facility care.

Reimbursement

Medicare does not recognize day care as a separate identifiable service for its beneficiaries. However, specific services are covered by Medicare, including physician services, physical therapy, rehabilitative services, and social and psychological services. To receive Medicare reimbursement, the individual must be in need of skilled rehabilitation under a plan of care established and periodically reviewed by the physician. Care that is classified as maintenance is not reimbursable.

Medicaid, a joint federal and state health insurance program for low-income persons, allows states the option of reimbursing adult day care in their state Medicaid plans. Programs conducted by a hospital or programs that are recognized as clinics under state law are eligible for Medicaid reimbursement. Under the Medicaid guidelines, the reimbursable medical services that day care centers might offer include medical services supervised by a physician, nursing services by a professional nursing staff, diagnostic services, rehabilitation services (including physical, speech, occupational, and inhalation therapy), self-care services oriented toward the activities of daily living, recreation therapy, dietary services, and transportation services. Most centers do not provide all of these services. However, the Medicaid guidelines indicate that the services available to an individual must be a combination of some or all of these and must be delivered under an individual plan of care. Each state has established a required package of services for reimbursable day care. To find out about Medicaid reimbursement, contact the local public assistance office, state Medicaid, or welfare office.

For veterans, the Health Care Program Amendments of 1983 (PL 98-160) authorized the Veterans Administration to provide adult day care services to eligible veterans through Veterans Administration (VA) hospitals and through contracts with non-VA facilities. As of February 1986, there were eight adult day care programs operating through the Veterans Administration.

THINGS TO REMEMBER

Adult day care centers are in short supply in many communities. Long waiting lists may exist.

Every adult day care participant should be assessed and given an individual plan of care upon commencing services at an adult day care center. The plan of care should be reassessed periodically.

If there is more than one program in a community, observe several programs and interview staff as well as participants and their family members.

CONSUMER CHECKLIST

____   Is the adult day care center certified or licensed?

____   Is the medical staff adequate? Can they perform CPR? What is the ratio of staff to clients?

____   Do staff routinely monitor clients' progress and consult with family members?

____   Are policies and procedures for emergencies, complaints, and refunds clear?

____   Are meals available for special diets?

____   Does the calendar demonstrate a variety of frequently available activities?

____   Is financial aid available?

____   Are there extra fees for activities and transportation?

SOURCE: Article by Maggie Bendicksen. Reprinted from the *AARP News Bulletin*, April 1989.

Multipurpose Senior Centers

The notion of clubs for older persons has been prevalent for over a century, as a place for persons of similar interests, needs, and ages to get together. From this concept has emerged the idea of senior centers, which are designed to provide services and activities to older persons in a given community. Senior centers have become, in many communities, the focus of all programs and services for older persons, serving, if not as the provider, at least as the coordinator or the conduit for programs and services.

Key Data

- In 1970, there were 1,200 senior centers; by 1985, there were over 10,000 senior centers.

- Senior centers are the most widely used community service among the older population. A study conducted in 1986 indicated that about four million older persons use senior centers.

What are senior centers?

Senior centers are community centers at which older persons can come together for services and activities that may enhance their independence and encourage their involvement in the community. The range of services and activities offered is broad and the success of senior centers rests largely on their ability to respond to community needs. Participation is voluntary; older persons can choose whether they want to participate and in what way.

Senior centers emerged from the notion of senior clubs, a phenomenon dating back to post–Civil War days. In the early 1940s, the first known senior center was formed in response to a need recognized by workers in the New York City Welfare Department. The idea spread fairly rapidly, as locally supported and directed institutions were established by units of local government or nonprofit groups. The common thread among these centers was the desire to be responsive to local needs.

Senior centers have grown precipitously since the 1970s, when federal legislation made more funds available for the development of senior centers. In particular, the Older Americans Act provided resources for "community facilities for the organization and provision of a broad spectrum of services." By 1977, it was estimated that more than five million older Americans, between the ages of 60 and 95, participated in activities at over 5,000 senior centers. In any two-week period, 6 percent of all older Americans attended a senior center.

Senior centers differ from senior clubs in several key ways. Clubs tend to have regular members, organizational bylaws, and scheduled meetings. Clubs are less likely to have a permanent physical structure and usually offer a narrower range of services. Clubs, such as those affiliated with fraternal organizations or veterans' groups, may also limit membership to a single sex, whereas senior centers provide men and women equal access. In general, their purposes are different. Senior centers are designed to serve the broadest population possible within the community; senior clubs are designed to serve their members.

What kind of activities do senior centers offer?

Activities in senior centers depend largely on the participants in the center. The range of possible activities is almost limitless.

Common offerings include arts-related activities, such as drama, music, films, and crafts; educational activities, such as nature and science, book clubs, speakers, lectures, forums, and round-table discussions; physical activities, such as dance and exercise programs; social activities, such as bridge and other table games and excursions; and community service projects.

What kind of services do senior centers provide?

Unlike activities, which depend largely on the desires of the participants, the services a senior center can provide depend largely on the facility, the community support, and the resources of the center. Some services are provided by center staff or volunteers; others are provided by other centers in the community. The types of services fall into several categories.

Most senior centers offer information and referral services, particularly for employment (job referral and retraining), housing, and living arrangements. Many offer health-related services, such as health screening, pharmaceutical services, health education, and specialized services, including podiatry and dentistry. Health programs connected with senior centers are often organized by doctors, nurses, a hospital, or the local health department. Some senior centers offer protective and legal services, including assistance in locating legal services, in will preparation, in providing information on eligibility for public benefits, and in determining alternatives to guardianship.

A major service of senior centers is meals, as many senior centers serve alternatively as congregate meal sites (see the section titled "Meals on Wheels and Nutrition Services"). In fact, the strong interest in developing congregate meal programs spurred the development of senior centers as the obvious location for such meals. Senior centers also often serve as the headquarters for home-delivered meals.

Another category of services involves community outreach. Senior centers often serve as the coordinator or conduit for community-based services, including friendly visiting and telephone reassurance, homemaker services, adult day care, handyman or fix-it programs, and transportation programs. Other sections of this book consider these various programs in detail.

The most frequently offered services and activities at senior centers are transportation to the center, arts and crafts, lectures, employment counseling, health screening, and friendly visiting.

The services with the highest rates of participation are meals and information and referral, while those that elicit the greatest amount of enthusiasm tend to be the trips and excursions. It is important to recognize that participants are able to select those activities and services that meet their needs and desires; there is no prescribed program. Similarly, centers are likely to focus on providing the services and activities that will best meet the needs of the community. This is particularly true in rural areas, where the primary service of a senior center may be transportation to the center, to health facilities, and to stores.

Although senior centers are most often run under the auspices of a nonprofit board of directors, they very often have both advisory councils and participants' councils. These councils advise the center on both outreach and programming. Often the councils will have committees with responsibility for programs, finances, public information, hospitality, and service. These committees provide participants an opportunity to influence the focus and direction of the center and to help it remain responsive to community needs.

When is a senior center appropriate?

Senior centers are appropriate for persons who need companionship or social interaction or who are in need of services. The centers generally target a broad population within the community, so there are likely to be activities and services for everyone. Some senior centers are beginning to develop programming that meets very specific needs, such as special programs for persons who are blind and lip-reading programs for those with hearing impairments. However, this is the exception rather than the rule. It is often thought that senior centers are not designed to serve those who are frail or those who may suffer from mild depression, although this may not be true of all senior centers. Certainly, there is increased emphasis, in planning community services, on serving the needs of those who are frail.

How does one find a senior center?

Senior centers are most often operated by local government or nonprofit organizations. To locate a senior center in a community, contact the local office on aging or the mayor's office. Senior centers will also be listed in the telephone book, under "Elderly," "Aging," or "Human Services."

Senior centers are usually located in areas that are convenient to transportation, possibly in a neighborhood that is accessible to the target population. Ideally, they have lots of parking and are accessible to the handicapped. About half of the senior centers are separate buildings designed as senior centers or converted to a senior center from some other use. Often, unused schools are converted to senior centers, as they tend to be well located for such use. However, senior centers may also be located in churches, synagogues, recreation centers, government facilities, and housing authority sites.

How much does a senior center cost?

In general, use of the facilities and activities at a senior center is available at no cost to the participant. However, some services such as meals may charge a nominal rate. Often fees are charged on a sliding scale so that persons are not turned away because of an inability to pay.

Funding for senior centers comes from a variety of sources, including federal funds through the Older Americans Act, state funds, and local and private funds. Often the activities and services are undertaken largely by volunteers, thereby reducing costs.

THINGS TO REMEMBER

Senior centers are designed to serve community needs.

Participation in senior center activities is voluntary; you may participate in only selected activities and services either on an intermittent or a regular basis.

Many senior centers provide transportation between home and the center and to other activities in the community.

Activities and services may vary among senior centers in a given community.

CONSUMER CHECKLIST

____ What services or activities would be most beneficial? Are these provided at the local senior center?

____ Does the senior center provide transportation services?

____ Would the opportunity for social interaction and finding support systems be beneficial, even on an intermittent basis?

____ Is the center convenient to transportation?

____ Are there talents and skills you could bring to the center?

____ Are there any costs involved in taking advantage of some services and activities? Is there a sliding scale?

Transportation Programs

For older persons to have access to necessities such as food, health care, and social activities, they must have adequate, affordable, accessible transportation. In many communities, this is not available. Rural elderly and, in some cases, older persons who live in suburban communities are often stranded without access to transportation services. Without transportation, important links cannot be made between an older person and the community. Social interaction and community involvement is hampered.

Key Data

- In 1986, about 1.2 million older persons took advantage of special transportation services.

- It is roughly estimated that in 1984, 7 million to 9 million rural older persons lacked adequate transportation services.

- Approximately 58 percent of the older population have their driver's licenses (1982).

What are transportation programs?

Many communities lack a public transportation system. As a result, a number of types of transportation programs have emerged to fill the gap for older residents of a community. These take many forms, including van pools, dial-a-ride programs, and reduced fares. They generally fall into two categories: those that respond to demand and those that respond to needs. Demand-responsive systems respond to overall perceived demands for service by a broad population of older persons. Need-driven services respond to individual needs to enhance independence and maintain a life style.

Federal Involvement

There has been some impetus from the federal government for communities to become more involved in serving the transportation needs of their older residents. The Urban Mass Transit Act of 1964 established, as a national policy, that elderly and handicapped persons have the same rights to transportation as other persons, that is, that they be able to utilize mass transportation facilities and services. A decade later, the National Mass Transportation Assistance Act required transit authorities to reduce fares by 50 percent for elderly and handicapped users in offpeak hours. By 1974, 145 cities had already instituted half-fare programs. Reduced fares are thought to be successful in increasing the ridership of older persons on public transportation, yet, ridership is still low.

There are also federal dollars available under the Urban Mass Transit Act, Section 16(b)(2), in the form of grants to assist nonprofit organizations in providing services to the elderly and handicapped when mass transit systems are not available or are not appropriate. By 1977, over 1,400 organizations had purchased over 3,000 specialized vehicles. More than three-quarters of these vehicles were 10- to 16-passenger vans for older persons.

Federal involvement is also present under the Older Americans Act, in which access is a major thrust. Title III of this act requires the provision of transportation for clients to and from nutrition sites if transportation is otherwise unavailable.

Community Solutions

A significant number of diverse transportation systems has emerged. In an 89-county area in Missouri, for example, vans and buses provide a variable-route, variable-schedule program in which participants must send in a postcard or call for a reservation a week in advance. In other communities, six-passenger vans are dispatched with a 24-hour advance reservation. Another approach is to provide fixed-route, fixed-schedule, dial-a-ride services, with seats reserved a week in advance. These transportation programs generally provide service to shopping, health facilities, or a nearby city.

In some states, school buses may be used for purposes other than transporting schoolchildren in off-school hours. Unfortunately, school buses present some real obstacles in terms of accessibility as they have high steps and are inappropriate for many older persons.

Some communities have also experimented with taxicab-based systems, in which shared rides by older persons in taxicabs are available for a very nominal cost. Generally, rides must be booked several hours in advance.

Escort Services

Escort services arrange for people to not only provide transportation but to accompany older persons to and from their destinations. These are often provided informally by family members or friends. However, some communities have more formal programs that will limit the availability of escort services to trips for essentials such as medical appointments and social services. In others, escorts will help with shopping, participation in social activities, or in visiting friends or relatives. Depending on the program, volunteers or paid escorts are used. In some cases, escorts assist in negotiating public transportation; in others, they use their own car or an agency vehicle.

When are transportation programs appropriate ?

Transportation programs are designed to serve several needs and, therefore, may be appropriate when these needs are present. They are appropriate for persons who might otherwise be isolated, in enabling them to reach needed services. They also provide access to medical and mental health care services that older persons may require, and they allow older persons access to shopping for food and other necessities.

Escort services may be appropriate for persons with mobility impairments or for those who are visually or memory impaired.

They may also be appropriate for persons who feel insecure travelling alone or who are unable to speak English.

How does one find transportation programs?

Special transportation programs can be found through the local department of transportation or the local office on aging. In some communities, a local nonprofit agency has been formed to coordinate all the transportation resources and services.

How much do transportation programs cost?

One major impetus behind the establishment of transportation programs was the prohibitive costs of public transportation systems for persons on fixed incomes. Therefore, most special transportation programs are available at a very low cost to participants. Public transportation systems have reduced fares during nonpeak hours. The reduction must be at least 50 percent below the regular fare.

In some cases, Medicaid will reimburse the elderly poor for transportation costs to medical facilities. Each state Medicaid plan must include provisions for assuring the availability of transportation to such services. In general, the problem with transportation services is not the costs, but the availability of programs.

THINGS TO REMEMBER

There are a number of different types of possible special transportation programs for older persons. Look into what is available.

Some programs may have restrictions, providing transportation only for essential trips such as medical appointments.

Although many are, not all transportation programs are accessible to those with mobility impairments.

Reservations are often required in advance.

CONSUMER CHECKLIST

___ Is service availability and cost information available?

___ Is transportation only available to certain destinations or will the service respond to a particular need?

___ Is the transportation service wheelchair accessible?

___ What kind of notice is required in order to take advantage of the transportation service?

___ What are the costs of the transportation?

___ Are escort services available should companionship be preferred?

Care Management

As the availability and variety of community-based services expand, and as individual needs for these services grows, it is becoming increasingly critical that a system be established for coordinating these services. The process of assessing needs and finding or negotiating for services to meet those needs has become a complex maze. No two communities are alike and services are fragmented in their availability, eligibility, and sponsorship. Care management has emerged to try to coordinate these services in concert with the needs of an individual.

Key Data

- Over one-half of all states currently operate state-funded care management programs.

What is care management?

Care management is a system under which the responsibility for locating, coordinating, and monitoring a collection of services falls with a person or institution. It is comprised of a number of ways of matching services to an individual's needs. Among these are screening and assessment, development of a plan of care, authorization and arrangement for service delivery, and monitoring and reassessment of needs. Within these broad categories are a variety of techniques and methods for conducting care management.

Specifically, care managers may help an individual determine his or her need for services, determine his or her eligibility for services, help with applications for government assistance, suggest alternative living arrangements, and arrange for a given service or simply locate a service. The care manager may be put in a position of being a coordinator for services, arranging for services, authorizing services, and/or controlling payment for services. Similarly, care managers may serve as advocates for an individual, assuring that appropriate services are received and providing a check on the quality of services provided. Care managers may be counselors, assisting individuals and their families in solving problems and in meeting needs. They may also be gatekeepers in containing costs and in justifying expenditures of funds. Some care managers will be more comfortable with certain of these roles than others.

What does care management entail?

Screening is a preliminary evaluation of an individual's need for care management. Screening will involve looking at the immediacy and the magnitude of the need. Some people will not need care management services, if all they need is a single service to which they can be referred. Assessment is a process that determines actual eligibility for care management. It includes a review of informal support systems such as family, the need for protective services and health-related services, and an assessment of the individual's living arrangement.

Care planning is the development of a plan to establish goals for the individual, a list of services needed to achieve these goals, the responsibilities of the care manager and service providers, and payment methods. The resulting plan of care outlines services to be provided, the frequency and the duration, and who will provide them.

Service delivery, or the arrangement thereof, is another key component of care management. The care manager arranges for or authorizes services to fulfill the plan of care. Arrangements are made either through collaboration with agencies or through the use of purchase-of-service agreements. Service delivery may also involve coordinating the help already provided by friends and family. In situations in which the care manager works for a service provider, service delivery may simply entail ordering services from the agency.

Monitoring is critical. Monitoring involves maintaining regular contact with the persons who are providing the care. The result will be an opportunity to regularly assess whether the services are of high quality and appropriate to meet individual needs. Care managers are also responsible for periodic reassessment to determine the ongoing appropriateness of the plan of care and the extent to which goals have been met. Reassessment may well end up in termination of the care management arrangement when services are no longer needed, either due to a change in condition, death, or relocation of the individual.

When is care management appropriate?

Care management is designed to serve those likely to need multiple services over a long period of time. People who take advantage of care management are often those who do not have informal support systems, such as family and friends, in close proximity. They are often persons who, without access to community-based services, would be at risk of institutionalization. They may be in a crisis situation and in need of immediate help, or they may have reached a point at which there are too many obstacles to daily living. While care management is not designed to take away an individual's or a family's decision-making ability, it is designed to help persons through the process of assessing, finding, and negotiating for care and services. It is often tapped by adult children who are interested in having someone monitor their parents' well-being in a distant city. It may well maximize an individual's ability to make more informed decisions.

How does one find care management services?

Care management is provided by community organizations such as home health care agencies; Area Agencies on Aging; local social service or health agencies; private, nonprofit, social service agencies; and, a relatively new phenomenon, social workers in private practice. Care management services can be located through hospitals, local offices on aging, or social service agencies. There is a growing network of care managers, known as private geriatric care managers, who are in private practice. They are often social workers, gerontologists, or nurses. They can be located through their association, the National Association of Private Geriatric Care Managers (see Chapter 5).

How much do care management services cost?

There is tremendous variety in the costs of care management services. Private care managers will charge from $50–$125 an hour (1989), often with an additional fee of $100–$500 for the initial assessment. Public agencies may provide care management services at low or no cost to an individual.

Costs are largely dictated by the responsibilities that the care manager assumes, the geographic area being served, and the size of the caseload that a care manager is handling. It is important to remember that the costs of care management are above and beyond the costs of the in-home, direct services themselves.

Although care management is usually not covered by Medicare, Medicaid, or private insurance, there are a few exceptions. Targeted care management is on the list of covered optional Medicaid services that a state may offer. As of October 1987, 14 states were offering some form of care management under Medicaid. These programs are restrictive, as they primarily serve persons who are eligible for Medicaid and meet the level of care requirement of a nursing facility. In some cases, eligibility is limited to those with acquired immune deficiency syndrome (AIDS).

A number of states have added general revenue funds to expand the population that is eligible for care management beyond that covered by Medicaid. They have both broadened the economic limits and expanded the functional limitation portion to include persons who might not be nursing home eligible. It is estimated that about one-half of the states have some type of care management program.

Care management may also be available in some communities with local funds. Generally, under these circumstances it is provided in conjunction with direct in-home service.

Care management is also now a component of some long-term care insurance policies (see the glossary). To monitor and regulate home health care benefits, in particular, long-term care insurance carriers have been exploring the use of care managers.

THINGS TO REMEMBER

Care management can provide a clear and single point of access for an individual in negotiating the community service network.

Care managers are responsible for helping to arrange and schedule care, as well as for monitoring the quality of the care.

Care management may reduce your autonomy, by varying degrees.

The size of the caseload of a care manager may affect their ability to manage individual cases effectively.

You can refuse the care plan or a portion thereof and can withdraw from the process at any time.

The cost of care management service is in addition to the costs of direct service care.

A care manager affiliated with a service provider may not be in a position to shop around for the most suitable service, but may limit referrals to the affiliated agency.

CONSUMER CHECKLIST

____ Is there a need for multiple services over a long period of time?

____ Will services be tailored to you and your family?

____ Is the care manager affiliated with one nursing home, home health agency, or homemaker service? Is there a possible conflict of interest?

____ Is Medicaid reimbursement available? Have eligibility criteria been examined?

____ Is the care manager in a position to serve as an advocate or will financial or organizational constraints limit this role?

____ What are the care manager's credentials? What is his or her education and experience? Does the care manager hold a professional license?

___ How are fees established?

___ Is there a contract that establishes the fees and their ability to increase over time?

___ Are you at liberty to negotiate the plan of care?

Telephone Reassurance and Friendly Visiting

Very often, older persons living alone suffer from depression resulting from social isolation. The lack of companionship is often difficult to compensate for. Several types of voluntary-based community services have evolved to fill the void of loneliness and to provide a periodic check to be sure all is well. These are generally known as telephone reassurance and friendly visiting programs.

Key Data

* One-third of persons 65 or older live alone. Women are over twice as likely to live alone as men.

* Among women over age 80, over three-quarters live alone.

What are telephone reassurance and friendly visiting?

Telephone reassurance and friendly visiting are among the oldest social service programs for older persons. However, in previous decades, the support was provided by a network of friends and neighbors in face-to-face visits. With the advent of telephones, visits were often replaced by frequent telephone calls to check on the well-being of an older individual.

Telephone reassurance and friendly visiting are now part of the more formal network of community-based services for older persons. They are frequently under the sponsorship of voluntary or public agencies. More often than not, volunteers perform the services for the sponsoring agency, under the supervision of a professional staff. Staff provide training, coordination, and consultation. Volunteers working in these programs are trained to detect potential problems through their frequent contact with older clients. These problems are then reported to the staff so that appropriate steps can be taken.

The formal telephone reassurance programs are generally targeted to the more frail or vulnerable older persons who live alone. While they do not have the advantage of face-to-face contact, it is possible to have more frequent contact over the telephone. The calls provide friendly contact, but can also serve as a reminder to take medication or an opportunity to do a quick assessment of an individual's emotional state. Telephone reassurance programs generally involve a daily call at a specified time. If contact is not made, a personal visit is made to the home.

When is telephone reassurance or friendly visiting appropriate?

These programs are appropriate for individuals living alone who may be frail and who wish to have the security of knowing that someone is in touch with them on a regular basis. They are also appropriate for persons who wish to have some social contact or companionship.

How does one find a telephone reassurance or friendly visiting program?

Telephone reassurance and friendly visiting programs have become a part of the formal network of community-based services for older persons. While they may not exist in every community, a good place to begin one's search is the local office on aging, listed in the telephone book. As they are often sponsored by churches, synagogues, or other voluntary organizations, these potential sponsors can be contacted for information as well.

How much do telephone reassurance or friendly visiting programs cost?

These are volunteer programs, with very little operating costs. There is, therefore, no cost to the consumer. There may, however, be some eligibility requirements, such as being alone or housebound or residing within a certain geographic area.

THINGS TO REMEMBER

It is not necessary to feel completely isolated and alone if you are frail and basically housebound.

Frequent contact with a volunteer can be made through these programs.

The security and companionship of daily contact with someone interested in your well-being does not have to cost money.

Sponsors are generally nonprofit groups, religious organizations, or public agencies, which are providing a service. They do not have a financial interest.

CONSUMER CHECKLIST

____ Is the sponsoring organization a trusted group in the community?

____ Will volunteers visit or call as often as you would like?

____ Are there specific tasks you would like a volunteer to help you with, such as reading to you or helping with correspondence?

____ Can you screen the volunteer before you make a commitment to regular visits?

____ Is there a waiting list for the service?

Personal Emergency Response Systems (PERSs)

A frequently mentioned concern of older persons who live alone is the possibility of not being able to summon assistance when needed in an emergency. Whether emergency assistance is ever needed is often less important, however, than knowing that assistance will be available immediately. This security can be obtained through personal emergency response systems. Although relatively new, they are slowly growing in acceptability and availability.

Key Data

- There are 15–20 personal emergency response systems on the market.

- One-third of the population age 65 or over lives alone.

What is a personal emergency response system?

A personal emergency response system (PERS) is a two-way communication system that, when triggered, indirectly links users to help. They can be literally a lifeline, signalling for help when needed in an emergency. More than simply providing help in an emergency, however, a personal emergency response system can provide the 24-hour reassurance that help will be received when needed.

Each system has two parts: a small transmitter (portable help button) that is carried by the user and a console or receiving base connected to the user's telephone. If a person using such a system falls or, for example, experiences chest pains, he or she can call for help by pressing the button. The button is portable and has an effective range of approximately 200 feet. It can send a radio signal from almost anywhere in an average-size home to the console.

The console is an automatic dialing machine. When the help signal is received, the console dials a preselected emergency telephone number. Most systems can dial out even if the phone is off the hook.

The centers that emergency response systems are preprogrammed to call are usually electronically coded to quickly identify a file on the caller. The file might contain information on medical history, medications, and names and phone numbers of persons who are to be notified in an emergency.

There are several ways in which the center responds. They will try to determine the nature of the emergency by telephoning the user. Some systems have speaker phones as an added feature built into the console. They can then talk to the user directly about the emergency. All systems can quickly send emergency services to the user's home. In most systems, the situation will be monitored until the emergency is over. In one system, the console sends a second help-needed message if assistance is not received within an allotted time.

There are a few systems that send a message directly to municipal emergency services (911 for example), rather than through a response center. Other programs have up to five separate telephone numbers to be called automatically if the button is pushed. These systems operate without a response center, sending a preprogrammed distress message to the persons called.

With these systems, however, one can't be sure that the message has been received.

There are also emergency response systems that are hardwired; that is, they are hooked into the home's wiring system. This means that the user must be in close proximity to the pull cord in order to activate the system. This is a distinct disadvantage for active users.

Features of Personal Emergency Response Systems

All portable help buttons are lightweight and battery powered. Some are worn around the neck or wrist. Others are carried on a belt or in a pocket. Most systems allow for two users. Very little pressure is needed to engage a help button, although this is a feature that should be tested. Most transmitters are water-resistant but not waterproof.

Consoles will work with any private telephone line and usually require little rewiring, unless there is more than one telephone extension. Consoles use lights and sounds to signal users that the button has been pressed. If the button has been pushed mistakenly, there is a switch to deactivate the call for help. Most emergency systems have a battery pack that will power the system for several hours if the electricity goes out.

Another feature is an inactivity timer, set for an 8- to 24-hour cycle. It will automatically send out a call at the end of the cycle if the user has not used the telephone or pushed a special button. This is particularly important if a user falls and cannot reach the button.

Response centers fall into two categories: those that are provider-based (a local hospital or social service agency) and those that are manufacturer-based (monitored through a national center). Where the response center is depends on the system selected. In either case, personnel answering the calls are trained to provide prompt attention. It is important to realize, however, that these staff are not doctors or nurses.

Most systems have not undergone testing to meet the standards of Underwriters Laboratory (UL). UL is a national testing service that focuses on product safety and performance standards. Although the lack of independent testing could be problematic, there is currently no evidence to show that these systems are not reliable.

When is a personal emergency response system appropriate?

These systems may be appropriate for individuals living alone who are concerned about their ability to signal for help in an emergency. However, the benefits of a PERS can extend beyond those who are frail, disabled, or infirm. They can provide psychological comfort to persons who are alone and are fearful of a fall, fire, or criminal intrusion, as well as to caregivers or distant loved ones.

How does one find a personal emergency response system?

Personal emergency response systems (PERSs) are generally linked to a hospital. To find out if such a system is available in a given area, contact the local hospitals. One might also contact the local office on aging to see if they are aware of such a system. This is still a relatively new technology, and, although they are available nationwide, the local hospital may not service the system.

PERSs are developed and sold to participating medical facilities and a few retirement communities by several national companies. A publication that lists the major companies that market nationally, *Meeting the Need for Security and Independence with Personal Emergency Response Systems,* is included in Chapter 6.

It is advisable to pick out two or three systems to test prior to making a commitment to buy or lease. Call the companies or a medical center and ask for a demonstration. Consumers should test the products themselves prior to making a selection.

How much do personal emergency response systems cost?

These systems can be rented, purchased, or leased. Rental agreements can be for several years or months or on a month-to-month basis. Rental fees can be as high as $50 a month. The normal rental fee is from $15–$30 per month, but will vary depending on the type of equipment and monitoring services. Lease agreements vary from company to company.

The purchase price of a system can range from $200 to more than $1,000. In addition to the purchase price, users may be required to pay a monthly monitoring fee of $10–$45 (1989).

Consumers are often better off renting the equipment rather than purchasing it, not only for cost reasons but for ease of maintenance and repair.

A few insurance companies cover these costs when the system is recommended by a doctor for medical use. Some hospitals and social service agencies will cover fees for low-income users. Medicare, however, will not reimburse these costs.

THINGS TO REMEMBER

Personal emergency response systems have been on the market for about 20 years. New companies are emerging and the technology is changing.

Test any product before deciding to rent, lease, or purchase. Features vary slightly from product to product.

Find out about the response center and how calls will be handled.

Read any contract before making a commitment on equipment that is being purchased or secured with a long-term lease. Details about the warranty should be readily available.

Technology is changing rapidly. Ask about the availability of features in which you are interested that may not appear to be standard items.

CONSUMER CHECKLIST

____ Are there several transmitter styles to choose from?

____ Can the button be easily pushed?

____ Is it easy to change the battery? Does this need to be done frequently?

____ How far can the signal be transmitted? What will block it?

____ Can the system be triggered if the phone is off the hook?

____ How is the help button worn?

____ Is there a two-way voice capability with the console? Can it be heard from all parts of the house?

___ Is the button on the console easy to depress?

___ At the emergency center, what files are kept on users?

___ Who will be receiving the calls?

___ Will prompt, reliable attention be received? What procedures are followed?

___ How will equipment repairs be handled?

___ What is the initial cost of the system? What is the ongoing cost?

Chapter 2

Home Maintenance
and Adaptations

Most homes are not constructed or designed with older residents in mind. Rather, they are designed to be suitable for younger families. However, most persons "age in place," that is, they remain in their homes as long as they possibly can. As they grow older, their homes may not be as safe or as suitable as they might like. They may be harder to maintain, may present safety hazards, or they may simply become too big or empty to feel secure.

There are many things that can be done to a home to make it more suitable as a person ages. Some involve taking advantage of community services that will assist with maintenance and repair, some involve structural changes to make spaces more suitable for persons with activity limitations, and others address changes in living arrangements. While the purposes and outcomes may vary, the options presented in this chapter look at a home as something that can be altered to suit individual needs, rather than as a stagnant structure.

Home maintenance and adaptations speak to the issues of safety and security in the home. They can provide assistance with something seemingly as minor as changing a light bulb to as major as adding a ramp to provide access for a wheelchair. In short, they can make it possible for persons to remain in and maintain their homes when they might otherwise have to move.

Sharing a home or adding an accessory apartment are changes in life style within a home. In both arrangements, private space is maintained, but additional people live within the home. When an accessory apartment is created, a homeowner adds an additional self-contained unit within the home that can provide companionship, help with daily tasks, and rental income. In a shared housing arrangement, the common space in a home is shared, creating a "family of choice." The benefits are similar.

Most of these options require the user to take an active role in their creation. Home sharers must be selected carefully, as must tenants to occupy an accessory apartment. Home adaptations call upon users to assess their needs and abilities and anticipate changes over time so that appropriate modifications can be made to the home. All can be extremely beneficial in maximizing independence in the home.

Home Repair and Maintenance Programs

For many older persons, keeping up with the repair and maintenance needs of a home can be difficult. Not only do many older persons live in older homes (i.e., those built before 1939), but even seemingly minor repairs can become burdensome if frailties or chronic illness are present. It is generally believed that many older persons would prefer to remain in their homes if maintenance and repair assistance were available.

Key Data

- 50 percent of the elderly live in dwellings built before 1939.

- Fewer than 5 percent of elderly homeowners and 10 percent of elderly renters live in dwellings built after 1970.

- Housing for some 244,000 older homeowners and 506,000 elderly renters has two or more structural deficiencies.

What are home repair and maintenance programs?

Home maintenance and repair programs provide assistance in making repairs to the homes of older persons, readily addressing problems that affect the recipient's health and safety. They range from weatherizing cold rooms, installing grab bars, or changing a light bulb to fixing a broken step or replacing a frozen pipe. Other repairs that these programs will often address include minor plumbing and security concerns or minor painting and carpentry. Some home repair programs will provide chore services, such as washing windows and other heavy housework. Others may help negotiate a major job, such as roof repair, with a contractor. The overall goal of home repair and maintenance programs is to reduce the need for larger and more expensive repairs. As an added benefit, they may also improve the market value of a home. These programs generally serve elderly, sometimes disabled, households.

Most programs provide call-back assistance and emergency services. Call-backs are generally made because of unsatisfactory work, new problems, or incomplete work. Emergency assistance is provided to address urgent health and safety problems, to correct problems considered life-threatening, and to contain problems that might otherwise cause further damage.

Federal Programs

The Farmer's Home Administration (FmHA) of the U.S. Department of Agriculture sponsors a home repair program for rural homeowners who need work done to bring their homes up to standard or to remove a health or safety hazard. Under Section 504, subsidized loans are made available to persons who are age 62 or over and/or are from low-income households. For very low income persons, grants, rather than loans, are provided. Rural areas are defined as those in the open country or places with a population of 10,000 or, in some cases, 20,000 or less. Section 504 loans may be made in amounts of up to $7,500 and are repayable over 20 years. Applicants must demonstrate that loans are not available from any other source. Applications and information are available from the local Farmer's Home Administration office.

The U.S. Department of Housing and Urban Development (HUD) provides community development block grants to entitled communities for a number of activities aimed at neighborhood revitalization and economic development. Communities have the latitude to decide what programs are necessary, but at least half of the activities must benefit low- and moderate-income residents. Home repair programs are often funded through community development block grants. Older persons head 60 percent of the households receiving home repair services funded as a result of community development block grants. Programs operated with these funds can be located through city or county community development offices.

HUD also operates a nationally available program known as the Title I Home Improvement Program. It provides insurance to local lenders to guarantee the repayment of loans made under the program. Loans are made to finance major or minor improvements, alterations, and repairs of individual homes and nonresidential structures. Lending institutions approved to participate in the program determine applicants' eligibility requirements. Class 1a loans are for alterations, repairs, and improvements that substantially improve or protect the livability, safety, and utility of homes.

Local Programs

Under the auspices of the Older Americans Act, state or local offices on aging may offer home repair programs to older persons in their service areas. These programs may take a number of forms, but generally they target basically sound housing stock, concentrating on minor repair and maintenance jobs.

Some home repair and maintenance programs fall under the category of home repair insurance. Enrollees in these insurance programs pay an annual fee based on income. This entitles them to home repair materials costing no more than a predetermined amount, say $50, and manual labor to complete the necessary repairs. During the year, the client may request up to two or three repeat visits for additional repair services. If further repairs are needed, the program sponsor may help negotiate for lower rates with a local contractor.

Other home repair programs are akin to home repair audits. Using retired construction workers to conduct audits, estimates are made of the scope of work required and the approximate costs. The program sponsor maintains a list of contractors who have conducted satisfactory home repair work in the past. The program does not actually perform the repair work, but helps identify needed repairs and negotiates for the work to be done.

Home repair programs may also actually perform the work on a first-come, first-serve, pay-as-you-go basis, rather than under a prepaid arrangement. Often these programs are referred to as handyman programs. A limit is set on how much can be spent on each job. These limits may be in the range of $200 to $300, which is a figure often negotiated with the local building trades union. Eligibility generally goes to those who are resident home-owners, who are age and income qualified, or who have jobs that fall within certain simple repair categories. Often these cate-gories will limit jobs to those that do not require a permit. Participating homeowners pay a modest hourly rate or pay sim-ply for materials. In many cases, there is a fund for persons who need repairs but are unable to pay for them. Sometimes, but not always, the work is provided by retired plumbers, electricians, and carpenters.

Home repair programs may also operate tool banks that lend tools to individuals to perform work themselves.

Home maintenance and repair can also be arranged as a ser-vice exchange, although this is generally done on an informal basis among persons within a church or synagogue or under the auspices of a neighborhood or community organization.

How are these programs organized?

In all these programs, there is generally a central coordinator and a repair supervisor. The supervisor is responsible for the day-to-day activities associated with providing the actual maintenance and repair. They may conduct an inspection to determine what home repair needs should be addressed. The inspection may un-cover more needs than available resources, requiring the supervi-sor and client to prioritize repairs. Those programs that don't inspect rely on the homeowners to identify their outstanding needs. They supervise the work crews, individual tradesmen, or, in some cases, subcontractors. They also coordinate the repair schedule and materials acquisition. The repair services are then rendered by a repair staff, subcontractors, or volunteers. Typi-cally, these persons are generalists, or tradesmen, able to perform a broad assortment of repairs. Work is performed by crews of two or three.

When are home repair programs appropriate?

Home repair and maintenance is appropriate when there are defects that make a house unsafe or unsuitable for residence or if there are conditions that will lead to deterioration. Often, persons who have lived in a home for a number of years fail to notice defects and simply compensate for them or adjust to them in their day-to-day lives. For this reason, it is sometimes necessary or appropriate to have an independent assessor, a knowledgeable friend or relative, review the home to determine what, if any, repairs are needed. The assessor will check the home's structure, windows, doors, electrical system, water systems, insulation and heating, masonry, and outside siding. The "Consumer Checklist" will provide early indicators that some repairs may be needed, but an independent set of eyes may provide a more thorough assessment.

How does one find a home repair program?

Home repair programs are sponsored by a myriad of organizations, including:

Area or local offices on aging

Public housing authorities

Religious organizations

Nonprofit neighborhood or community organizations

County or city departments of housing and community development

Social service organizations

Private for-profit organizations

To find out about loans provided by the Farmer's Home Administration (FmHA), contact the local FmHA office and talk to the FmHA county supervisor. HUD field offices can provide a list of lenders approved to offer Title I Home Improvement Loans.

How does one select a maintenance or repair contractor on one's own?

When working directly with a building contractor, a list of all the work to be done should be put in writing before contractors are contacted. Asking friends, neighbors, or a local office of consumer affairs for recommendations of reliable contractors who perform quality work and are reasonably priced is a good idea. The local office of consumer affairs may also be able to provide information on whether licenses or permits are required for the work to be performed. From among those recommendations, at least three contractors should be asked to submit bids based on the work to be done. The bids should be submitted in writing and should indicate the amount of time required to do the project, or the start and completion dates. It is important to hold the contractor responsible for completing the project on schedule. Also, each contractor submitting a bid should supply three references. Consumers should talk to the references to see if the contractor has performed satisfactorily in the past. References should be asked: Were cost forecasts realistic? Was the contractor easy to work with? Were his or her assistants capable and were projected schedules met?

For large projects, such as those over $2,000, it is not uncommon to provide some of the payment up front. Consumers should not pay all of the money up front. It may be reasonable to set up a payment schedule of 30 percent up front, 30 percent after the work has been substantially completed, and the remaining 40 percent upon completion of the project to the consumer's satisfaction. It should be clarified at the outset who pays for materials.

How much do home repair programs cost?

Costs to participants vary depending on the nature of the repair and the structure of the program. Home repair insurance programs provide services for a fixed annual fee of $25–$50 (1988), for eligible homeowners. They provide about three visits per year per subscriber to make repairs. Handyman services generally provide repair for reduced labor costs or provide free materials.

Deferred-payment or low-interest loans may also be available for home repair. These are generally sponsored by local government. Typically, these loans do not have to be repaid until a homeowner dies or sells the home. Age and income are often criteria used for eligibility for these programs, although sometimes program guidelines specify that, in addition, the loans must be used to bring the homes up to building codes and standards. These loans may not be used for cosmetic changes to the home. Deferred-payment loan programs offer loans at low interest rates or interest rates on a sliding scale, depending on income and on one's ability to pay.

In programs that will help clients negotiate with a home repair contractor for large jobs, the program coordinator will seek bids from several contractors and recommend the most reasonable one. The advantage of having a home repair program coordinator help in seeking bids and selecting a contractor is that they are familiar with what most repairs should cost and can determine the reasonableness of fees charged. (The bulk of the fees likely will be labor costs.) The coordinator might also have developed a list of reliable and reputable contractors with whom he or she feels comfortable doing business.

In the Farmers Home Administration programs, eligibility is based on age and income. Loans carrying interest rates as low as 1 percent as well as arrangements in which part of the loan principal does not have to be repaid are not uncommon for persons who have low incomes. For those with higher incomes, there are programs that provide loans that must be repaid in full but are available to those who might not otherwise qualify for a loan. The county FmHA supervisor can help determine the type of assistance that is appropriate for each individual. Grants have no repayment terms, whereas for loans or loan-grants, any loan of $1,500 or less must be repaid within 10 years, $2,500 must be repaid within 15 years, and larger loans within 20 years. For persons with higher incomes, loans may be negotiated for larger amounts and for as long as 25 years, with interest rates from between 1 and 3 percent. Recipients of grants must agree not to resell their homes within three years.

THINGS TO REMEMBER

Home repair programs are sponsored by a variety of local organizations. Persistence is necessary in a search to meet individual needs.

There is tremendous variation among programs in eligibility requirements and in the scope of jobs that can be done.

If you decide to select a home repair contractor on your own, get recommendations from neighbors and friends, ask for bids from several contractors, do not pay for all the work in advance, and monitor the work closely to be sure it suits your needs.

CONSUMER CHECKLIST

To assess the nature of, and extent to which, repairs may be needed, the following checklist may be helpful.

____ Are the basement walls or floor wet after it rains?

____ Are the window frames rotting? Do the windows open and close? Do they permit cold air to come into the home?

____ Are there storm windows and doors?

____ Does the roof leak?

____ Do the toilets flush properly? Does the tank or bowl leak?

____ Does the furnace adequately heat all the rooms of the house? Has the furnace been converted from coal to gas, oil, or electricity? Do any of the radiators leak?

____ Does using certain appliances blow fuses or throw circuit breakers? Has the main power box been upgraded recently?

____ Does the water heater provide enough hot water for multiple baths or showers?

____ Are there cracks in the masonry steps or sidewalks that might cause an accident?

____ Do the door locks work properly?

____ Do the gutters and downspouts carry rain away from the house properly?

Home Adaptations

Home adaptations are changes or modifications to a home or residence to make it more suitable for a person with limited mobility or vision, hearing, or memory loss. Most housing is designed for able-bodied persons. As a person ages, however, changing physical conditions make some mundane tasks more difficult. And homes that were once very comfortable can rapidly lose their utility and become unsafe, full of barriers and obstacles, or simply impossible to negotiate.

Considerable work has been done by some design professionals and architects to determine ways in which homes can be easily adapted. Today, most homes with adaptations or adaptable features have been specially built or remodelled to meet the needs of people with disabilities. However, most homes lend themselves to changes to make them more usable over a persons' lifetime.

Key Data

- One out of five U.S. residents age 15 and over (or 37.3 million persons) has difficulty performing one or more basic physical activities. The activities include seeing, hearing, speaking, walking, using stairs, lifting or carrying, getting around outside, getting around inside, and getting into or out of bed (U.S. Bureau of the Census, 1986).

- About 19.2 million people had difficulty walking a quarter of a mile, and 8 million were unable to walk that far (U.S. Bureau of the Census, 1986).

- Of those who have trouble performing at least one function, 15.5 million were age 65 or over; 7.5 million persons age 65 or over are completely unable to perform at least one function (U.S. Bureau of the Census, 1986).

What are home adaptations?

Most older people live in homes that were designed without their needs in mind. In order to make their homes more suitable, home adaptations are often necessary. Adaptations can meet some very specific needs, such as the addition of a ramp to make an area accessible to a person with mobility impairments. Adaptations can also borrow from the principles of adaptable design and try to add the kind of flexibility that will make a home meet needs as they may change over time or from resident to resident.

Adaptable design or adaptable housing refers to a living environment in which features of a home are adjustable, depending upon the needs of the resident. It does not look different from other housing, but simply has flexible features. For example, sinks, counters, and grab bars are installed so they can be readjusted to different heights for different people. These kinds of features help persons of short stature, as well as those who are in wheelchairs. The appearance of the home remains unchanged, but the home becomes imminently more usable for all persons.

Adaptable design comes out of efforts to make all environments generally accessible, that is, free of barriers for persons of all levels of ability and disability. If homes, in particular, are designed to be adaptable, they will have several key accessible features as well. The growing emphasis today among designers, architects, and policymakers is on adaptability and more universal design concepts. In fact, the Fair Housing Act Amendments of 1988 prohibit discrimination on the basis of handicap. Landlords are required to make the necessary adaptations to apartment units to allow for residence by a disabled individual.

What are some adaptations that can be made?

Getting from one room to another can be difficult for a person in a wheelchair or walker. Thresholds in doorways of older homes can be hazardous, the doorways themselves may be too narrow to permit passage, and locks and door knobs may be unworkable. Following are some suggested modifications to alleviate these and other problems.

Corridors and Doorways

The standard door width is 32 inches, although some doors may be narrower. A standard wheelchair is 24–27 inches. When room is added for fingers, knuckles, and inaccurate maneuvering, the clear opening must be about 32 inches. Rather than replace the entire door and frame, it is possible to replace the existing hinges on doors with swing-clear hinges. They enlarge the clear opening of the door by 1½ to 1¾ inches, which may be enough to allow for more easy passage by a person in a wheelchair. If it is a swinging door, the wooden doorstops can be removed and re-installed up to 3 feet above the floor, adding an additional ¾ inch to the clear opening width of the doorway. Another possibility is to remove doors altogether.

Rather than changing the hinges or removing the doors altogether, it may be preferable to replace the doors. Sliding doors, pocket doors, or folding doors provide some alternatives, depending upon the structure of your doorway.

Hardware on doors can be particularly problematic for persons with hand dexterity limitations caused by arthritis or other chronic conditions. Most locks require fine dexterity and finger strength, as do most door knobs. It is easy to replace door knobs with levers, but it is less easy to find a lock that provides the degree of security desired but can be easily operated. Pushbutton locks may work, as may slide bolts or magnetic card readers, or a combination of these measures. It should not be necessary to compromise one's personal safety for accessibility.

Removing thresholds may eliminate a real safety hazard for persons in walkers or for those who simply have difficulty in lifting their feet when they walk. When thresholds are removed, it is often necessary to patch the flooring.

Doormats and throw rugs are well-known hazards that lead to dangerous falling accidents. It is advisable to secure them to the floor with tacks, staples, or double-sided tape.

Stairs

A high percentage of the accidents that occur in the home happen on stairs. Risers should be 6–7 inches and treads should be wide enough to allow the foot to rest comfortably. Unfortunately, if steps are particularly steep or narrow, it is difficult to modify them without replacing them altogether. Open staircases are also dangerous.

Nosings on stair treads that project can cause tripping. They can be modified by adding a wedge below the nosing.

Adding hand rails to stairs is something that can be done more easily. To achieve maximum support, hand rails should be installed on both sides of stairs so that persons with strength on only one side will have support going up and coming down the stairs. Hand rails should extend beyond the top and bottom of the stair to provide support getting on and off the last step. A rounded hand rail is much easier to grasp than a rectangular or square one.

Lighting on stairs can prevent accidents. Light switches placed at both the bottom and top of stairs will allow the user to light his or her way.

For persons with severe mobility impairments, stairs may be altogether impossible to negotiate. Ramps are commonly used in place of or in addition to outdoor stairs. It is important that a ramp not be too steep. Exterior ramps should have a slope of 1 inch of rise for every 20 inches of length. Interior ramps can be a little steeper, with a slope of 1 inch of rise for every 12 inches of slope. Landings are necessary at the top and bottom of ramps, and hand rails should be placed on both sides.

Sinks and Bathrooms

Three critical elements of a sink are the clearance underneath, the height of the sink, and the hardware. All are fairly easy to adapt. For persons in wheelchairs, removing the doors or the entire cabinet below the sink will allow them to get as close as possible to the basin. It is important, however, to cover the pipes with pipe insulation to avoid scalding legs and knees. Sinks can also be made in which the cabinet below the sink is simply removed altogether.

Sinks and cabinets can be placed on adjustable brackets, to allow for raising and lowering depending on the height of the user.

The same philosophy applies to faucets as applied to door knobs. Levers are preferable for persons with hand dexterity or strength limitations and are easy to install. Single-lever faucets need only be operated by one hand, and they provide a mixed water temperature from one tap.

Toilets can be adapted by installing grab bars. There are several different types of grab bars that suit different needs. Whatever type of grab bar is selected, be sure they are firmly secured on to studs in the wall to prevent instability.

Bathtubs are the subject of considerable controversy, because they are the cause of more accidents and accident-related deaths in the home and because they are inherently difficult to get into or out of. Bathtubs can be made safer with the addition of grab bars on the wall or tub itself, tub seats, rubber mats, and lighting. Lever controls on faucets are preferable.

If a tub or shower is being replaced altogether, roll-in and transfer showers make bathing easier for persons in wheelchairs.

Hand-held showers are a useful and inexpensive addition to an existing tub or shower.

Kitchens

There are many ways to modify a kitchen to make it more usable for a person with physical limitations. Some involve structural changes, some involve the purchase and installation of new appliances, and others simply involve ingenuity and the purchase of assistive devices. These are low-cost items that can make daily tasks easier, such as touch-control light switches and wider grips for handles of pots and pans.

As in bathrooms, putting cabinets and countertops on adjustable brackets so they can be raised and lowered can make a kitchen work area more usable. In addition, different counter heights can be created by installing folding or pull-out surfaces, such as cutting boards, at different heights.

Remove the door in the cabinet in front of the sink to allow maximum access to the basin. If the basin is too deep, install a wooden, wire, or plastic rack to raise the working level to a more comfortable level.

Purchase a range top with front or side controls so it is not necessary to reach over hot burners. Hard-to-turn controls can be adapted with add-on handles.

Wall-mounted ovens are ideal for persons in wheelchairs who cannot reach the long distance over a standard oven door. They may be difficult to find, however, except as microwave ovens.

Storage is always a problem in a kitchen. Lazy susans, rolling carts, and door racks for brooms or canned goods may help make space more accessible. There is also a wide range of inexpensive shelving components that can improve storage.

No two persons will age in the same way or face the same problems. For this reason, understanding the basic concepts of home adaptations is important as a basis for making modifications that will suit individual needs. There is no prescribed formula for home adaptations that is appropriate for all users. Remember that these are all decisions based on your needs, interests, and life style.

When are home adaptations appropriate?

Because adaptability is flexible and designed to suit different needs, adapting one's home can be done at any time. It can be done in anticipation of a dramatic change in physical condition, when an individual finds that he or she can no longer function safely in the home, or simply as a person becomes more frail yet is still mobile and able to live independently. Adapting a home is not necessarily age related. Few, if any, of the modifications described above are inappropriate for a younger, more able-bodied person. They are likely, in fact, to make a home safer and more livable for residents of all ages. However, if a home is not adapted in advance of a change in physical condition, it may become less a matter of choice than a necessity in order to remain living in one's home.

How does one find programs to assist with home adaptations?

There are a few programs and services around the country that are dedicated to assisting people in making modifications to their homes. Generally, these are nonprofit, community-based organizations that can conduct a thorough evaluation of not only the home, but also the individual's ability to function in the home. They will also generally oversee the work that is done. Unfortunately, there are only a handful of these programs.

Physical and occupational therapists can also be useful in helping to identify changes that are needed to make the home function better for a resident. Also, by contacting the state chapter of the American Institute of Architects, one may be able to locate an architect who specializes in adaptable design. Finally, there are a growing number of contractors who are experienced in accessibility and adaptability in home modifications.

To find these programs and individuals, contact the local office on aging or office of handicapped affairs. Frequently, at the state level, the governor will have an office of disabilities or handicap affairs that may be a good source of information.

Other good sources of information are the specific consumer-related organizations, such as:

American Cancer Society

Muscular Dystrophy Association

Multiple Sclerosis Society

Cerebral Palsy Society (individual societies in metropolitan areas)

The Arthritis Foundation

Lighthouse for the Blind

If it is necessary to hire a contractor to get the job done, follow the guidelines in the previous section ("Home Repair and Maintenance Programs"). It is likely to be difficult to find a contractor who is familiar with the kinds of adaptations required. It will, therefore, be necessary to work along with him or her. For example, try out hardware before it is installed to be sure it will work. Make sure the results are suitable, both in terms of quality of workmanship and usability.

How much do home adaptations cost?

The cost of making modifications to a home varies tremendously, depending upon what is done. Some changes can be done with little more than a trip to the hardware store, some require the services of a handyman, some may require ordering special products, such as a roll-in shower, and still others may require a contractor to move walls or make structural changes. It is important to do a thorough assessment of one's needs and expectations before undertaking major renovations, to make sure they will, in fact, create a more livable environment.

The federal funding sources described in the section titled "Home Repair and Maintenance Programs" apply to modifications as well. These sources of low-interest loans may be extremely beneficial. In addition, the Veterans Administration provides low-interest loans to veterans to modify their homes.

There may also be a number of local programs, particularly for the elimination of barriers for low-income persons. Some communities have below market rate rehabilitation loan or deferred payment loan programs for home adaptations. Others may have programs targeted at specific modifications, such as an exterior ramp program. Such programs can be identified by contacting the city or county office of housing or community development.

The Internal Revenue Service (IRS) allows individuals to deduct equipment, furnishings, and permanent changes for access to the home as medical expenses, should these and other medical expenses exceed 7.5 percent of household income. IRS Publication 907 describes this further.

THINGS TO REMEMBER

Modifications in your home can be made to suit individual needs, and do not need to meet public building standards.

Do a thorough needs assessment and functional assessment before contacting a contractor, so it is clear exactly what you are looking for someone to do.

Although they may be hard to find, there are professionals who can help guide you through the process. Be resourceful in locating such people.

Adapting a home need not be an extremely expensive undertaking. There are many small things that can be done at little cost that will make a large difference.

Check local and state government offices for programs that may help reduce the costs of adaptations.

CONSUMER CHECKLIST

____ Has an assessment been conducted of not only the home, but also your ability to function in it?

____ Are some spaces, rooms, or appliances no longer functional because of a change in your physical condition?

____ Does the decision about whether to stay in the home or move depend on the ability to make modifications to the home?

____ Has the office of handicapped affairs been contacted and have available reference materials and resources been obtained?

____ Have minor adaptations that will improve the livability of the home been considered?

____ Is an effort being made to improve the safety of the home? Have hazards been identified and are corrections being made?

____ If adaptations are not currently necessary, is it anticipated that they will be in the future?

____ If additional financing is necessary, have the sources for financing (home equity loans, reverse mortgages, low-interest or deferred-payment loans, or grants) been identified?

Accessory Apartments

Home adaptations can take the form of not only altering the barriers or suitability within the physical environment, but also changing the physical environment itself. One way of doing this is by creating a second dwelling unit within a single-family home, to be lived in by a tenant, a service provider, or a family member. This kind of arrangement, known as an accessory apartment, can provide companionship, security, and income.

Key Data

- It is estimated that 57 percent of homes with five rooms or more are occupied by persons age 55 or older, usually with households of one or two persons (1979).

- During the period 1973–1980, 27.7 percent of all new housing units came from conversion and other nontraditional sources. It is not known how many of these are accessory apartments.

- It is estimated that, in 1979 alone, as many as 500,000 illegal conversions of accessory apartments took place.

What is an accessory apartment?

An accessory apartment is a complete, self-contained living unit within an existing single-family home. It has its own kitchen, living area, sleeping area, and usually a separate entrance. There are a wide range of terms used to describe accessory apartments: accessory dwelling units, mother-in-law suites, single-family conversions, and mother-daughter residences. They all refer to an independent unit that shares, at most, an entrance, a yard, and parking with the single-family home. Accessory apartments are not a new phenomenon; they have existed for many decades in some communities.

Renting an Accessory Apartment

Renting an accessory apartment, as opposed to a room in one's home, can be a significant source of income. Because it is an independent unit, an accessory apartment can command more rent than simply a room, even if the room is furnished. It is also generally rented on a landlord/tenant basis, which involves drawing up a formal lease or rental agreement. The lease or agreement must comply with local landlord/tenant laws or with the ordinance that applies to accessory apartments.

Leases

Standard leases are available from real estate agents or the library, and a copy of the accessory apartment ordinance may be available from the local zoning office. If special arrangements are made with a tenant for, for example, service exchanges, these should be written into the lease. If the changes are complicated, an attorney's assistance might be sought.

It is wise to opt for a short-term lease of six months to one year. This allows for changing tenants with greater ease, raising the rent, or amending the lease. If the arrangement is mutually satisfactory, the lease can simply be renewed.

As a landlord, one will also be required to handle security deposits, select tenants, and check references. These may be new, although not insurmountable, responsibilities with which the homeowner is not familiar.

Finding Tenants

One can find tenants through the traditional ways of advertising in newspapers, placing notices on bulletin boards, and by contacting tenant referral services. The last should be listed in the telephone book or can be located through the office of landlord/tenant relations. Rents for accessory apartments should be competitive. The newspaper can be a good source of information about what kinds of rents are being charged.

Screen tenants carefully to be sure that expectations are compatible. References from previous landlords may be a useful indicator of the potential for the prospective arrangement to be successful. Although living quarters are separate, personal relationships often evolve. Having someone trustworthy close by to call upon in emergencies or to occasionally help with chores may not necessarily mean a reduction in privacy, but can be an added benefit of an accessory apartment.

When is an accessory apartment appropriate?

An accessory apartment can be a source of income for homeowners to help meet rising maintenance and living expenses. It may prevent them from having to move to a smaller, less expensive home or from having to sell their home altogether and become a renter. The tenants may provide, in addition to income, some services, such as yard work, transportation, or even shopping assistance, in exchange for reduced rent. For older persons who feel uncomfortable living alone, a tenant in an accessory apartment may provide a source of companionship and reduce the fear of criminal intrusion or personal accidents.

How does one create an accessory apartment?

Accessory apartment designs will vary, both in looks and in costs. Some people prefer to hire an architect to help them with the design. While this will add to the up-front costs, it may be a worthwhile investment in the long run. At a minimum, it is best to avoid the expense of installing new sewer, electric, or gas lines, or of moving existing ones. Try to work around the existing structure, as necessities like heat, air conditioning, and doors are expenses that may not be avoided.

Creating an accessory apartment that is adaptable, that is, that can accommodate a person with mobility impairments, may be extremely beneficial in the long run. Not only does it expand the options for finding a tenant, but also it may provide a place for the homeowner to reside should an adaptable environment be preferable in the future. Adaptability does not add to the cost; it simply may change some standard dimensions and ways of thinking. For example, doorways and bathrooms should be made wide enough to accommodate a wheelchair, steps should be avoided, and the kitchen and bathroom should have enough space so that a wheelchair can turn around. (See "Home Adaptations" for more information.)

Zoning

Zoning can be a barrier to creating an accessory apartment. Neighborhoods designed for single-family homes generally prohibit a second living unit such as an accessory apartment. Restrictive convenants may also prohibit their use. Prohibitions often rise from concerns linking accessory apartments to increased congestion and decreased property values. There are often fears that traffic and parking problems will increase, that the appearance of the neighborhood will change, and that accessory apartments will overload the existing infrastructure, including sewer, water, and other systems.

Zoning typically is less restrictive in rural areas than in urban or suburban areas. Where permitted, accessory apartments are allowed with a special exemption variance or special requirements to alleviate these concerns. Included may be off-street parking requirements, requirements that one unit be owner occupied, limits on the number of tenants per unit, or requirements that the appearance of the neighborhood not be changed as a result of the addition of an accessory apartment. Most communities also require building permits and inspections for any renovation, to be sure that codes are met. In contrast to these fears are the results of several studies that have shown that accessory apartments have had no noticeable impact on communities and, in many cases, they go unnoticed.

The four methods used to permit accessory apartments are zoning ordinances, variances, licensing, and special use permits.

Zoning ordinances are enacted by a local government. They may permit accessory apartments in specified zones, allowing conversion of a single-family home in those zones at any time.

A *variance* allows a homeowner to be exempted from a particular zoning ordinance by a local government entity. Variances are generally granted to a parcel of land rather than to a homeowner.

Licensing of accessory apartments provides local government with a mechanism for ongoing review through periodic renewal requirements.

Special use permits require local governments to review each case individually by conducting a public hearing. The permit is generally granted to the applicant rather than the property.

To get a special use permit, it is usually necessary to submit a formal request to the local zoning board, notify neighbors, and appear at the zoning board hearing at which the request is being considered. If the special use permit is granted, a fee is likely to be charged, ranging from $50–$300.

Selecting a Contractor

Extreme care should be exercised in selecting a contractor, as fraud and complaints about home repair contractors are common. (See the section titled "Home Repair and Maintenance Programs" for information about selecting a contractor.)

How much does an accessory apartment cost?

The biggest financial cost involved in creating an accessory apartment is the modifications that may have to be made to a home. Converting a walk-out basement, a recreation room, or an upstairs area into an accessory apartment could cost anywhere from $10,000 to $25,000 or more. The costs depend on the design of the home, the scope of the work involved, and construction costs in the community.

The costs will also vary from one house to another. Generally, the costliest additions are a bathroom and a kitchen. If the plumbing is already present, either because of a wet-bar in the basement or a partial bathroom in the recreation room, the costs will be less than if it is necessary to start from the beginning.

Additional costs will involve financing the construction, advertising for tenants, maintenance, additional utilities, insurance, and taxes. The rent charged will offset some of these ongoing costs, and, depending upon the size of the original outlay, the accessory apartment may pay for itself within a few years.

Financing

Some communities have developed loan programs to assist with the installation of an accessory apartment or to make other changes in homes. Low-interest loans or deferred payment loans (those that don't have to be repaid until the borrower dies, moves, or sells the home) sponsored by government agencies are generally the least expensive form of financing. However, they are often limited to costs of major alterations or repairs that will bring a home up to building codes and standards.

If a commercial loan is secured, potential borrowers should check with a number of lending institutions, as interest rates and terms may vary. The longer the loan term, the lower the monthly payments will be.

Adding an accessory apartment will improve property and is likely to increase the market value of the home. The increased value, however, may result in an increase in property taxes. One study of townships with accessory apartments indicated an average increase of $24 in property taxes per year.

Impact of Rental Income

The income received from an accessory apartment may increase a homeowner's monthly income. However, it may also have an impact on eligibility for public benefit programs and on taxes. The income from an accessory apartment is taxable, so one's taxable income will increase. If the increased income places a homeowner above the income and asset limitations for Supplemental Security Income (SSI) or Medicaid, it may affect the ability to receive these benefits.

There are several tax advantages to managing rental property, including the ability to depreciate the property and deduct the maintenance costs associated with the rental unit. Internal Revenue Service (IRS) Publication 527, *Rental Property*, outlines the details of these tax provisions. It is important to keep accurate records of income and expenses, including remodeling and maintenance costs.

THINGS TO REMEMBER

> Adding an accessory apartment requires that a homeowner take on the responsibilities of being a landlord.
>
> Income from an accessory apartment may affect eligibility for public benefits and will increase taxable income.
>
> Zoning may be a problem. Check local ordinances, but remember that the same ordinance may not apply to all residential districts within a community.
>
> Not all homes may be suitable for conversion to an accessory apartment.

CONSUMER CHECKLIST

____ Has it been determined that second units are permissible under existing zoning laws?

____ Does the house lend itself to conversion to an accessory apartment? Will building a separate entrance, another bathroom, and/or a second kitchen be a sound investment?

____ Will the benefits of renting the accessory apartment compensate for the cost of conversion?

____ Is there an agency or organization in the community that is involved in the development of accessory apartments?

____ Would an arrangement of service exchange with a resident be an optimal situation? What kind of services would be performed and in exchange for how much of a reduction in rent?

____ Is there adequate parking available for both households?

____ How will utility payments be shared?

SOURCE: Reprinted from *Your Home, Your Choice,* 1989, with permission from the American Association of Retired Persons.

Shared Housing

To save money and share chores, people often have adapted their living arrangements, joining with other individuals in a shared household. Today, shared housing is becoming a more viable and acceptable option for persons of all ages, but it may be particularly attractive to older persons. Shared households are established on the basis of a match between persons who have similar or complementary housing needs.

Key Data

- It is estimated that there are 400 shared housing programs in 42 states. Over half are match programs; the rest are group residences (1989).

- In shared housing arrangements, over 70 percent of participants had incomes of $10,000 or less.

- 1 percent of the elderly live with a nonrelated person; 33 percent live alone; 11 percent live with a relative; and 56 percent live with a spouse.

What is shared housing?

Shared housing, or homesharing, is an arrangement by which two or more unrelated people share a dwelling within which each retains a private space. It might involve an owner and a renter or two or more people renting a house or an apartment together. No two homesharing arrangements are alike; each must meet the needs of the individuals involved. For example, some homesharing arrangements may involve an exchange of services in return for reduced rent. Some may entail a straight rental arrangement. Many shared homes are intergenerational, while some are peers sharing a home. Homesharing arrangements may also be comprised of a group residence, in which three to eight people rent or purchase a house, each person having his or her own bedroom and sharing common areas. It is important when considering homesharing as an option that its many possibilities be explored.

When is shared housing appropriate?

Just as homesharing can take many forms, so, too, can it serve many functions. A homesharing arrangement may be attractive because it may either provide the homeowner with a source of income or provide the homesharer a living arrangement with a reasonable rent. Homesharing may also be appealing because of the companionship it affords or because of the opportunity for service exchange. Service exchange refers to the possibility of sharing tasks, such as yard work or meal preparation, in exchange for reduced rent. Sharing a home with someone who can help out with these tasks might be a real asset.

Homesharing arrangements are often intergenerational. Particularly in neighborhoods that are close to universities, homesharing arrangements often involve a college student living with an older person. In exchange for a modest rent, the student will do the grocery shopping, laundry, or other household chores.

The income from a homesharing arrangement can help defray property taxes, utility costs, maintenance and repair expenses, or simply supplement a homeowner's income. Income may not be the primary reason for exploring a homesharing arrangement— the companionship, increase in personal safety, or opportunity to have someone help keep up the house can be very beneficial.

Sharing a home with an unrelated person is not for everyone. The single factor that can contribute to the success or failure of a given homesharing arrangement is compatibility. It is important, therefore, that persons considering homesharing assess their patterns of relating to other people prior to becoming involved in a homesharing arrangement. In addition to life style preferences, characteristics such as ability to communicate, to confront problems and look for reasonable solutions, to be sensitive to other people, and to be flexible and compromise should be assessed. When analyzing any particular homesharing arrangement, it is worthwhile to weigh what may be particularly difficult about a person or situation against what may be the advantages or strengths of a homesharing situation.

It is always a good idea to get to know the other person(s) well enough in advance to decide whether a shared arrangement will work. One should explore differences and similarities and avoid extreme differences that would make living together unwise.

A trial period is advisable. Depending upon what is feasible, a trial period can last a week, a weekend, or a month or two. Any time that can be spent together before making a commitment will be beneficial in the long run.

Once a homeowner and homeseeker have decided to live together, it is important that they have an open discussion about their expectations and individual needs. It is also wise to repeat that discussion periodically, to establish a forum for resolving conflict should it arise or for simply comparing schedules or plans. Some communities have homesharing counseling or match programs (described later) that can assist in this process.

A homesharing arrangement is likely to be successful if the two parties have complementary needs. This may mean someone with a small income or someone who wishes to save money sharing with someone whose needs are for services rather than income. It may mean someone with a car moving in with someone who can no longer drive but needs to make regular visits to a physical therapist. Or it may mean two widows who desire companionship but respect one another's need for privacy. It is important in a shared housing arrangement that people feel they are each benefiting from the situation.

How does one find shared housing?

There are a number of ways to locate shared housing arrangements. The most direct way is probably through a network of match programs. These are generally nonprofit, community-based agencies that match homeowners (or home providers) and homeseekers (or tenants). They conduct an in-depth home interview to determine needs, expectations, and characteristics of each party. This information is then used to match people with complementary interests. Match programs often facilitate introductions and help negotiate contracts or agreements. Some agencies charge a fee; others do not. Often those who do not charge a fee will accept contributions. Many match programs will monitor the shared household for several months, or periodically, to help iron out differences that may arise. To find a match program in a particular area, interested consumers should contact the local or county office on aging or the National Shared Housing Resource Center (listed in Chapter 5).

In spite of the time and effort the match program may put into trying to create a successful match, shared households do not always work. There are always issues or peculiarities that cannot be anticipated.

Shared housing arrangements can also be formed through roommate or housemate referral services. These almost always charge a fee and are often for-profit organizations. Once the match is made, little or no contact is maintained with the referral service. Such an agency can be located in the telephone book.

Another way of finding a shared housing arrangement is through advertisements in local newspapers or on bulletin boards at a church, synagogue, library, or university. These may be more risky, as there is not a third party who has done at least a modest amount of screening. It is important in these situations that individuals do their own screening. A list of questions to ask the person who has advertised for a homesharer should be assembled in advance. References should be requested. And, again, taking time to get to know the person before making a commitment is likely to pay off.

Will zoning be a problem?

In some communities, or in neighborhoods of some communities, there are restrictions on the number of unrelated persons who can occupy a home. Often this is delineated in the way *family* is defined in the zoning ordinance. Family can refer to those who are related by blood, marriage, or adoption, or it can refer to those who are a family of choice. A shared housing arrangement is the latter. Zoning ordinances may also prohibit shared housing because of the code category into which shared housing falls, because of density and parking controls, or because of fire and safety regulations. It is wise to check with the local department of planning or the zoning commission prior to pursuing a homesharing option, to make sure it is permitted under local zoning laws.

Is a lease needed?

The answer is a resounding yes. Whether the homesharer is found through a formal program or on a bulletin board, a lease or a written agreement to share will formalize the arrangements that are otherwise made verbally about rent, services, space, and other matters. The American Association of Retired Persons has developed guidelines for a lease in a homesharing arrangement (see *A Consumer's Guide to Homesharing* in Chapter 6).The National Shared Housing Resource Center has model leases that can be used as examples in drawing up one's own lease (see Chapter 5).

In addition to naming the parties to the lease, a lease in a shared housing arrangement should include the following:

Restrictions on the use of the home

Beginning and ending dates of the agreement

Rent to be paid or services to be performed in lieu of rent

Portion of utility costs to be paid by each party

Use of phone and any costs involved

Right to terminate the lease

How much does shared housing cost?

Because there is so much variety in shared housing arrangements, it is difficult to pinpoint a cost figure. In general, in a shared housing arrangement one can expect to pay considerably less than the cost of an apartment in the area, sometimes as much as 50 percent less. In an arrangement in which services are performed, the rent may be reduced even further. Less rent is paid, but the homesharer is giving up having his or her own living room, dining room, and kitchen, as well as other common areas in the house.

A homeowner or renter wishing to share his or her home may incur the costs of advertising for a homesharer, fixing up or painting the room(s) the homesharer will occupy, and any agency costs, if the homesharer is found through a match agency (see "How Does One Find Shared Housing?"). It is important to realize that sharing a house may have a negative impact on one's eligibility to receive public benefits such as food stamps or SSI (Supplemental Security Income—see the glossary). Individual circumstances can be checked with the local Social Security office, food stamp office, or legal services office.

THINGS TO REMEMBER

Shared housing arrangements are not for everyone. Individual situations and expectations should be considered along with your ability to be flexible.

Zoning is not always favorably inclined toward shared housing arrangements. Check local codes.

Your eligibility for public benefits may be affected by moving into a shared housing arrangement. This may include food stamps, Supplemental Security Income, as well as state or local benefits such as utility assistance. Check eligibility requirements carefully.

CONSUMER CHECKLIST

Following is a list of questions for those considering sharing their homes or apartments.

____ Why do you want to homeshare with someone?

____ Is your home or apartment suitable for sharing? (Is there a private room for sleeping and an easily accessible bathroom? Is there adequate closet or storage space? Are there structural barriers, such as stairs, that might limit who can live in your home?)

____ What must you do to make the space ready for another person? Will the space be furnished or unfurnished?

____ How much rent do you need?

____ Do you need help with household tasks? If yes, which tasks and how much help?

____ If the homesharer is to provide services, by how much should you reduce rent?

____ Are you comfortable sharing your living room, dining room, and kitchen?

____ What household responsibilities do you want to share (housework, gardening, trash removal, laundry, etc.)?

____ What are you looking for in a housemate? Do you have a preference as to age or sex? Would you consider living with children? Do you object to smoking or drinking? How do you feel about pets? What are your housekeeping standards?

____ What kind of relationship do you want with a housemate? Are you looking for a friendly companion or simply a landlord/ tenant relationship?

____ What qualities do you have that might contribute to a shared housing arrangement, and what are your shortcomings for such an arrangement?

Following is a list of questions for those who are interested in sharing someone else's home or apartment.

____ Why do you want to share a home with someone else?

____ What kind of neighborhood do you want to live in?

____ Do you need space that is furnished or would you prefer to take your own furniture?

____ How much rent can you afford? Are you willing to provide services in exchange for a reduced rent?

____ What is essential to you in a housemate? Do you have a preference as to age or sex? Would you consider living with children? Do you object to smoking or drinking? How do you feel about pets? What are your housekeeping standards?

____ What kind of relationship do you want with a housemate? Do you want to be a tenant in a home or are you looking for a companion?

____ What kind of living space do you need? How much private and common space do you need? Do you need space that is free of barriers?

____ Do you need assistance from the person with whom you will be sharing?

____ What qualities do you have that would contribute to a shared housing arrangement, and what are your shortcomings?

SOURCE: Reprinted from *A Consumer's Guide to Homesharing,* 1987, with permission from the American Association of Retired Persons.

Chapter 3

Financial Assistance

For many persons, the problem in their later years is not their ability to physically maintain their homes and their independence, but their financial ability to do so. With reduced incomes in retirement and high costs of maintenance, repair, and utilities, older persons are often strapped financially. A number of programs and services can help, and these are addressed in this chapter.

In surveys of the older population, property taxes, utility and maintenance costs, and high rents are frequently mentioned as burdensome. There are programs that specifically address these high costs and help to reduce them. Some are offered in the private sector by banks or utility companies, some by local governments, and others primarily by the federal government, such as rental assistance.

Home equity conversion programs provide, for the most part, a source of income that is discretionary and can be used to pay any number of day-to-day living expenses. These programs are limited to homeowners, as they are based on tapping the equity in the home.

As with the services and options described in previous chapters, financial assistance programs can really promote independence and help improve quality of life.

Utility Assistance Programs

Many older persons face rising or unpredictable energy costs. Because of the importance of maintaining adequate heating and cooling in the homes of older persons, who may otherwise be subject to health problems, the incidence of high utility bills is problematic. A range of public and private responses to alleviate this burden are among those known as utility assistance programs.

Key Data

- Total fuel-related expenses (home heating/cooling and gasoline) account for more than 10 percent of the total Social Security check of elderly households, whose sole source of income is Social Security, which is slightly higher than the percentage spent by the population as a whole (1988).

- The budget share that older persons spend on fuel-related expenses rises with advanced age.

- Older persons consume less energy than any other age group, but spend a greater proportion of their income on energy consumption. They also pay more per capita than any other age group for energy.

- The elderly account for almost half of all victims of residential hypothermia, which can set in at temperatures that are in the mid-60s. Heat stress is also a problem.

- In 43 states and the District of Columbia, average energy costs in the winter exceeded $100 per month; in 13 states and the District, winter month bills were $150 or more (1988).

What are utility assistance programs?

Utility assistance programs refer to an assortment of programs and services designed to assist with instituting energy conservation measures and in paying utility bills. They are sponsored by local, state, and federal government; by private utilities; and by nonprofit organizations. These programs proliferated in the 1970s, when energy prices soared. They have remained a strong presence among community-based services and have taken hold under the auspices of a number of utility companies.

Energy-related programs range from energy assessments or audits to financial assistance programs to weatherization of homes. The federal approach has fallen under the auspices of two major programs: Low Income Home Energy Assistance Program and the Weatherization Program. The state and local government role has been primarily to implement the federal government's programs, while the private sector response has been varied.

Low Income Home Energy Assistance Program (LIHEAP)

LIHEAP was authorized under Title III of the Crude Oil Windfall Profits Tax of 1980. It provides block grants to states to assist eligible households to offset home energy costs that are excessive in relation to household income. In some states, LIHEAP funds are also used for weatherization. It is administered by the U.S. Department of Health and Human Services. Basic eligibility for the program is limited to those whose income is 150 percent of the existing poverty level. In addition, states have been given broad flexibility in administering the program and have instituted other eligibility criteria as they have deemed appropriate. The maximum amount of assistance allowed per household is $750. Household income, energy costs, and climate are used to determine assistance payments. In fiscal year (FY) 1988, the average benefit nationally was $194, which covers 5.5 to 45.3 percent of annual residential energy costs, depending on the state. Funding for LIHEAP is always limited. It is not an entitlement program; that is, not all those who meet the eligibility criteria are served. However, there are relatively high participation rates among the elderly; 37 percent of participating households contain at least one person aged 60 or over (1987).

Weatherization Program

The Weatherization Program was authorized under Title IV, Part A, of the Energy Conservation and Production Act of 1976. It is administered by the Department of Energy. It was initiated as a way to cushion low-income persons from high and rising energy costs while promoting conservation. The elderly are a priority group in the program. It is a mechanism for low-income persons (persons whose income is 125 percent of the poverty level or less) to have their homes weatherproofed. Weatherproofing refers to insulating, caulking, and other methods of making a home more energy efficient. It is available to both homeowners and renters. The maximum amount allowed for weatherizing a household is $1,000, which includes the cost of materials, support activities, and administrative costs. The Weatherization Program is implemented through federal grants to states, which generally contract with local community action agencies for program operations. Waiting lists for assistance under the federal government prevail.

Weatherization of a home is generally considered to be a good investment that pays off in a number of ways. However, there is great variety in the size of the annual rate of return on the investment and in the years that the payback on the investment takes. At a minimum, weatherization improves the energy efficiency of a home, thereby reducing consumption and, hopefully, creating a more comfortable environment. On a broader scale, improvements made by weatherizing a home are long-lasting. The savings continue to benefit residents long after their weatherization investments, thereby helping to reduce energy consumption and energy bills in the long run. One estimation is that for an average investment of $968 (in 1980 dollars), energy consumption can be reduced by 26 percent and households can realize savings of up to 27 percent in energy bills.

Guaranteed Service Option

Several states have implemented a guaranteed service option. This is a statutory requirement that low-income households that are having trouble meeting their energy bills and that qualify based on other criteria can pay a percentage of monthly income toward their utility bill to guarantee continuation of service. These are often called PIPs (percentage-of-income plans) and are likely to become increasingly available. In some places PIPs operate in conjunction with LIHEAP; that is, the difference between the assigned percentage of income from the household and the actual fuel bill would be covered by the LIHEAP benefit paid on behalf of the household. The other formulation of PIPs carries the unpaid amount as a debt of the household but does not lead to loss of utility service or interruption in fuel deliveries. Similarly, some states have instituted a disconnection moratorium that prohibits utilities from disconnecting service in the winter for nonpayment.

Public and Private Utility Companies

Public and private utility companies have an interest in reducing energy consumption among their residential customers. They have instituted a number of programs, some in response to a public policy mandate, such as lifeline rates, and some in the interest of conservation, public purpose, or improving public image.

The Public Utility Regulatory Policies Act of 1978 required that state public utility commissions investigate and, if warranted, adopt lifeline electric rates. Lifeline rates establish a minimum number of kilowatt hours required for conducting basic necessities and a corresponding special low rate for these kilowatt hours. A number of utilities have adopted such rate structures, although the trend seems to favor a guaranteed service option, described above. One utility offers a rate reduction to persons age 62 or over who use less than 500 kilowatt hours of electricity per month.

Other utilities have adopted time-of-day rates or offpeak rates, to provide lower electricity prices to those households using electricity during offpeak generating hours. This allows customers to reduce their use of electricity during peak generating hours and fulfill their energy needs using less expensive power.

Emergency credit programs and fuel assistance programs assist those who are unable to meet their utility bills. Some involve the establishment of a special budget payment plan. Others request donations from customers and match those donations on the basis of an established ratio. The money collected is used to pay utility bills for customers who are unable to pay.

Many utility companies also encourage weatherization and conservation. A number of utility companies employ financial incentive programs to encourage people to weatherize. They provide no-interest loans, with no repayment for 10 years or until the house is sold, or partial or total weatherization grants for eligible customers. These financial incentive programs are most common in the Northwest for households that heat with electricity.

More frequently, however, utility companies will conduct energy assessments or audits of the homes of customers. This can either be done by a walk-through of the home to look for leaks, insulation, and sources of energy waste or it can be done through the mail with a home heating audit questionnaire, followed by a free computer analysis. Audits or assessments identify areas of energy waste and make suggestions for ways to reduce excess usage. They are generally done at little or no charge to the customer and include recommendations on how to improve the thermal and equipment efficiency in the home.

If a person needed attic insulation or a new oil burner, some utility companies will loan an individual up to $1,500 at a below-market interest rate to make those home energy improvements. Others will provide automatic thermostats at cost, which lower temperatures at night and raise them in the morning. Another alternative is offering free insulation and storm windows, for which the company must be reimbursed without interest when the home is sold. Others will install insulation on electric water heaters at no cost to the customer, weatherstripping, plastic storm windows, or caulking.

Utility companies may also offer incentives and rebates for the purchase of energy-saving equipment, such as the cost of installing insulation; the purchase of energy-efficient water heaters, air conditioners, or heat pumps; or fix-up weatherizing. These may apply in particular, for example, when a customer replaces an old central heating system with a modern, high-efficiency gas furnace or boiler or when an existing gas water heater is replaced. Utility companies also conduct conservation education programs to teach their customers conservation measures to reduce energy consumption.

When are utility assistance programs appropriate?

People who have trouble meeting their utility bills or who anticipate trouble in months or years ahead should consider the assistance programs outlined above. These programs are also appropriate for people concerned about conservation who wish to improve the energy efficiency of their homes. Older people in particular are subject to hypothermia, a condition in which body temperature is abnormally low (i.e., below 95 degrees Fahrenheit), and hyperthermia, and might readily benefit from energy assistance programs.

Eligibility criteria vary considerably. Some programs have no eligibility criteria other than residing within the service area of a given utility. Others have stringent criteria with respect to age, income, or average fuel bills.

How does one find a utility assistance program?

The federal weatherization programs are generally administered under the auspices of a state energy office or a local community action agency. These are listed in local telephone directories under services or government agencies. The Low Income Home Energy Assistance Program is administered by the U.S. Department of Health and Human Services at the federal level and energy offices at the state level. Inquiries can be made to local offices on aging, the state energy or community development office, or local utility companies.

Utility companies often publish pamphlets or brochures about their programs. They frequently distribute these in the monthly bills. The office of public or consumer affairs at each local utility company can provide information about programs. Although not all of these programs are targeted specifically for the elderly, the state or local office on aging is likely to be familiar with those programs that are. Addresses of the state offices on aging are included in Chapter 5. Public service commissions are also likely to be familiar with state laws and programs related to energy assistance.

How much do utility assistance programs cost?

Costs vary depending on the nature of the program. Energy audits are generally free of charge. Loans may range from no-interest to below-market interest rates, depending upon ability to pay. Others may provide labor at cost, but the customer will have to pay for equipment, or vice versa. Consumers should be sure to find out what costs are involved before committing to a program or service. Financial assistance programs generally don't cost the consumer, but have well-defined eligibility criteria.

THINGS TO REMEMBER

Improving the energy efficiency of a home can save money in both the short and long run.

Every utility company has taken a slightly different approach to serving the energy conservation and fuel assistance needs of its customers. Contact the local utility's office of consumer or public affairs for information specific to your utility.

State governments have, in many cases, taken steps to encourage action by utilities. Check with your public service commission for any incentives or mandates that may have been enacted.

Financial assistance programs and weatherization programs are available to those who qualify.

CONSUMER CHECKLIST

Following is an energy-saver checklist to improve the energy efficiency of your home. Many of the suggestions involve little or no cost and can be put into practice immediately.

Attic

____ Check doors and windows for cracks that may need weather-stripping.

Kitchen and Laundry

____ Use major appliances during offpeak hours. Some utilities charge higher rates for peak hour energy usage. Learn your utility company's policy.

____ Check and compare energy efficiency ratings before buying new appliances.

____ Allow dishes in the dishwasher to air dry.

____ Use cold water to flush garbage disposal.

Stove

____ Have pilot lights adjusted so that they burn blue, not yellow, conserving gas.

____ Line burner wells with aluminum foil to reflect heat and cook more efficiently. They can be cleaned more easily too.

____ Cook several small dishes in the oven at one time—store them and reheat later. Or use countertop appliances, as they often use less energy, for small cooking needs.

Refrigerator/Freezer

____ Close a dollar bill in the door of the freezer, the refrigerator, and the oven. If it pulls out easily the appliances are wasting energy and their seals should be replaced.

____ Defrost the freezer when ice is one-quarter inch thick.

____ Clean the coils on back of refrigerator frequently.

____ Let dishes come to room temperature before storing them in the refrigerator or freezer.

Washers and Dryers

____ Vent dryers to the outside.

____ Run full loads or adjust washer water level accordingly.

____ Close laundry room doors when air conditioning is on. Cool this room with fans.

____ Hang clothes outside to dry on nice days.

Bathrooms

____ Fix leaking water faucets. A leak filling a 4-ounce cup in 10 minutes wastes 1,642 gallons a year.

____ Install a flow restrictor in showerheads and aerators in all faucets.

Other Rooms

____ Close doors, heat, and air conditioning vents in unused rooms to minimize energy waste.

Floors

____ Carpet as much floor area as possible to provide comfort and protection from cold flooring, as well as to reduce heat loss. Use rug pads between the carpet and the floor for added protection.

Fireplace/Heating Stoves

____ All fireplaces and furnaces should have an intake valve that supplies the fire with outside air rather than air from within the room.

____ Close the damper when fireplace is not in use.

Lights, Radios, and Televisions

____ Install fluorescent fixtures where possible—they use less energy than incandescent ones.

____ Turn off lights, radios, and TVs when you are not in the room.

Water Heaters

____ Set temperatures at 120–140 degrees.

____ Drain sediments 3–4 times a year.

____ Consider buying a do-it-yourself insulation refit kit or blanket-type insulation for your heater. A $20 investment can pay for itself in 1–4 years. Check instructions carefully.

Heating/Cooling Systems

____ Clean or replace filters regularly.

____ Have your furnace and air conditioner serviced yearly.

____ Have a service technician measure the carbon dioxide in your gas burner. The higher the carbon dioxide, the greater the efficiency of the unit. A 9 percent level is good.

____ Use room air conditioners sparingly. They are the largest consumers of energy dollars in most homes.

Windows and Doors

____ Install storm windows/doors or double-paned glass to reduce energy loss. Staple clear polyethylene plastic film around windows and unused doors in lieu of storm windows/doors.

General

____ Check to see if weatherstripping and caulking are needed by moving a moistened finger slowly around windows, doors, air conditioning units, and attic door. If the finger chills, air is leaking. Weatherstrip or caulk the openings.

—   Set your thermostat at 78 degrees in summer; lower it in the winter to 68 degrees. REMEMBER: Older people often are vulnerable to extreme temperatures. Don't endanger your life by a too high or low thermostat setting. Turn the heat down or the air conditioning up when you are gone for several hours at a time to conserve energy.

—   Don't set a higher temperature to warm up faster or a lower temperature to cool quickly. It only wastes energy.

—   Feel for air drafts around electrical outlets. Inexpensive pads are available, as are plugs for unused sockets.

—   Arrange for trained technicians to conduct a check of the insulation in your attic, walls, and crawl spaces. Installing insulation can be very expensive and professional advice can help determine if it is a worthwhile investment. Check with your area consumer agency or state energy office for possible programs or recommended technicians.

SOURCE: Reprinted from *At Home with Energy,* 1984, 1986, with permission from the American Association of Retired Persons.

Property Tax Relief

Instituting policies to help older persons remain in their homes for as long as they wish is consistent with the high value placed on stability, independence, and homeownership. In keeping with this philosophy, all 50 states and the District of Columbia have instituted some form of property tax relief for older persons. Table 3.1 shows availability of three major types of program by state. In some cases, these programs are applicable to renters as well as homeowners.

Key Data

- Property tax revenues represent 40 percent of all local government revenues.

- The District of Columbia and all states except Hawaii have instituted some policy for property tax relief for older persons and/or persons of limited incomes.

Table 3.1   Property Tax Relief Programs, 1989

STATE	HOMESTEAD EXEMPTION OR CREDIT	CIRCUIT BREAKER	DEFERRAL PROGRAM
Alabama	X		
Alaska	X		
Arizona	X	X	
Arkansas		X	
California	X	X	X
Colorado	X	X	X
Connecticut		X	
Delaware	X		
District of Columbia	X	X	X
Florida	X		X
Georgia	X		X
Idaho	X	X	
Illinois	X	X	X
Indiana	X		
Iowa	X	X	X
Kansas		X	
Kentucky	X		
Louisiana	X		
Maine		X	X
Maryland		X	
Massachusetts	X		X
Michigan		X	X
Minnesota	X	X	
Mississippi	X		
Missouri		X	
Montana	X	X	
Nebraska	X		
Nevada		X	
New Hampshire	X		X
New Jersey	X		
New Mexico	X	X	
New York	X	X	
North Carolina	X		
North Dakota	X	X	X
Ohio	X	X	
Oklahoma	X	X	
Oregon		X	X
Pennsylvania		X	
Rhode Island		X	
South Carolina	X		
South Dakota		X	
Tennessee		X	X
Texas	X		X
Utah	X	X	X
Vermont		X	
Virginia		X	X
Washington	X		X
West Virginia	X	X	
Wisconsin	X	X	X
Wyoming	X		

- Property tax burdens began to rise dramatically in the 1950s and 1960s, when urbanization and the baby boom placed pressure on local governments to provide additional public services, such as elementary and secondary schools.

- In 1975, over nine million families in the United States received some form of property tax relief, totalling $450 million. The average payment per recipient family was $150 per year.

- 26 percent of the older population are renters.

- Renters typically spend a greater percentage of their income on housing than homeowners.

What are property tax relief **programs?**

Property tax relief measures have several objectives. They either reduce the regressivity of the tax, that is, they reduce the unequal burden of a tax on persons who may be paying a greater percentage of their income for property tax than others, or they protect low-income persons from sizable tax liabilities. Other, more indirect benefits are evident in enabling older persons to retain their homes. Property tax relief may also prevent neighborhoods from deteriorating by reducing the amount of income older persons must pay for property taxes and thereby freeing income for home repair.

The property tax relief measures vary from state to state and, in some situations, within a state. Because local governments rely so heavily on property taxes as a needed source of revenue, relief programs have attempted to preserve the property tax while altering its applicability to populations who might be unduly hurt by it. Among these populations are farmers, low-income persons, elderly people, and disabled people.

Homestead Exemption

The Homestead Exemption is the oldest form of property tax relief. It is usually a fixed percentage reduction in the assessed valuation of the primary residence (homestead) of the eligible taxpayer. It can also be in the form of a fixed reduction in the tax bill. While income is not used in calculating the amount of relief to be provided, it may be a criteria in determining eligibility. Generally, ability to pay is not a factor in determining either eligibility or amount of relief.

Homestead exemptions or credits are provided to homeowners in 34 states and the District of Columbia. Two-thirds of these programs are limited to older persons. Some give older persons a greater benefit than the general population; others do not impose any age restrictions. Financing sources vary. Most are locally financed, a lesser number are financed by the state, and fewer still are jointly financed by state and local governments.

Circuit Breakers

While not the oldest form of property tax relief, the circuit breaker is the fastest growing type. A property tax circuit breaker directly reduces the amount of property taxes paid in excess of a percentage of household income. Both income and property tax payments are used in determining eligibility and the amount of relief. When property taxes exceed a prescribed percentage of household income, either the property tax bill is directly reduced or the taxpayer receives a refundable credit against state income taxes or a cash rebate. Sliding scale circuit breakers rebate a percentage of property tax liability, with the rebate being larger for low-income persons. Threshold programs rebate the amount of property taxes that exceed a percentage of income; for example, a threshold program might provide for the rebate of property tax that exceeds anywhere from 3–8 percent of income, depending on the state.

The circuit breaker is generally part of the state income tax process, although several states have chosen to administer it differently. As part of the former process, the applicant files a supplemental statement with the income tax return, listing all forms of income. The state then computes the excessive amount of property tax and either credits the amount or sends a refund check.

Thirty-one states and the District of Columbia have circuit breaker programs. The majority are expanded circuit breakers that are also applicable to renters. They are generally state-financed programs. Most limit participation to older persons, and some give greater percentages to older persons.

Circuit Breakers for Renters

The underlying rationale for providing property tax relief to renters is that a percentage of the rent paid by tenants is dedicated to paying the landlord's property taxes. Renters are, therefore, in some cases afforded the same relief from the property tax burden as homeowners.

This most often applies in circuit breaker programs, in which renters are afforded relief from property taxes when the percentage of rent considered to be devoted to property taxes exceeds a prescribed percentage of their income. For a renter, the percentage of rent that is reasonably expected to go toward payment of property taxes is from 17–30 percent. Once this percentage exceeds the prescribed percentage of their income (ranging from 3–8 percent), the circuit breaker goes into effect.

Relief takes the form of a refundable credit against state income taxes or a cash refund. In the former case, a renter files a supplemental statement with his or her income tax return listing all forms of income. The state determines the excessive amount of property taxes and either credits the amount of relief against the income tax or sends a refund check. In those states in which there is no income tax, and in several additional states, the program is administered separately from any income tax.

States have different income ceilings and may have limits on the amount of rebate or on the amount of eligible property tax liability. States may also have provisions requiring the most relief to be applied to the most needy persons.

Property Tax Deferral

Property tax deferral programs allow older persons who are eligible to defer payment of their property taxes, or a portion of their property taxes, until the home is sold or the homeowner dies. The deferral is secured by a lien and, upon transfer of the home, the taxing jurisdiction collects the unpaid taxes plus accrued interest. The interest rate charged is generally a below-market rate. Homeowners who choose to defer payment of their property taxes are not considered delinquent taxpayers, because they are, in effect, borrowing money from the government to pay taxes. Unlike most loan programs, however, neither points nor fees are charged.

In some states, borrowers must file an application before paying taxes. The state then sends a check to the local tax collector in the individual's behalf or it sends a check to the borrower, made payable jointly to the borrower and the tax collector. In other cases, participants may file an application after they pay their taxes and a check is subsequently sent to the participant in his or her name. Local programs frequently credit the property tax obligation as paid rather than issuing a check after payment. In every case, a lien is placed against the property to secure the debt that is owed.

Eighteen states and the District of Columbia offer property tax deferral programs. The majority are limited to older persons and in most cases eligibility is based on income. They differ in terms of the type of agency that offers them, the manner in which money is handled, and the amount of money that can be borrowed, as well as in criteria for eligibility. Generally, the home must be owned with little or no debt against it. Most property tax deferral programs are state-financed, although a few are authorized by the state, with a local option for participation.

Property Tax Freeze

A freeze is primarily a local program that, in effect, excuses eligible older persons from any future tax increases on the home. The freeze holds fixed the tax rate existing when an individual reaches a certain age—usually 63 or 65 years of age. Any subsequent changes in the locality's tax rate are not imposed on the individual's tax bill unless these changes are less than the base year maximum rate.

When are property tax relief measures appropriate?

Older homeowners who live in areas that have enjoyed high rates of home value appreciation often see their property tax bills rise proportionately. For these individuals, property tax relief may mean the difference between moving and being able to remain in their homes and familiar neighborhoods.

Property tax relief may also be appropriate for persons who wish to free some income to pay for day-to-day expenses, repairs on the home, or a hospital bill. It may add some flexibility for persons who live on fixed incomes.

Most property tax relief programs are an annual election. Each year, on the income tax form or special property tax form, homeowners can decide whether to take advantage of a relief measure. Depending upon individual circumstance, this may change from year to year.

Property tax relief programs are beneficial for renters who are struggling to meet increasing rents. Because it is assumed that landlords pass on their property taxes in the form of higher rents, the circuit breaker program can reduce the amount of one's income devoted to rent.

How does one find property tax relief **programs?**

The best source of information about property tax relief programs in a given state is the state department of revenue or taxation. Local offices to whom taxes are normally paid may also have information about both state and local programs. Both of these offices should be listed in the telephone book under "Government Agencies."

How much does property tax relief **cost?**

Property tax relief is designed to reduce the burden of taxes to individual homeowners. With the exception of property tax deferral, there are no direct costs. It is simply a matter of finding the program or programs that are available and determining one's eligibility.

Property tax deferral programs charge interest on the deferred taxes. Interest rates are generally set, by law, at below-market rates of 6–8 percent and the taxes do not have to be repaid until the home is sold or the homeowner moves or dies. Although most programs allow eligible homeowners to borrow the full amount of their property taxes in any one year, they place a limit on the total amount that can be borrowed against the home. This limit is generally some percent of the home's value or of the amount of equity (value minus debt) that is in the home.

THINGS TO REMEMBER

There are three major types of property tax relief. Some states offer more than one, with six states and the District of Columbia offering all three.

Eligibility criteria differ across states and programs.

Guidelines for these programs change periodically, so it is important to maintain contact with the department of taxation.

Participation in a property tax deferral program could limit your ability to borrow against the home for other purposes.

Renters can avoid paying higher rent, a portion of which is considered to be devoted to property taxes.

You need not pay income taxes to participate in a circuit breaker program if you live in a state in which circuit breakers are extended to renters.

CONSUMER CHECKLIST

____ Are property taxes an increasing burden, causing undue hardship or forcing reductions in expenditures for other necessities?

____ Are rent increases causing an undue hardship on personal financial security?

____ Has the possibility of taking advantage of a relief program to which you may be entitled been fully explored?

____ If the state offers property tax deferral, is the presence of a lien on the property of concern?

____ Is full or partial repayment of deferred property taxes possible with no penalty?

____ Is the amount of income to be released as a result of participation in property tax relief worthwhile?

Rental Assistance

For the older population of renters, keeping up with rent increases, displacement due to condominium conversions, and maintaining a suitable residence can be seemingly insurmountable problems. Federal initiatives over the years have sought to address the needs of renters through various forms of rental assistance programs, including direct payments of rent and construction programs or incentives for the development of low-income housing.

Key Data

- In 1987, about 25 percent of the older population rented.

- In 1987, about 1.3 million families lived in public housing units; about 45 percent of these were elderly.

- About 1.7 million elderly renters with incomes under $5,000 devoted 35 percent or more of their income to housing (1985).

What are rental assistance **programs?**

Rental assistance programs are largely sponsored by the federal government to provide assistance to individuals and families unable to meet the high costs of rent. They take the form of Section 8 certificates, housing vouchers, and public housing. A few states have initiated programs to provide rental assistance directly to their residents, but the availability of these programs is not widespread.

The federal government's involvement in housing assistance for low-income families through the public housing program began in 1937. The goal of housing policy, in general, was set forth in legislation 12 years later that called for the realization of a decent home and suitable living environment for every U.S. family. This goal has been reaffirmed in subsequent legislation enacted in more recent years.

Public Housing

The original of the housing assistance programs, public housing, has been around for five decades. Low-rent projects have been developed, owned, and operated by Public Housing Authorities (PHAs) throughout the country. PHAs are state-chartered, local bodies authorized to provide housing with federal assistance.

PHAs also lease units in existing housing developments or in newly constructed, privately owned buildings.

In recent years, there has been little new construction of public housing units, although there has been some rehabilitation of existing units needing to be brought up to code. Nonetheless, public housing currently houses approximately 1.3 million families, many of whom are elderly. A number of public housing authorities operate public housing specifically for the elderly, rather than for an age-segregated population. Other public housing is targeted to native Americans. In public housing, as in other rental assistance programs, tenants pay no more than 30 percent of their income for rent.

Section 8

An effort to develop alternatives to public housing resulted in a rent-supplement program funded by HUD (the U.S. Department of Housing and Urban Development) that provides greater choice of housing location and type. This program was targeted to elderly or handicapped families, those moving from substandard units, or those forced to relocate by government action or disaster. This rent-supplement or rent certificate program is known as Section 8. Congress sought to eliminate the gap that previously existed among eligible households, which prevented assistance from being given to those whose incomes were too high for entrance into public housing but too low to meet the basic market rent payments.

Section 8, as originally established, is a demand-side subsidy made on behalf of a tenant to a landlord. Prospective tenants must apply for eligibility at a Public Housing Authority. After receiving a certificate of eligibility from the PHA, tenants find their own units. Certificates are for a 15-year term. The payment to the landlord is the difference between the tenant's rent payment (30 percent of income) and an approved contract rent. Contract rent, with few exceptions, cannot exceed a HUD-established fair market rent (FMR). The fair market rent is an amount established based on comparable new and existing units in the community (see the glossary). Units can be publicly or privately owned (although not in a public housing project), but the emphasis is on private ownership. In general, the owner is responsible for all management.

By the end of fiscal year (FY) 1987, 2.2 million units were eligible for receipt of a Section 8 subsidy payment. Over half of those in existing housing and over two-thirds in newly constructed units were designated for the elderly and handicapped.

Housing Vouchers

The Housing Voucher, while part of the Section 8 program, is a more recent twist to providing rental assistance. In the voucher program, HUD pays the difference between 30 percent of the tenant's income and a rent standard, which is the same as the fair market rent. The contract rent, however, is negotiated between the tenant and landlord and the tenant pays the difference between the contract rent and the voucher amount. Depending upon whether the contract rent is higher or lower than the rent standard, this rent may be more or less than 30 percent of income. Thus, the HUD payment or voucher amount is fixed and the tenant payment depends on the results of the negotiation between landlord and tenant. (In the Section 8 program, on the other hand, the tenant's rent payment is fixed at 30 percent of his or her adjusted income and HUD pays the difference between that amount and the contract rent.)

The maximum term for a voucher is five years. The landlord is not prohibited from raising the rent to cover increased costs, but if adjustments to the voucher amount are not made by the PHA the tenant has to meet the additional payment. Since its inception as a demonstration program in 1983, over 100,000 vouchers have been issued.

Housing for the Elderly and Handicapped

This program, commonly known as Section 202, was authorized in 1959. It is the principal program serving lower income elderly and handicapped persons and families. HUD provides low-interest loans to nonprofit developers to build or convert existing structures to rental units. All units built since 1974 have rental assistance through the Section 8 program. In other words, at least 20 percent of residents of Section 202 housing pay no more than 30 percent of their income for rent, and the remainder is subsidized by HUD. Residents must be age 62 or over, or else handicapped, and have incomes under 80 percent of the local median income adjusted for family size. All Section 202 projects are designed to house the elderly and handicapped and include ramps, grab bars, and intercoms to call for assistance, if needed.

Sponsors of Section 202 projects are often religiously affiliated or community organizations. As of the end of fiscal year (FY) 1986, 152,000 units had been completed with commitments of Section 8 certificates in over 2,500 projects.

Congregate Housing Services Program

In 1978, Congress authorized funding for congregate services to be provided in Section 202 projects or public housing for the elderly. Congregate services include meals, transportation, housekeeping, and care management services. The aim of the services is to enable the elderly to live more independently. It has, in fact, been shown to avoid premature placement in a nursing home. Because of minimal funding, the Congregate Housing Program has only been able to serve residents of 63 projects.

Farmers Home Administration

The Farmers Home Administration administers a direct loan program known as the Section 515 program, Rural Rental Housing. Unlike the 202 program, sponsors must be developing housing in rural communities and are not restricted by a nonprofit status. Sponsors may be individuals, public or private nonprofit corporations, public bodies, or profit-making bodies. Under the 515 program, direct loans are made at a market interest rate. Residents have no limits in terms of income or assets, except those related to Section 8. Section 8 may be used in conjunction with these projects. Community size is limited to 20,000 or less if located outside a standard metropolitan statistical area or to 10,000 or less for communities that are rural in character but fall within a standard metropolitan statistical area.

Other Federal Programs

The federal government also provides insured mortgage loans under Section 231 as an incentive to develop new low-income facilities. There are no restrictions on the type of housing sponsor. Residents are not restricted by income or assets unless the project is connected with the use of Section 8 rent subsidies.

When is rental assistance appropriate?

Rental assistance is designed for those who, because of very low or low incomes, have trouble otherwise paying rent. Eligible households are those with incomes no higher than 80 percent of the median in the area, adjusted for family size. In addition, rent assistance programs serve those with very low incomes, that is, under 50 percent of the median. In an attempt to target aid to the most needy, 75 percent of all Section 8 projects subsidized before 1983, and 90 percent of all projects subsidized after that year, must be rented to very low income families. Preference is given to families who occupy substandard housing, are involuntarily displaced, or are paying over 50 percent of their income for rent.

In order to be eligible for occupancy in a Section 202 project, one member of the family must be 62 years of age or handicapped. Single persons over age 18 who are handicapped are also eligible for a Section 202 apartment. If two or more elderly or handicapped persons are living together, or if an elderly or handicapped person is living with someone determined by HUD (based on a physician's certificate) to be essential to his or her care or well-being, then that person will also be eligible.

How does one find rental assistance?

Public housing, Section 8 certificates, and housing vouchers are issued or managed by Public Housing Authorities. Most communities or counties around the country have Public Housing Authorities (PHAs). The address and phone number should be listed in the telephone book.

Once the local PHA receives an allocation of rental assistance payments from either the HUD field office or a state housing finance agency, it is responsible for informing prospective families of the program, processing their applications, and certifying their eligibility. If an applicant is eligible, he or she will be given a unit, a rent certificate, or a housing voucher or will be placed on a waiting list. It is important to realize that there are many more people eligible for and in need of rental housing than there are certificates or units. Waiting lists are not uncommon.

Certificates for Section 8 and vouchers are valid for a limited time, usually 60 days, during which the eligible family or individual is expected to lease a dwelling unit. If one is unable to locate a unit within that time, it is often necessary to return the certificate and lose the opportunity to obtain a subsidized unit.

Low-income housing or facilities for the elderly can be found by contacting the local office on aging or the state office of the American Association of Homes for the Aging (addresses are listed in Chapter 5).

How much does rental assistance cost?

With the exception of voucher programs, tenant rent payments are currently set uniformly at 30 percent of adjusted income. This rent includes both shelter rent and payments for utilities (except for telephone). If units are metered separately so that the tenant pays his or her own utility bills, adjustments are made in the rent paid to the landlord.

THINGS TO REMEMBER

Long waiting lists often plague rental assistance programs. Be prepared to wait for a unit or certificate.

Housing vouchers require that the recipient negotiate a rent payment level with the landlord. Determine what you can pay before discussing the potential rent with the landlord.

Having a live-in caregiver will not eliminate your eligibility for Section 202 housing.

The Public Housing Authority has the responsibility of inspecting units to be sure they conform to HUD standards.

CONSUMER CHECKLIST

____ How much of your income is currently spent on housing?

____ Is there a waiting list for public housing units and rent certificates? Has an application been filed to be placed on this list?

____ Have other housing projects been located and an application been filed with each administrator?

___ Periodically check with the Public Housing Authority or Section 202 project administrator to learn about your progress on the waiting list.

___ Are services available in the project being considered? (In all but a very few Section 202 units, services are unavailable. It is expected that residents will live independently. Consequently, residents must locate the services they need in the community. No two projects are alike in this regard, so it is important to request information from the facility administrator regarding what additional services may be available.)

Home Equity Conversion

Home equity conversion is a mechanism that allows older homeowners to convert the equity in their homes into a cash resource while continuing to live in their homes. For most older persons, their house is their single largest financial asset. Many, however, find themselves in a position of being unable to meet day-to-day living expenses because of low incomes and large expenses. The equity in their homes could assist them in meeting these expenses. Until home equity conversion was introduced almost a decade ago, the only way older persons could access the equity in their homes was to sell the home and move. This is not the preferred housing choice of most older persons, who wish to remain in their homes for as long as they can.

Key Data

- 74 percent of the older population (age 65 and over) are homeowners. Over three-fourths of these homeowners own their homes free and clear of mortgage debt.

- The average equity locked in the homes of older persons is in excess of $60,000.

What is home equity conversion?

Home equity conversion is a term describing two basic types of financial instruments: loans and sales. Like all financial instruments, they have costs and they involve some degree of risk.

They are also not yet widely available, although there is increasing interest among policymakers, state governments, and private lenders in making these more accessible.

Loan Plans

Loan plans fall under two general categories: special purpose loans and reverse mortgages.

SPECIAL PURPOSE LOANS   These are the most widely available and most frequently used home equity conversion plans. The proceeds from the loans must be used for specific purposes, such as home repair or property tax deferral. However, what also distinguishes them from other types of loans is that they do not have to be paid back until the borrower dies, moves, or sells the home. They are usually offered by government agencies or private non-profit organizations.

The deferred payment loan is designed for repairing or improving a home. There is generally no interest or very low interest charged on these loans. The obligation to repay the loan is deferred until the borrower leaves the home, either because of death, sale, or voluntary relocation.

Deferred payment loans are most often made by government organizations and they vary from jurisdiction to jurisdiction as to availability, eligibility, interest rates, and specific purpose for which the funds may be used. Generally, income and assets of a potential borrower must be below certain levels. There may also be limits on the value of the home and the amount of debt against the home. In some programs, there is a minimum age. In most states, deferred payment loans can be used for repairs and improvements to make a home safer, more accessible or usable, or more energy efficient. These loans are usually not for cosmetic changes or interior decorating.

Deferred payment loans are generally offered at below-market interest rates or no interest, with no loan fees or points. The types of repairs allowed might increase the value of the home, so that even at a nominal interest rate the deferred payment loan might pay for itself. The biggest drawback is availability and eligibility. They are not widely available.

PROPERTY TAX DEFERRAL   The most widely available deferred payment loans are property tax deferral programs, described in

"Property Tax Relief." These let homeowners borrow money against their homes to pay for property taxes. The money borrowed does not have to be repaid until the borrower dies or sells the home.

REVERSE MORTGAGE   The most widely known type of home equity conversion is the reverse mortgage. It works much like a standard mortgage loan, only in reverse. To be eligible for a reverse mortgage, a borrower must own his or her home free and clear of mortgage debt, or nearly so. The reverse mortgage is paid out either in monthly payments over a period of years or as a line of credit. The money received, plus interest, does not have to be repaid until a predetermined period of time, often until the borrower dies or sells the home. At that time, the loan advances plus interest must be repaid.

There are several different types of reverse mortgages, although they all have certain characteristics in common. These are rising debt loans, meaning that the total amount owed grows larger over time. This is because additional payments are received each month and interest is compounded on those payments. Over a long period of time, the growing nature of the reverse mortgage balance produces a substantial amount of debt.

Reverse mortgages are also similar in that the amount of money that can be paid out in monthly advances or in a line of credit is related to the amount of equity in the home, the interest on the loan, and the loan term. In general, the more equity one has the greater will be the loan advances. However, the higher the interest rate and the longer the loan term, the smaller the advances can be.

Reverse mortgages will generally provide a larger lump sum payment at the outset. Often, this is used to pay off existing debt or any fees associated with the reverse mortgage. All forms of reverse mortgages are due and payable when the borrower dies, sells, or moves away from the home. In some cases, the reverse mortgage will be due before any of those events, after a predetermined number of years has past.

Most reverse mortgages are limited by the value of the home, that is, they are nonrecourse loans. This means that the lender cannot require repayment from any assets other than the home. The borrower keeps title to the home with a reverse mortgage; at no point does the home change hands. Also, because the borrower does not owe anything until the end of the loan term, he or she cannot miss a payment and, therefore, the lender cannot foreclose on the loan.

TERM REVERSE MORTGAGE   The term reverse mortgage provides monthly loan advances for a fixed number of years, usually at least three but no more than twelve. All principal advances and interest are due when the term of the loan is over. Ordinarily, this requires sale of the home. There are three key features of a term reverse mortgage. The amount one can get from a reverse mortgage depends upon the value of the home; when interest rates are higher, loan advances must be lower; and the shorter the loan term, the larger the monthly payments can be because the same amount of money is being spread out over a shorter period of time.

Because the loan is due and payable on a specific date, it is important that the borrower make plans for living and financial arrangements before taking out the loan. These loans are best suited for people who need more monthly income for a limited and definite period of time and who expect to sell their homes when that period is over.

SPLIT TERM REVERSE MORTGAGE   In the split term reverse mortgage, loan advances are guaranteed for a fixed term of years and are scheduled to stop on a specific date. But, unlike the term reverse mortgage, loan repayment is not due until the borrower dies, moves, or sells the home. This means the borrower can remain living in his or her home long past the loan term. In one split term reverse mortgage offered by the state of Connecticut, the term is always for 10 years. In another, offered by the state of Rhode Island, borrowers can select a term of either 10, 15, or 20 years.

OPEN-ENDED REVERSE MORTGAGE   The open-ended reverse mortgage is distinguished from the others in several ways. It provides monthly loan advances for as long as the borrower lives in the home and defers all repayment until the borrower dies, moves, or sells. In exchange for this open-ended nature and payment guarantee, the borrower, in some cases, must agree to share some of the future appreciation in the home's value. In other cases, the lender may charge a substantial upfront payment that may be financed along with the loan balance. These costs are in addition to the interest charged on the monthly payments. It compensates the lender for the risk that the borrower could live so long and the home could appreciate so little that the loan balance would exceed the home's value.

When appreciation is shared, before the loan is made, the borrower decides what percentage of future appreciation will be paid to the lender when the loan is over. The greater the percentage selected, the higher will be the appreciation paid to the lender, and the higher will be the monthly payments to the borrower.

There are similar reverse mortgages that provide payments for as long as the borrower resides in the home but do not require the borrower to select a percentage of the appreciation they will share at the outset. Instead, these programs evaluate the value of the home when the loan is over for repayment. In other words, appreciation is not shared unless the loan balance exceeds the original value of the home.

LINE-OF-CREDIT REVERSE MORTGAGE   Another kind of reverse-mortgage is referred to as a line-of-credit reverse mortgage. The line of credit works like a revolving credit plan except that no repayment is required of principal or interest until the borrower dies, sells, or moves. The money borrowed is generally used for emergency or periodic expenses, such as property taxes, hospital bills, or home repair.

In a line of credit, the amount of money a borrower can withdraw is generally limited in several ways. First, a borrower can only make a certain number of withdrawals a year. Second, the amount that can be withdrawn at any one time will be limited, and third, the total cumulative amount that can be withdrawn is also limited. The total limit is related to the value of the home; it is likely to increase as the borrower gets older.

INSURED REVERSE MORTGAGE   In the fall of 1989, the federal government began to insure reverse mortgages on a demonstration basis. The insurance provides lenders and borrowers with greater protection against the risks of reverse mortgage lending and borrowing and has encouraged more lenders to get involved. The insurance has established guidelines for the monthly advances or lump sum payments that can be made in relation to age, marital status, and home value. A corresponding premium is charged on each reverse mortgage and placed in an insurance account. If a borrower lives so long or the home appreciates so little that the borrower would otherwise owe more than the home is worth, the insurance account would compensate the lender for some or all of the difference. No repayment is required of borrowers of insured reverse mortgages until the borrower dies, moves, or sells the home. Because the borrower is assuming some of the costs of insurance, payments tend to be lower than in non–federally insured reverse mortgages.

Sale Plans

Home equity conversion sale plans allow the borrower to remain living in the home while receiving purchase payments from the buyer. There are two basic sale plans: the sale leaseback and the life estate.

SALE LEASEBACK   In a sale leaseback, the homeowner sells his or her home to a buyer, who then leases it back for life. The owner becomes a renter in his or her own home with a lifetime lease. The amount paid each month for rent is less than the monthly purchase payment received from the buyer, so there is a net gain in cash received each month. In addition, the seller is no longer a homeowner and, therefore, not responsible for property taxes, insurance, major maintenance, or repairs.

The most difficult part of a sale leaseback has been finding a buyer willing to buy a home and delay taking possession of it indefinitely. The tax advantages of owning rental property have become less attractive from an investor's point of view in recent years. This means that the likely investors are family members or investors who expect there to be substantial appreciation in the home. Once an investor is found, it is necessary to retain an attorney to help carry out the transaction. Three related issues must be negotiated: the lease, the sale, and the financing of the sale.

The terms of the lease are particularly important. It is important to have a lease that includes a contract giving the seller the right to automatically renew the lease for life. It is also important to determine the rate of rent to be paid and the ability of the buyer to raise the rent in future years. Additional lease items are the right to sublet, the responsibility for utility payments, and minor maintenance and repair.

The purchase price of the home generally falls within a market range, that is, what the home would sell for on the open market, with some compensation for the leaseback provision. In some situations, it may be advisable to use a down payment toward the purchase of a deferred payment annuity to insure the seller a lifetime source of income. When payments on the home cease, the seller's income would otherwise be reduced. A deferred payment annuity that takes effect at that time would compensate for that loss of income.

Sale leasebacks, while often difficult to negotiate, allow an older person to remain living in his or her home with a cash resource and without the responsibilities of home ownership.

LIFE ESTATE   In this type of home equity conversion sale plan, the homeowner remains the owner of the home until he or she dies. What is sold is the right to ownership upon death. The real estate term for this is a life estate, and the remaining interest is sold. This means that ownership begins when the homeowner dies. Because life estates do not offer the same tax advantages as a sale leaseback, life estate plans are usually offered by nonprofit organizations, such as hospitals, colleges, and universities. In most cases, these plans include some element of charitable donation; they do not pay the full cash value for the remainder interest. Rather, it is expected that the homeowner will donate all or part of the value of the remainder interest to the nonprofit organization in exchange for gift tax deductions. The advantages and disadvantages of any life estate plan depend largely on the specific details of the plan.

When are home equity conversion **plans appropriate?**

Home equity conversion is designed for older homeowners who wish to remain in their homes but need additional cash to do so. They are appropriate for persons who do not have immediate plans to sell their homes and move and for those who are not concerned about leaving the full value of their estates to their heirs and need cash. Different home equity conversion plans serve slightly different needs within these broad categories, as described above.

How does one find home equity conversion plans?

Reverse mortgages are offered by some private banks, savings and loans, and mortgage companies. In some cases, reverse mortgages are offered by state housing finance agencies. A consumer can contact his or her local office on aging for a list of participating lenders. The American Association of Retired Persons' Home Equity Information Center tracks existing and emerging programs and can provide a list of participating lenders in a given area. The National Center for Home Equity Conversion can do the same (see Chapter 5). For a list of lenders participating in the federal government's reverse mortgage insurance demonstration program, contact the HUD regional office or AARP.

How much do home equity conversion plans cost?

Home equity conversion plans are financial transactions and, therefore, are not without costs. Costs take several forms, depending upon the particular plan. Interest, compounded monthly, is charged. In some cases, additional costs are borne in the form of forgone appreciation. Closing costs are generally financed and do not have to be paid for out-of-pocket by the borrower. However, there may be application fees. In sale plans, there may be sales commissions. The costs of a home equity conversion plan can be very low or very high, depending upon how long the borrower lives and how much the home's value changes.

THINGS TO REMEMBER

Home equity conversion plans are financial transactions and cost money.

The more equity you have in your home, the more you can convert; the more you convert, the less equity will be available in the future.

Homeowners with a large amount of remaining mortgage debt are generally not eligible for home equity conversion.

Each plan works differently and has different costs and benefits.

It is possible to retain some of the equity in the home and not borrow the full amount, if this is desirable.

CONSUMER CHECKLIST

____ For what purpose is a home equity conversion transaction being considered? Are there other ways to achieve the same end?

____ If a deferred payment loan is being considered, do the program's rules allow for the type of repair or improvement needed?

____ How much longer do you intend or expect to remain in your home?

____ Would a deferred payment loan make you ineligible for some other type of home equity conversion in the future?

____ Is it important to leave the home, or a portion of the home, to your heirs?

____ Will the proceeds received from a reverse mortgage affect eligibility for public benefit programs to which you may be entitled? (Note: They will not affect eligibility for SSI or food stamps but may for other benefit programs. It depends whether proceeds from a loan are treated as income.)

____ If a term reverse mortgage is being considered, have plans been made for a living arrangement at the end of the term? (Even if there is sufficient equity remaining in the home, the lender is under no obligation to extend the loan.)

____ Have the advantages and disadvantages of sharing appreciation been fully considered? How much appreciation would be shared?

____ Will the amount of money that could be received from a reverse mortgage or other home equity conversion plan be sufficient to meet your needs? Is it worth the cost?

____ Is there a local home equity conversion counseling service available to help you evaluate whether this option is appropriate?

Chapter 4

Options for Relocating

For an older person who chooses to relocate, a variety of housing options are available, ranging from those that cater to very independent individuals to those that serve a more frail, dependent group. Some options, like condominiums, cooperatives, and manufactured homes offer a limited number of services (such as recreational activities) but a secure environment. Others, such as congregate and assisted living facilities, continuing care retirement communities (CCRCs), and nursing facilities provide a wide range of both housing and services designed to meet various needs, including nutrition, health care, and personal and financial security.

This chapter begins at one end of the spectrum with options most appropriate for independent, mobile older persons and ends with options suitable for those older persons requiring constant care. The first group of options discussed—condominiums, cooperatives, and manufactured homes—are alternatives that usually appeal to independent older persons who want the advantage of homeownership in a safe, secure environment where maintenance is taken care of by someone else.

The next group of options discussed includes congregate housing, assisted living facilities, and continuing care retirement communities. These alternatives represent arrangements that combine varying levels of supportive services, depending on an individual's needs and preferences, in specialized environments. These options are most appropriate for those persons in need of some assistance in order to maintain maximum independence. Finally, nursing facilities are discussed for older persons in need of comprehensive long-term care.

Although the number of options has grown over the past several years, each one needs to be reviewed and assessed, taking into account an individual's needs, preferred life style, and budget.

Condominiums

Strictly speaking, a condominium (often referred to as a condo) is a form of real estate ownership, not a style of housing or living. Unlike a cooperative arrangement, described in the next section, condo owners have separate ownership of an individual living unit. The total cost of owning and maintaining a condo is usually less than buying a home. Condos usually appeal to independent, older persons who may want the advantage (especially the tax deduction) of owning their unit in a safe, secure environment where maintenance is taken care of by someone else. Two important differences between condos and co-ops should be noted:

1. Condo owners are usually responsible for any and all repairs to the interior of the individual unit. Co-op owners may bear such costs collectively.

2. Condo owners are generally not responsible for a neighbor's default.

Although condos differ from co-ops in terms of ownership, neither are likely to offer supportive services.

Key Data

- Condominium owners own real property and hold deeds to the units they purchase plus a fractional interest in the undivided common elements.

- Condominium owners mortgage their property, pay real estate taxes and interest on their mortgages, and deduct them on their tax returns.

- Condominium owners form associations and elect boards of managers to make policy decisions and administer the property.

- Actions of the board of managers and the unit owners are governed by the declaration of condominiums, the bylaws, and the condominium rules and regulations.

- Condominium owners are charged a monthly assessment for maintenance and operations of common areas. They own the interior of their units and a proportional interest in common areas.

What is a condominium?

A condominium is a particular type of real estate ownership. Each owner has full title to his or her individual living unit, plus a share in the grounds, recreational facilities, and other common elements in the complex. The condominium concept has enjoyed popularity in Europe and South America for many years, although it is a relatively recent phenomenon in the United States. Early condominiums date back to ancient Rome. Brazil has had a condominium law since 1928.

Condos come in different forms, from attached row houses and cluster homes to high-rise apartment buildings to mixed housing developments that include some detached houses. Many condos provide community facilities such as swimming pools, tennis courts, and recreation halls. Most complexes are built by developers, but there is a growing trend in some parts of the country toward conversion of existing rental apartments into condominiums.

In addition to holding the deeds to their units, condo owners are responsible for the mortgage, taxes, and maintenance. Each owner pays a share of taxes and maintenance assessments on the common areas. Owners are not responsible for their neighbors' debts. If a neighbor defaults on mortgage payments or fails to pay taxes, the other owners are not affected. All owners in the condo complex are members of the condominium association. The members elect a board of directors that runs the complex. The responsibilities of the association include contracting for the repair and maintenance of common areas, including painting, sewage, garbage disposal, grass cutting, gardening, snow removal, etc.; determining and collecting assessments to pay common expenses and accumulate reserves; managing the unit owners' investments; enforcing the regulations established by the association; and assisting with resident relations in the common environment. The board may choose to hire a professional manager to assist with these responsibilities. The manager attends to the details of maintaining the common areas, leaving individual condo owners free from the maintenance chores of all but their own units.

The basic document that defines and creates the condominium is called the master deed or declaration. This deed defines the separate ownership of individual units and is an affirmation of the shared obligations for the common areas. Deed owners are required to carry adequate insurance protection for the normal risks of fire, liability, and other hazards. There is usually an additional packaged insurance policy on the common areas of the condominium. The master deed also establishes the owners' percentage in the common areas, the number of votes in the condominium association, the amount of assessment for maintenance and operation of common areas, the real estate tax assessments, and the ability to obtain financing from a lending institution. The formulas for these items are specified by state law. Any changes to the master deed must be brought about by unanimous agreement of the condo association. Those considering purchase of a condominium should have an attorney review the deed and other pertinent documents well in advance.

When is a condominium appropriate?

Today, condominiums are proving to be a popular option for smaller families, single and divorced people, and retirees who do not want their lives revolving around the upkeep of a big home. Older persons are often attracted to specific condominium developments because they provide the convenience of low maintenance and services along with amenities such as swimming pools, golf courses, and social activities that match their personal interests. Older persons might also give high priority to the security that may be offered by a condominium development.

However, the very thing that may attract some condominium buyers, for example, communal interest and organization, can be a drawback for others. Condo owners must be prepared to live by the rules and regulations of the condominium association. Prospective buyers are encouraged to check all restrictions to make sure they can live with them. They should pick up a copy of the condominium association's newsletter, talk to some unit owners, and find out how amenable the board is to change and how influential owners are at affecting policy.

How does one find a condominium?

The most obvious place to start shopping for a condominium is with a trusted real estate agent. One can also refer to the real estate section of the local newspaper for a listing of condominiums available for purchase. There are two ways to buy a condominium: Choose a new unit or purchase a previously owned one. Each has advantages and disadvantages. Buying in a new project means there is little financial history to examine. Nonetheless, buyers are wise to check the builder's past ventures and inspect the budget for the current project. Compare the budget to those of similar condominiums in the area.

When considering a used unit, be sure to check the audited financial statements and current budget statements for interest or debt payments. Condominiums are legally required to make their records available for inspection by owners (if they don't have such records something is definitely wrong). Buyers should have their accountants review the audited statements and the bylaws of the condominium association with them prior to making a final decision. One should pay close attention to the item in the audited financials called the reserve fund or the capital replacement fund. This fund shows reserves set aside for repairs and replacements that are the responsibility of the condominium. The balance in the fund should be at least one-half of the current year's budget.

Conversions

Some renters find themselves dealing with condominium conversion. Simply, condominium conversion is the changing of a rental apartment into a unit that is for sale as part of a condominium building. When apartments are converted into condominiums, renters often have the opportunity to purchase one of the condo units at a discount. Tenants who do not want to buy or cannot afford to do so usually face the prospect of moving as the units are sold.

Whether any particular conversion plan is a good deal for tenants depends on many factors: the location and condition of the building, the price, the availability of financing, and alternative accommodations. Usually tenants will pay more for their apartments than the owner or developer did, but less than the price paid by other people buying into the complex. Some cities have passed ordinances that require conversion landlords to continue renting to their older tenants. Experts recommend that tenants undergoing a conversion form a tenants' association and hire an attorney. Such groups enable the tenants to share information about the conversion and discuss the needs of the residents. An association may also provide residents with more leverage in negotiating with developers. Prospective buyers in a conversion should take the same precautions as outside buyers of used units.

How much do condominiums cost?

Some real estate experts estimate the cost of a condo at 10–30 percent less than the cost of a single-family house. The cost for a condominium is lower than a single-family home because less land is allocated for each individual unit of comparable value and because some common walls and facilities are used. The same tax advantages of the conventional home are available to condo owners. These include a tax deduction for interest paid on the principal of a mortgage and for property taxes.

In addition to the costs associated with the purchase, the unit owner will be assessed a monthly maintenance fee. Maintenance fees are usually set annually by the condo association and pro-rated on a monthly basis. Monthly maintenance fees vary greatly from one project to another. What is included in the maintenance fee significantly influences the cost of condominium ownership. Facilities that have an abundance of luxuries and amenities will have higher maintenance fees. Buyers should decide in advance what amenities are important to them and shop for a condo accordingly. For instance, those who plan to go swimming only a few times a year may not be willing to help pay for a swimming pool, the liability insurance, the lifeguard, and other costs that go with it. Such individuals may be better off in a project without that amenity and its costs.

Buyers also need to consider insurance. Prospective buyers should check the deed or bylaws for provisions requiring hazard or liability insurance. The insurance policy should also be checked to determine the amount of coverage and deductible amount. The condo association needs liability coverage for the entire premises, on personnel such as garage attendants, and also on machinery. Individual owners are responsible for maintaining comprehensive insurance on their own units.

Financing

Financing a condo is no different from financing a single-family home. Buyers must qualify for a mortgage, pay closing costs and legal fees, and continue to pay taxes on their units. Conventional mortgages and Federal Housing Administration (FHA) and Veterans Administration (VA) loans are generally available to qualified buyers. Banks, savings and loan institutions, and insurance companies are all permitted to lend to condominiums. Because there are many more risks for lenders due to such things as maintenance, insurance, and condo association decisions that are beyond the lenders' control, some lenders will not handle condos and others require larger down payments.

Mortgage lenders usually require mortgage insurance to protect them for as much as 25 percent of the unit price in case a buyer defaults. Conventional mortgage insurance is supplied by a mortgage insurance company chosen by the lender. FHA insurance is the most widely known form of federal mortgage insurance.

Developers of new condo complexes may be able to arrange financing for buyers, but it's important to shop for the best deal on a mortgage. Prospective buyers should start with the financial institutions where they do most of their banking. These institutions may have a good mortgage product and certainly would not want to lose a loyal customer's business to a competitor.

A minimum of a 5 percent down payment is required to qualify for a conventional nongovernment mortgage. VA loans have the lowest rates and best terms, requiring no down payment.

However, as the name implies, VA mortgages are exclusively available for qualified veterans.

THINGS TO REMEMBER

A condominium is a business in which you buy shares. Your decisions about purchasing a condo should be based on the same kind of information you would need when buying shares in any company.

Don't rely just on the appeal of a particular unit and community facilities. Do some extensive research, compare several developments, and consult with a lawyer who is experienced in condominium purchases to look over the details before buying.

Talking with other buyers and with people who already live in the development may help you learn more about the community than just talking with the board or developer.

Be sure to obtain copies of the legal documents, operating budgets, yearly financial statements, bylaws, and regulations. For conversion projects, get an engineer's report on the existing building and what repairs and construction might be required. Once you are an owner, you will probably end up subsidizing these repairs through your monthly condo fees.

CONSUMER CHECKLIST

Personal Housing Questions

____ What kind of life style is important to you? How important are leisure, privacy, community, family?

____ What type of housing would you like? What type do you need?

____ What is your housing budget?

____ What about location? How close do you want to be to shopping, neighbors, family, and transportation?

____ Are you ready to participate in a homeowners' association?

____ What type of professional help will you need to get the best buy? Legal? Financial? Engineering?

Legal Aspects

DECLARATION OR MASTER DEED

____ Does the declaration give a complete description of the land, buildings, and units?

____ Is there a description of the common elements? Does the association own them or lease them?

____ What is your percentage of ownership of the common elements? Will there be any change when the project is completed?

____ Can the units and buildings be used for a variety of purposes?

____ How are the units assessed, or what are the maintenance charges? How are monthly fees set, and how can they be changed?

____ Is there a cap on how much these fees can go up during any one calendar year?

____ Is there a management contract in place?

____ What process is in place for amending the declaration?

____ Are there any restrictions on the sale or rental of the units?

____ Are accurate financial records readily available?

Condominium Association

____ How does the association function? Is it possible for the developer to control the association?

____ What are the responsibilities of a condominium owner?

____ Can you abide by the rules and regulations of the bylaws?

____ What percentage of the owners is required for a change in the bylaws? How many owners does this represent?

____ What happens if a condo owner defaults on his or her fees?

____ Are the common elements covered by fire and damage insurance?

____ Are floor plans available? Does the layout suit your needs?

____ Are the floor plans signed by an architect or licensed engineer?

____ Is the living area satisfactory? Floor space? Room size? Storage?

Builders and the Development

NEW CONSTRUCTION

____ What is the developer's track record? Does the developer have adequate funding to complete the project?

____ If the project is not built yet, does the builder have other condominium complexes available for you to tour?

____ What kind of guarantees are available on appliances such as furnaces and water heaters?

CONVERSION

____ Is the development comprised of existing rental apartments that are being converted to condominiums?

____ What is the past record for maintenance? (Examine the written records not just the developer's verbal explanation.)

____ What is the condition of mechanical elements such as plumbing, heating, air conditioning?

____ What is the condition of structural elements such as the roof, insulation, and windows?

____ Is the kitchen equipment new or in good condition?

CONDOMINIUMS IN GENERAL

____ Will the developer retain ownership of any units?

____ How many? How long?

____ Does the developer retain ownership of the recreational facilities, or does ownership pass to the owners' association?

Financial Aspects

____ How much does the unit cost? Is this firm or can it go up by closing time? How much do desired options add to the cost?

____ Is the deposit placed in escrow until closing time? Is it refundable if you cannot get a loan?

____ How available is financing? Are FHA, VA, or conventional mortgages available? How difficult will financing be for a would-be buyer if you decide to sell later?

____ Are extra costs involved for the recreational facilities? Are costs apt to increase?

____ Does the developer retain ownership of them and have the ability to raise the rental fees?

____ Is there an additional charge for their use, for example, membership in a swimming club?

____ Does the condominium owner have any tax advantages? How are joint property taxes assigned? What is the assessed value and tax rate on the unit you are considering?

Attorneys

Before signing anything, have an attorney familiar with condominium documents go over them with you.

____ Have the above questions been answered, especially the legal ones?

____ Have all the state requirements been met?

____ Have all the local code requirements been satisfied?

____ Is the surrounding zoning compatible?

Cooperatives

Unlike with condominiums, an older person buying a cooperative does not own his or her unit outright but shares in the corporation that owns all the property. Co-op owners hold proprietary leases on the specific apartment unit occupied within the complex and pay a proportionate share in the co-op's expenses.

Co-op living is attractive to independent older persons who want some of the financial benefits of homeownership along with a convenient, secure environment that may offer some services. Co-ops tend to be less expensive than the traditional single-family home and more economical to maintain. As mentioned in the introduction to the condominium section, co-op owners are usually not responsible for repairs to the unit. Such costs are usually borne collectively by all the owners; however, co-op owners may be held responsible if a neighbor defaults.

Key Data

- Cooperative (or co-op) owners hold shares or certificates in a corporation rather than holding individual titles to their apartments.

- About a half million people live in co-ops, mainly in the Northeast and in a few large midwestern cities such as Chicago and Detroit.

- Co-ops are operated by homeowners' associations that may employ a management company to handle day-to-day operations.

- Co-ops operate under bylaws that govern the operation of the building and the actions of their board of directors.

- Co-op homeowners are charged a monthly assessment for maintenance and operation of common areas.

- Co-ops are usually financed with cash or personal loans.

- Co-op boards generally have the right to approve or reject prospective shareholders.

What is a cooperative?

Housing cooperatives are nonprofit corporations that own and operate living facilities for the benefit of the occupants. Cooperative housing can be viewed as the middle ground between homeownership and renting. It carries with it many of the advantages of owning a home, including individual control over the unit, but as in rental housing, the responsibility for the maintenance of the building and grounds is left to others. There are two kinds of cooperatives: conventional—where the funding is private—and publicly assisted—where private funding is supplemented by government grants. Cooperative owners do not own their units. Rather, each co-op owner is a shareholder in a cooperative corporation. Owners share the cost of mortgaging, maintaining, and operating the structures, elect directors and officers, and have voices in establishing and enforcing a cooperative policy.

Cooperative housing can consist of one or a combination of the following: high-rise buildings, a group of low-rise or garden apartments, or a group of single-family or duplex homes. Most common is one or more multi-unit buildings on a single lot or on an adjacent parcel of land, often containing 100–300 individual units. Some cooperatives are newly constructed, but others are existing apartment buildings that have been converted or other types of buildings rehabilitated into co-op housing, such as a group of manufactured homes. From 1945–1960 the most popular type of shared environment housing in the United States, not including rental, was the cooperative. This is still true in New York City, but elsewhere the trend is now toward condo ownership.

Co-op owners receive membership certificates in the corporation rather than deeds as in the purchase of a condominium. Each co-op owner has one vote in the corporation that owns the building. Owners also receive proprietary leases that give them the right to occupy their apartments. The leases are usually good for the life of the co-op corporation. The leases specify owner obligations, which are mainly to pay a proportionate share of the corporation's operating expenses, property taxes, and mortgage payments. There is one single blanket mortgage on the building. The mortgage and property taxes are paid by the owners on a pro-rata basis according to the size and value of their units. Co-op shareholders may deduct a proportionate share of the corporation's mortgage, interest, and property taxes from their federal income taxes. The co-op is governed by a board of directors that ranges in number from 5–15, depending upon the size of the project. The board usually has the right to approve or reject prospective buyers of shares, i.e., residents. Co-ops are controlled by state laws, which differ from state to state.

The day-to-day management of the project is usually handled by a professional management company. Responsibilities of the manager include hiring and firing employees, assigning and supervising jobs, collecting rent and fees, keeping records, ordering supplies, securing insurance, paying taxes, and more. The manager oversees maintenance and services and keeps the projects running smoothly. He or she is responsible to the board president.

All leases should grant the shareholders the right to inspect the co-op's corporation, books, records, and papers during business hours. The articles and bylaws should be available. The lease should also ensure that the building is covered by insurance against liability and property damage.

When is a cooperative appropriate?

A cooperative may be a good solution for older people looking for smaller, economical, supportive living arrangements with some of the financial benefits of homeownership. Cooperatives are also convenient because exterior maintenance is usually provided by the building management. Co-ops can also offer an older person services in a secure environment.

One possible disadvantage of a co-op is that the owners are closely tied to each other. If a co-op owner defaults on his or her payments, for instance, the rest may have to make up the deficit. For this reason, financial requirements to become a co-op owner may be very stringent and one may have to make a large cash down payment. All co-op shareholders are responsible for managing the property and are bound by the decisions of the group. If a majority of the owners want a swimming pool all the shareholders will have to pay for it even if some never use it. On the other hand, if the majority refused to pay for repairs, the value of the property may decline. This kind of living may not suit those who do not like meetings and negotiating with neighbors.

How does one find a cooperative?

Those interested in finding a co-op should start by looking for a listing of cooperative organizations in the yellow pages under "Consumer Cooperative Organizations" or "Apartments." One may also ask the local board of realtors, inquire at an area office of the U.S. Department of Housing and Urban Development, or write to the National Association of Housing Cooperatives (see Chapter 5) or to one of its regional or state associations.

How much do cooperatives cost?

The prices of cooperatives vary greatly from one part of the country to another, but are usually in line with local real estate markets. The purchase price of an apartment and monthly fees are dependent upon the number of shares of stock issued for that apartment and are specified in the lease.

Financing

Borrowing money to purchase a co-op may prove to be difficult because buyers do not really own property and therefore do not have a deed to pledge as collateral on a loan. Co-op owners have stock certificates and leases to offer as security to creditors. However, the possession of stock and a lease does not grant occupancy until the would-be resident is approved by the co-op board according to its provisions in the bylaws. Often the prospective co-op buyer's own financial status becomes the basis for the loan. Buyers should start searching for co-op loans at a bank or savings and loan institution they patronize. They might also ask friends or relatives who live in co-ops for referrals. The bank offering financing will investigate the buyer's background and will request income statements and records going back three years, in the form of pay stubs or tax returns.

Lenders will also request copies of the co-op corporation's prospectus and bylaws, the subscription agreement or sales contract, and a statement from the co-op board allowing the use of the stock and lease to secure the loan. A package of all these materials should be assembled for each institution approached. Credit references, bank accounts, credit card accounts, etc., will be required.

Nowadays, banks will generally loan from 60–85 percent of the purchase price of co-ops. A co-op mortgage loan will typically be for a term of 20–30 years. Prospective co-op buyers cannot obtain new financing for their units, but must adhere to the provisions of the single mortgage on the building. If the original mortgage loan is 60 percent paid off, the buyer will have to pay 60 percent of the purchase price of the unit in cash to the seller. Furthermore, the co-op owners cannot refinance their units as condo owners can.

Co-ops can also be financed through government-assisted financing. The Federal Housing Administration (FHA) insures mortgages on cooperative housing projects for five or more dwelling units. FHA-insured funds may be used to build a new co-op housing project or to acquire and rehabilitate existing buildings. FHA also provides technical assistance to cooperative corporations and helps build and operate the project. Furthermore, with FHA insurance, down payments can be significantly reduced.

Sometimes a co-op seller will finance a sale personally with an owner take-back financing. The buyer signs a note with the seller agreeing to the repayment terms, which would likely include some payment of interest. Those interested in this type of agreement need to ask the co-op board what their policy is on owner take-backs.

THINGS TO REMEMBER

Investigate thoroughly all aspects of the co-op management and facts about the unit. It is a good idea to obtain the help of a professional experienced in cooperative operation.

No contract should be signed until a comprehensive physical examination of the property is made.

Check not only the physical condition of a particular unit, but also the physical and financial condition of the entire building.

CONSUMER CHECKLIST

PROSPECTUS/COOPERATIVE PLAN

____ Though complex, these documents contain virtually all of the information needed in order to make an intelligent purchase decision. Be certain you fully understand the purchase procedure described in the plan before you begin negotiating the sale.

FINANCIAL STATEMENTS

____ Check items affecting rent, such as mortgage debt service and the possibility of refinancing in the near future, expenditures made for repairs and improvements, the co-ops cash position, and whether any lawsuits or tax proceedings are pending.

MANAGING AGENT

____ Learn the operating history of the co-op, the nature of tenant complaints, the need for alterations and repairs to the building, what difficulties might arise if you wish to alter your unit, the prices obtained recently for comparable units, and the level of security available to tenants of the building or complex.

CORPORATE PAPERS

____ Determine if the certificate of incorporation and the bylaws comply with Section 216, Internal Revenue Code. Find out if the corporation has the right of first refusal to your shares if you decide to sell.

PROPRIETARY LEASES

____ Be certain of transfer requirements. Examine the use, occupancy, subletting, and default provisions and resolve whether the corporation or the tenant is responsible for repairs to units. Find out if there is an escape clause.

SHAREHOLDER LIST

____ Learn who will be your neighbors. Find out how directors are chosen and the names of directors whose approval is needed for purchase.

THE NEIGHBORHOOD

____ Check out shopping facilities, transportation, churches, and the availability of any other service important to you.

EXTENT OF SERVICES AVAILABLE TO CO-OP

____ Determine the availability of a credit union, optometry services, banks, stores, and medical, legal, and dental services.

Other Questions You Should Ask

____ Are floor plans of units available for inspection?

____ What cash investment is required?

____ Are copies of leases, bylaws, and offering plans available for your lawyer to read prior to signing a subscription agreement?

____ What major appliances are permitted in the apartments?

____ What are the maintenance responsibilities of tenants? Of management?

____ What decorating and furnishings are you expected to provide?

_____ To what extent can you rearrange floor plans or wall decor?

_____ What substantial alterations are allowed? Under what conditions may they be undertaken? Must you have the approval of the board of directors?

_____ How much of a down payment is required when the purchase agreement is signed? What are the conditions of its return?

_____ What is waiting time for a unit?

_____ What parking facilities are available? What are the rules and regulations for tenants? For guests?

Manufactured Homes

Over the last decade manufactured homes have come into their own. The major difference between a manufactured home and a traditional single-family home is that the former are produced in factories. Over half of manufactured homes are located in parks. Some of these manufactured home parks offer a wide range of services, especially if the park is geared toward a retired population.

Manufactured homes, like condos and co-ops, are favored by independent older persons who are attracted to this affordable housing option that provides them a secure living environment while allowing them the independence and privacy of a single-family home.

Key Data

- Approximately 840,000 households headed by older persons (those over 65) live in manufactured homes (1980).

- The average cost to purchase a new manufactured home is $30,000–$75,000.

- 98 percent of manufactured homes are never moved from original sites.

- 50 percent of all manufactured homes are located on rental property.

- There are about 38,000 manufactured home parks nation-wide.

- Monthly fees in manufactured home parks average $450.

- Older manufactured home owners are concentrated in the western states.

What is a manufactured home?

Manufactured housing is a generic term used to describe housing produced in a factory rather than at the actual site. These homes are built to a single national standard found in the federal Manufactured Home Construction and Safety Standards, adopted in 1976 and administered by the U.S. Department of Housing and Urban Development (HUD). This single national standard is referred to as the HUD Code. Manufactured housing is commonly referred to as mobile homes—a name resulting from their evolution from the travel trailers of the 1930s and 1940s. A manufactured home sits on its own foundation and comes complete with bedrooms and a kitchen and bath. It arrives at its site as a finished living unit and usually includes major appliances and furniture. All manufactured homes require installation and connection to appropriate services and facilities at the site, and many have additions such as porches and garages made onsite. Manufactured homes are not easily transported and few are moved after installation.

Manufactured homes have been an important source of housing since they were introduced to the U.S. market in 1930, because they are both economical and easy to maintain. Many older persons now living in manufactured homes sold their conventional homes, bought manufactured homes with cash, and used the remaining funds to supplement their incomes. Although there are now close to a million older persons living in manufactured homes, the proportion of older people in manufactured homes has remained constant (about 5 percent) since 1975.

Although manufactured homes may represent an important alternative for a large number of older persons, the industry has had its problems. For example, some manufactured home parks originally built on undeveloped land are now choice sites for development, which has led to decreasing numbers of park spaces available and increased tensions between park owners and residents.

Those considering a manufactured home should think carefully first about their own needs and what this kind of housing arrangement can offer. The following questions are a good beginning point.

How long can I live in this home?

If I need services will they be available?

Will I feel comfortable living in a manufactured home park?

Types and Styles

Manufactured homes come in all sizes and styles. There are two basic types of manufactured homes ranging in size from 400–2,500 square feet. The smaller of the two types is a single section home, which arrives from the factory as one complete unit. The walls, rooms, and roof are in place. The larger type is the multi-section home, which arrives from the factory in two or more parts that are bolted together onsite. One can purchase a manufactured home with many extras, including fireplaces, cathedral ceilings, sunken bathtubs, even jacuzzis and solar greenhouses. Some new manufactured homes are virtually indistinguishable from conventional homes.

Today, there are more than 180 companies producing manufactured homes in the U.S., with sales centers nationwide offering a wide variety of styles and types. Most manufacturers build homes only to the HUD Code.

When is a manufactured home appropriate?

A manufactured home may be appropriate when one has a limited budget and needs a reliable, steady, monthly shelter expense, wants to own a home, or is looking for a home that's low in cost to operate and has easy maintenance.

How does one find a manufactured home?

One should start shopping for a manufactured home long before the anticipated moving date. A listing of dealers can be found in the yellow pages. One may also contact the Manufactured Housing Institute (see Chapter 5) and ask for a list of dealers. Choosing a reputable retail dealer is key to a successful transaction. The dealer not only will help select a home, but also may be responsible for delivery and installation of the home and may arrange financing, insurance, and service warranties. People living in manufactured homes may be able to provide recommendations of reputable dealers. The local Better Business Bureau or office of consumer affairs may be able to indicate whether a particular dealer has a record of unresolved complaints on file. Buyers should not feel rushed. They should visit several dealers and get an idea of the types of homes in their price ranges. Sample floor plans should be studied by prospective buyers to determine if they will meet the buyers' needs.

Locating a Site for a Manufactured Home

Manufactured home buyers need to decide where the home will be located before the purchase is made. Basically, buyers have three alternatives to choose from:

1. Locate the home on land one owns or intends to buy. Zoning laws should be considered, along with hookup regulations and restrictive covenants. There may be some restrictions that could prohibit a buyer from locating a manufactured home on a particular parcel of land.

2. Locate the home on a leased site in a manufactured home park. If one chooses this option, the company managing the development will usually take care of zoning and regulatory matters.

3. Buy a home already onsite in a planned community.

Manufactured Home Parks

More than half of all manufactured homes are located in manufactured home parks (defined as a group of six or more manufactured homes). Today, there are about 38,000 manufactured home parks across the country. Some parks have adults-only areas, while others have planned services and activities. Many have clubhouses for gatherings and parties. Some have tennis courts and swimming pools. A sense of community can be found in many.

Typically, in manufactured home parks the units are owned by the residents and the land and related improvements—streets, buildings, etc.—are owned by the park owner, to whom homeowners pay a monthly fee to cover lot rental, services and facilities, and real estate taxes. This difference in property status has led to a presumption of legal priority for the park owner and has often led to the homeowners' rights being subordinate to the park owner's rights. Because of this unequal bargaining position, some homeowners have been faced with evictions, excessive fee increases, and unreasonable policies. Some states have passed laws to protect manufactured home owners threatened with eviction. Laws vary from state to state. Buyers concerned with the possibility should check with their state attorney general's offices or Manufactured Home Owners Association (more than 20 states have formed such associations) before choosing a park. There is a small but growing trend toward cooperative or condominium corporation ownership by park residents.

Some parks are specifically targeted to adults or older persons only. The Fair Housing Act Amendments of 1988 prohibit discrimination against families with children and set 55 as the minimum age for 80 percent of the residents of retirement communities. It requires such communities to add "significant facilities and services," such as congregate dining, transportation, and health care, in order to be exempt from allowing younger residents.

Buyers should visit several parks before selecting one. They should ask the management of each park for a fee list as well as for a list of the park's rules and regulations.

How much do manufactured homes cost?

In 1987, the average sales price of a new manufactured home was $23,700. This price covers only the unit itself. In addition, there are several one-time costs buyers need to pay including:

Closing costs. State sales tax, recording fees, proof of insurance, etc. When securing the loan, one must be sure to ask how much closing costs will be.

Moving costs. Transferring the home from the factory to the site. This is sometimes included in the price of the home. One should ask the dealer before buying.

Setup costs. This covers the costs of having a crew actually set up the home. Dealers will provide the information on how much setup costs will add to the manufactured home price.

Furnishings. Manufactured homes will come with a stove and refrigerator and often also with basic furniture. Dealers will provide a description of what furniture is included in the basic price. Items like beds, carpeting, drapes, and extra cabinets may not be included.

Out-buildings. A storage shed or garage will be another one-time cost.

Extras. Extras like concrete steps, awnings, trees, or shrubs will all be additional one-time costs.

Manufactured homes are sold by approximately 10,000 dealers in the United States. These dealers operate similar to the way car dealers operate. They may sell homes built by one or more manufacturers. Dealers offer some or all of the following services: financing, transportation and installation, service and repair, accessories and parts, interior decoration, and home maintenance.

Financing

Before beginning to shop for a manufactured home, the consumer must answer the question: How much home can I afford to buy? One should begin by making a list of needs (the "must haves") *and* wants (the additional necessities). Next, one should determine which of the needs and wants are affordable. One may wish to sit down with a trusted relative or friend to determine his or her income and needs over at least the next five years. A list of monthly costs should include:

Manufactured home mortgage payment

Insurance (fire and theft)

Taxes

Utilities

Maintenance

Lot fees (if home is in a park)

Once the affordable monthly payment has been determined, the next step will be finding a way to finance the purchase. The single largest determinant of a manufactured home price is whether it is purchased with or without the land. This distinction is important in determining the basis for both financing and future financial responsibilities.

Because manufactured homes are not fixed to permanent foundations, they are legally defined as personal property. This means buyers may need to finance their purchases through consumer credit rather than mortgage credit. Some lenders are beginning to offer loans at rates competitive with home mortgage loans. The consumer should contact several local lending institutions to get the best interest rate. Buyers can also make use of Veterans Administration (VA) and Federal Housing Administration (FHA) programs. Use of either the VA or FHA programs may provide longer maturities, lower down payments, and often lower interest rates. Insurance can be financed with the mortgage payments or purchased directly. If financed, interest is paid on the insurance fees.

THINGS TO REMEMBER

Check with the local Better Business Bureau before buying any manufactured home. Ask the dealer for a list of people who have recently bought a manufactured home; give them a call.

The appliances should all be guaranteed under the appliance manufacturer's standard warranty. Refer to the owner's manuals to see what items are covered by which party. Ask questions if it is not clear and get everything in writing.

Make a list of errors or flaws, if any, when moving in and give this list to the dealer.

Check carefully any contract before signing. Be certain that the home delivered is the one that was ordered.

All manufactured homes must be built to the HUD code. Look for the red-and-silver plate placed on the outside of every home certifying that it was built in compliance with HUD standards.

CONSUMER CHECKLIST

Guidelines for Manufactured Home Buying

Be sure to shop carefully before choosing the manufactured home and the park where you will put it. Here are guidelines to follow.

____ Always have a space to put your manufactured home before you purchase the home. Get a written guarantee from the manufactured home park that there is a space reserved for you.

____ Check various brands of manufactured homes before buying. Check local owners' groups for advice. Don't be dazzled by fancy interiors of floor models. Instead, check for sound construction.

The American Association of Retired Persons gives this advice: "Look for wood rather than plastic, for thick walls, floors, and roofs, and for heavy insulation (in a moderate climate, insulation should be at least three-and-a-half inches at the ceiling and two inches in the walls and floors). Ask about the capacity of the water heater. Is the wiring copper? It should be. Do the doors have reinforcements against warping? Are the windows well caulked?"

____ Check the warranties. Though federal law requires a one-year warranty, some makers offer warranties of up to five years, sometimes at an extra cost. Find out what is covered by the warranty and what isn't. Ask for, in writing, the correct procedure for making a warranty claim. Make sure you understand what will be covered by the dealer who sells you the home, by the manufacturers, and by others, such as the company that made the appliances.

___ Check for extra costs. Find out if the sale price includes the cost of transporting the manufactured home to a park and setting it up.

___ Consider buying a manufactured home from an owner who is in the park. If the home is already on a lot, you will save transportation and hookup fees. But don't buy a manufactured home just to get into a park. Beware of parks that require you to buy a manufactured home from a particular dealer. The sale price may be higher than at other dealers.

___ Consider buying a used manufactured home, especially one already in place in an attractive park. The price will be cheaper, and again, you save money in moving and setup costs. Stick to models built since June 1976, when the U.S. Department of Housing and Urban Development began requiring manufactured homes to meet certain quality and safety standards.

___ Consider paying cash if you can afford it. This will reduce your monthly costs. If you need financing, shop around for the best terms. Look for 15-year loans insured by the FHA or, if you are a veteran, guaranteed by the VA. You can get longer-term loans for manufactured homes on permanent sites.

___ Check the taxes. Most states now charge personal property or other special taxes on manufactured homes. Homes on permanent lots may be charged regular property taxes.

___ Shop around for a modern, attractive manufactured home park. Drive around and look at the lots to make sure they aren't too close to each other. Check the streets, the kinds of homes that are parked in the community, the services, and the recreational facilities. Look around to see how far it is to stores, churches, theaters, and police and fire protection.

Also, talk to local real estate agents and find out if homes in the park are appreciating or depreciating.

___ Check all fees. Find out if the park has an entrance fee. Ask if it charges a fee to hook up a manufactured home to utilities. Find out how much you pay each month to rent your lot and for other facilities. Remember, the fancier the amenities, the more you'll probably pay. Make sure you get at least a one-year lease so that you can't be evicted without adequate cause. And check the lease to make sure your fees can't be raised without proper notice.

___ Investigate the park rules. Make sure they won't restrict your life style or your rights as a homeowner or home seller. Are there restrictions on having people visit or stay overnight, on pets, or on certain activities? Are there minimum size and age requirements for manufactured homes allowed in the park? Do homes have to be moved out after they reach a certain age?

___ Talk to current residents and learn if they are satisfied with the park management.

___ Take safety precautions. Make sure your manufactured home has a functioning smoke detector. Check with the local fire department for other safety tips for manufactured homes. If necessary, make sure your home is firmly anchored to protect against high winds.

SOURCE: Reprinted with permission from Michael Sumichrast et al., *Planning Your Retirement Housing,* 1984. Published by Scott, Foresman and Co., Glenview, IL, and the American Association of Retired Persons, Washington, DC.

Retirement Communities

Retirement communities, traditionally located in the sunbelt, are usually age-segregated and emphasize an active, leisure life style. Sometimes called adult communities or retirement villages, these complexes essentially provide only housing and, perhaps, recreational facilities and maintenance services such as gardening. Some communities do have health centers available but on a fee-for-service basis. Retirement communities are different from continuing care retirement communities (CCRCs), described later in this chapter. These communities appeal to older people in the 50–65 age range, whereas the average age of a person moving into a CCRC is about 75. Retirement communities, moreover, may or may not offer health care services on site and do not enter into a contractual agreement with their residents for health care services.

Key Data

- Retirement communities differ greatly but are usually designed for older persons interested in a leisurely but active life style in a self-contained setting.

- Retirement communities are aimed at healthy, usually affluent, older persons.

- Retirement communities often have emergency pull cords in the apartment units but no direct medical supervision.

- The average age of residential retirement community residents is less than 75 years.

What is a retirement community?

A retirement community is a large or small housing complex that provides some services, usually recreational, to its residents. Retirement communities vary greatly, incorporating a wide range of housing options geared primarily to healthy older people. These communities are often geared to adults only or residents of a certain age who can buy or rent all types of housing. An estimated 500,000 or more older persons live in retirement communities, most of them in the sunbelt. Often these communities are designed to be virtually self-contained, with a range of services available to their residents. Two of the largest and most popular are Sun City in Arizona and Leisure World in California.

For example, Sun City in Arizona is an unincorporated town with about 46,000 residents, most of whom are 55 or older (average age is 71). It is a self-contained community, with stores, restaurants, banks, and doctors' offices. It has a golf course, tennis courts, and swimming pools. There are over 130 clubs and activities established and run by residents. In addition, Sun City has a vast array of social, charitable, and civic organizations. Every week, the Sun City newspaper announces meetings, fundraising drives, and awards ceremonies held by the Rotary Club, the Women's Club, and the Civic Association. Residents reside in private homes, condos, and apartments. A new two-bedroom house in Sun City costs from $74,000 to $194,000.

The large retirement communities offer the most extensive network of recreational, commercial, financial, and, sometimes, medical services. Although these communities were not designed to offer extensive services, such as personal assistance, or health care to their residents, some are finding that it may be necessary or advantageous to construct health care facilities on the premises or nearby as their residents age. These types of retirement communities are typically built by large development corporations owning large parcels of land.

Leisure World in Silver Spring, Maryland, for example, has 4,000 residents living in 2,800 single-family homes, apartments, and semi-detached units. Residents must be 50 years old; the median age is 73. Prices of homes start at $60,000 with maintenance fees averaging $150 a month. A variety of educational and recreational programs are offered and a medical center provides routine outpatient services.

When is a retirement community appropriate?

A retirement community may be appropriate for older persons who enjoy living and socializing in a homogeneous community. These types of facilities cater to healthy, independent older people as opposed to those who may need more intense levels of care. Retirement communities offer the advantage of low-maintenance housing as well as a secure environment with plenty of activities. Some retirement communities feature owner-occupied homes or condominiums while others allow residents to rent either single rooms or apartments.

One disadvantage of this type of living arrangement is the lack of integrated age groups. Some older people feel that age-segregated housing will isolate them from the larger community. However, other older people find the companionship of friends with similar backgrounds fosters a comfortable feeling of belonging.

How does one find a retirement community?

There are several directories available (a few are listed in Chapter 6) to prospective residents of retirement communities. These guides usually give comprehensive descriptions of both the type of community and the services offered. One should always visit the community (and plan to spend a couple of days there) before making a final decision.

How much does a retirement community cost?

The cost of living in a retirement community varies with the housing and activities provided. Most require a resident to pay a monthly fee to support services such as grounds, upkeep, building repair, and maintenance. There are additional fees for special types of services and activities.

THINGS TO REMEMBER

If you are thinking of moving to a retirement community, there are several factors you should consider:

Costs both at the present time and in projected fees.

Geographical location, particularly proximity to transportation and family.

Services and facilities provided in the community.

Flexibility of the community to adapt to your needs as they change over time.

Implications and commitments involved in leases or contracts.

Management of the community and the extent to which you as a resident have a role in its governance.

CONSUMER CHECKLIST

Cost

____ Can you afford it? Can you afford to carry the mortgage, if you have one? Do you have a changeable interest rate in your mortgage?

____ Can you afford to pay the fee required to live in the community? What is the condominium fee, if you choose a condo at the retirement community? Who controls the fees—the developer or the owners' association? In estimating your monthly expenses, add 10–20 percent to what the developer suggests you will spend, just to be on the safe side.

____ Is the sales price comparable to other available housing? The cost per square foot should be about the same as for similar housing.

If your home is equipped with special provisions for older people, the cost may be 5–10 percent higher than other comparable housing.

____ Can you resell the units and get appreciation comparable with that of other housing? If they are in an older development, how have the houses appreciated in value over the years? How are they selling now?

____ Is the home you are about to buy fully energy efficient? Insist on knowing the insulation value (R-value), type of windows and doors, and cost of utilities.

____ Find out who has to fix what. Find out what your maintenance responsibilities are and what the owners' association will take care of for you.

Builder

____ Check the builder's reputation. Find out from others (people living there, the homeowners' association or condo association, or resale agents) if the builder has ever built a retirement community before. Has the company built anything before? Is it solvent? Does it pay its bills? What do financial people think of it?

____ Does the developer take care of warranty work? What is the developer's reputation for taking care of complaints promptly and fairly? One of the biggest problems for buyers is that many developers do not finish the units to the customers' satisfaction; they do not take care of the warranty.

____ Is the developer running the management or is the management of the community independent? Find out the management's reputation for running the community and responding to resident requests and complaints.

Don't Buy from Paper

Don't buy without seeing a model or making an actual visit to a house. If this is a condo or co-op and the building is poorly built, your monthly fees will help foot the bill if elevators, roof, concrete work, and so on need repairing or replacing.

____ What is the quality of the product? What do people who live in the community think about their homes? Are they satisfied or do they complain about inferior or unfinished work?

____ Are individual buyers or the community suing the developer for inferior work or unfinished work?

____ What is the durability of the housing and common facilities? Will there be a lot of renovation in the next two or three years? What is the life expectancy of roofs, carpets, appliances, elevators, heating and air conditioning equipment, and other items?

____ What kind of security does the community provide?

____ Insist on inspecting your home at least 14 days before settlement. Make a list of needed work. Go back again before settlement to see whether the work was done. Never go to settlement without all items being taken care of to your satisfaction.

____ Can you easily get from your car to the house? Is there public transportation close by in case you are unable to drive?

____ What is the distance to shopping facilities? Are they close enough that you could walk to get a few things at the grocery store, or must you drive?

____ Is the community very far from cultural activities? How far are you willing to travel to see a movie, a play, or an opera or to go to a good restaurant?

____ Are you willing to help pay for the clubs, recreational activities, and facilities you are least likely to use?

____ What is the development going to turn over to the owners' association after it leaves? What does that mean in terms of increased payments?

____ What restrictions are there on your activities and interests? What are the rules on inviting children and friends, on pets, on freedom to change the unit, on playing music? Are you still free to do the things you were used to doing? Can you live with the rules? Is it worth it?

SOURCE: Adapted from *Planning Your Retirement Housing*, 1984, American Association of Retired Persons.

Congregate Housing

A congregate living facility integrates shelter and services for older persons who may be frail, chronically ill, or socially isolated but do not need the 24-hour supervision provided by assisted living facilities (described in the next section). Whereas condos, co-ops, and manufactured homes attract independent persons from 65–75 years old, congregate housing facilities appeal most to those over 75 years of age who are semi-independent.

Congregate housing is sponsored by both government and private, usually nonprofit, organizations. Although there are a wide variety of styles and services offered by congregate facilities, all share two distinguishing elements: At least one meal a day is provided to the residents in a communal dining room, and access to social and recreational services is offered.

Key Data

- Congregate housing generally provides private living quarters, centrally located meals, and access to social and recreational activities.

- The majority of congregate housing facilities consist of apartment units in a single-story complex that contains space for congregate activities and services required by the residents.

- Occasionally there is a medical office on the premises, staffed by a nurse who is available for blood pressure screening, medical monitoring, and consultation.

- A social director may be available for group activities, assistance with shopping, and access to churches, social, and professional services.

- Linen service and heavy housekeeping will usually be provided or arranged for through management services.

- Residents in congregate housing tend to be 75 or older.

- Assistance with bathing, dressing, or other personal care may also be available, although this is not a routine service.

What is congregate housing?

Congregate housing serves older people who need some assistance in order to continue to live on their own but do not require 24-hour supervision and the kinds of custodial services that an assisted living facility or sheltered care facility provide. These facilities are apartment complexes designed especially for older persons. Some are equipped for handicapped residents, with special provisions for wheelchairs. Usually these complexes provide at least one meal per day, served in a common dining room, and may make available housekeeping and transportation services. Frequently, a congregate living facility will also have a number of health, social, and recreational programs. Although some sponsors include meal packages as part of the rent, most services are optional. Residents can use the services they need while retaining their independence. Although there are various definitions of congregate housing, emphasis is always on a semi-independent life style that inhibits premature institutional care. Congregate housing is seen by many experts as a practical way to achieve a balance between dependence and independence.

The majority of congregate facilities are sponsored by nonprofit organizations or government agencies and vary in size from 35–300 units. There have been hundreds of housing facilities constructed under both the Section 8 Program and the Section 202 Direct Loan Program of the Department of Housing and Urban Development, most without congregate services. Most of these federally financed projects are also sponsored by nonprofit charitable organizations, especially religious and fraternal organizations, and by some local governments. Recently, proprietary developers have begun to build congregate projects.

The Congregate Housing Services Program (CHSP) was authorized in the 1978 Housing and Community Development Act to demonstrate cost-effective assisted independent living to prevent premature or unnecessary institutionalization of elderly and disabled individuals. The program currently funds 63 projects, half of which are Section 202 sponsored and half of which are public housing. At least one meal a day is provided to eligible residents participating in the program, as well as a host of other support services. The program also funds a service coordinator who works with the local volunteer committee to assess the eligibility and needs of the participants. The 1987 Housing and Community Development Act authorized CHSP as a permanent program.

When is congregate housing appropriate?

Congregate housing appeals to a cross section of the older population. A variety of income levels and ethnic groups are represented in congregate projects. It is an excellent arrangement for an older person who wants security and companionship and immediate access to the range of supportive services provided. It is an economical and popular alternative for older people who do not require licensed health facilities but find home maintenance, shopping, cooking, and household duties difficult or impossible to manage.

Congregate housing does have some trade-offs that may make it less attractive to some people. These include changes in neighbors and location, some reduction in privacy, and the altering of one's personal schedule to accommodate group meals and other such activities.

How does one find a congregate housing project?

An older person interested in finding a congregate housing project in his or her community should begin by contacting the local housing department, religious or welfare organizations, or the Area Agency on Aging for information. Telephone numbers for these organizations are usually listed in the yellow pages of telephone directories.

How much does congregate housing cost?

The cost of congregate housing will vary with the type of facility and the number of services a person uses. However, one can expect to pay from $700–$2,000 per month or more. Units in federally sponsored programs for older persons with low incomes are considerably less. Generally, the greater the number of services offered, the higher the cost. In addition to monthly rent payments, at least one meal per day is typically an obligatory expense.

THINGS TO REMEMBER

Each congregate facility will have its own special feeling. Visit several facilities in your area before making a final decision, to see which one suits you best. Consider having some meals at the facility and dropping by at different times during the day.

Take tours of several different units to make sure that the building is generally in good condition before making a selection for an apartment.

Find out exactly what services are and are not covered by a monthly fee and get a listing of the fees for extra services.

Ask about the facility's policy on holding an apartment for a resident recovering from an illness in a nursing home or for someone who leaves the facility for several months for other reasons.

Read the lease carefully before signing to be sure it includes such information as the length and condition of residency, amount of security deposit, and the total monthly fee. Find out how often and how much fees may be increased and if the security deposit is returned upon departure. If the lease is terminated, what is the resident required to do?

CONSUMER CHECKLIST

Services and Costs

____ Make sure the congregate facility provides a complete list of services included in the basic fee and services that are provided at an additional cost.

____ Check to see that the services offered by the facility, either in the basic fee or for an extra charge, include meals and housekeeping, transportation, social activities, counseling, daily telephone monitoring, and recreational activities.

____ Review the lease or contract's provisions for rent increases so you can anticipate what your expenses will be.

Living Environment

____ Will you enjoy sharing meals with other residents?

____ Are meals wholesome and varied and can the kitchen meet your dietary needs?

____ Is there a warm atmosphere in the facility and will you feel secure knowing that there is assistance available when you need it?

____ Does the facility provide drapes and carpeting?

____ Are there restrictions on overnight visitors and are there accommodations for out-of-town guests?

____ Does the management assume responsibility for the security of your personal belongings?

____ Does the facility offer social activities?

____ Is there public or private transportation to and from activities you would enjoy?

____ Is there an activities director on staff or is there a consultant on activities to the facility?

____ Is there a resident council that meets on a regular basis?

Assisted Living Facilities

Assisted living facilities integrate shelter and services for older persons who are often frail and in need of 24-hour supervision. In contrast to congregate housing, assisted living facilities offer a more extensive package of services with an emphasis on meals and personal care. Although there is widespread confusion as to the accurate name for this type of housing alternative, the features found in all such settings are the provision of services and 24-hour supervision. Over the past decade, the assisted living industry has grown in response to movements to prevent institutionalization and provide a more supportive environment than congregate housing but one that is less medically oriented than nursing facilities.

Key Data

- Assisted living facilities vary widely in both style and size. The number of residents served can range from 2–3 people to 150–200 people.

- Assisted living facilities provide rooms, three meals a day, help with activities of daily living, medication monitoring, and some protective supervision.

- Monthly fees can range from $240–$2,500 per month.

- The majority have been operated for profit by individuals or couples. In recent years more nonprofit providers have started sponsoring such facilities.

- The average age of residents is 60–75 years old.

- Licensing requirements vary from state to state.

What is an assisted living facility?

Assisted living facilities (also referred to as adult homes or board and care homes, sheltered care facilities, personal care homes, residential care facilities, and domicilary care facilities) are community-based facilities that can serve as a bridge between congregate housing and nursing home placements. Assisted living facilities typically provide residents with a room, three meals per day (residents eat their meals together), transportation, laundry, housecleaning, 24-hour supervision, and personal assistance with activities such as bathing, dressing, and grooming. Some assisted living facilities provide care not only for older persons but also for physically and mentally disabled people.

The exact number of assisted living facilities in existence is difficult to determine because of the diversity of definitions for these types of facilities and because so many facilities are not licensed. In 1982, the inspector general of the U.S. Department of Health and Human Services estimated that there were 30,000 facilities nationwide, 5,000 of which were unlicensed. The number of facilities in individual states varies from more than 6,000 in California to less than 30 in Texas (U.S. Department of Health and Human Services, Office of the Inspector General, *Board and*

*Care Homes: A Study of Federal and State Actions to Safeguard
the Health and Safety of Board and Care Home Residents, 1982,
p. iv).*

When is an assisted living facility appropriate?

An assisted living facility may be appropriate for those who:

Are in need of help with daily tasks such as bathing and
dressing but want to maintain the highest level of independence

Require an arrangement that addresses both housing and
services needs such as shopping and transportation

Services

Although assisted living facilities have been around a long time,
the number of terms used to describe this living arrangement is
sometimes confusing. When considering this option, it is important to look at the services provided by the facility rather than
relying on the name. The services offered will depend on a resident's needs and the management's ability and willingness to
provide them. If residents are independent and mobile, there may
be fewer services offered. If a facility serves residents who require
constant attention, it will provide more extensive services.

In addition to meals, housekeeping, personal care, and transportation, some assisted living facilities also offer help with making appointments, organizing outings, and managing money.
Often community volunteers give some assistance with companionship or recreational activities. Some assisted living facilities
operated by the state may also offer moving assistance, counseling, health screening, and social support.

Assisted living facilities do not provide nursing care (although
some facilities contract with an outside agency for medical, nursing, and mental health services). Because assisted living facilities
are not medical facilities, the services provided usually are not
reimbursable by Medicare, Medicaid, or private insurance.

Facility Owners/Managers

The majority of assisted living facilities are operated as for-profit
businesses by individuals or couples. However, an increasing

number of facilities are operated by nonprofit organizations. State-operated facilities usually serve mentally handicapped individuals. The facility owner/manager plays an important role in the operation of the facility. He or she is responsible for the residents' well-being. Prospective residents should investigate the track record of the facility owner. Also, the credentials of the managers of any facility being considered should be thoroughly checked before a home is selected. Some owners/operators are required by states to take special training and pass tests before being licensed to operate an assisted living facility.

A "typical" facility manager is a white female in her late forties. Vacant rooms are rented to older persons who need personal care, thus converting her house into an assisted living facility. Some managers choose to live in the facility and assume day-to-day responsibility for the care of the residents. Other owners may hire outside help to run the facility or to perform tasks such as cleaning and cooking. And emerging in greater numbers are owners of businesses operating out of a corporate office, having signed a management contract with a firm responsible for the day-to-day duties of running the facility.

As with any housing arrangement, there is some potential for abuse and neglect in an assisted living facility. This abuse sometimes happens because the facility may be operating illegally and therefore escapes all inspections by regulatory authorities. Another area of abuse results from lack of enforcement of existing statutes.

One should not be misled because a facility is licensed; licensure may not indicate quality. Some residents do not know where to report problems and others may be afraid to turn in an owner/operator. The area where most abuse occurs is in mismanagement of the residents' money by the provider. It is not uncommon for the facility manager to handle the residents' finances. Some residents may even endorse their monthly income checks over to the facility manager, who may deduct the monthly fee and expenses and return spending money to the residents.

Licensing/Regulation

States have the primary responsibility for ensuring safety in assisted living facilities. The level of protection provided by licensure varies *greatly* from state to state, ranging from minimum standards of safety and protection to quality of care standards for resident services.

The variation in regulations is compounded by the fact that several different agencies may be involved in the licensing process. Departments of aging, health, mental health, and public welfare may all have some authority over assisted living facilities in a given state. This layered approach causes both confusion and ineffective enforcement in some states. Facility operators may close their doors when regulations become too onerous, or they may reclassify their facilities to ones that have less stringent regulations. This evasion of regulation makes it difficult for enforcement agencies to track problem facilities and take action.

Several aspects of the assisted living industry make enforcement of regulations difficult. Currently there are no clear professional standards and providers are unorganized. The sheer numbers and types of these facilities enable many to escape the attention of enforcement officials, and the existence of so many small facilities places a heavy burden on facility inspectors.

In the early 1970s, these problems began to receive national attention after a series of facility fires and the exposure of substandard conditions and some abuse of residents. The federal government designed a series of initiatives to help improve the industry. The Keys Amendment to the Social Security Act, in 1976, was the first of these measures. The Keys Amendment, though not providing for direct federal regulation of quality of care or safety standards, attempted to stimulate state efforts to regulate and monitor assisted living facilities. The amendment requires admission policies, safety, sanitation, and civil rights protection for assisted living facilities where three or more Supplemental Security Income (SSI) recipients reside.

Another measure by the federal government designed to strengthen state capability was an amendment to the 1978 Older Americans Act (OAA) that encouraged nursing home ombudsman programs to include advocacy for facility residents. Only a few states considered this voluntary program. Congress has since added a provision in the 1981 OAA amendments requiring state nursing home ombudsmen to investigate complaints about assisted living facilities.

Although the federal government has attempted to play a role in ensuring safety and quality of care for facility residents, no additional federal funds have been made available to the states to improve enforcement and oversight activities. The responsibility, therefore, remains with the states. As mentioned earlier, although a facility may be licensed by the state, it is no guarantee of safety or quality of care; if a facility is not licensed, it does not mean it is operating illegally. Some states do not require facilities with few residents to be licensed, so there may be some small excellent facilities that are not licensed.

Before visiting an assisted living facility, a prospective resident should check with the state's licensing agency to see that the facility is in compliance with all licensing requirements and that all necessary licenses are posted. If they are not, the facility may be operating illegally. Additionally, the long-term care ombudsman should be contacted to see if any complaints have been filed against the facility.

How does one find an assisted living facility?

The state's long-term care ombudsman's office can usually provide a list of local facilities and can answer questions regarding specific facilities, licensing, and regulations. The state regulatory office may also keep a list of facilities in the area and may be able to disclose information on facilities that have experienced licensing problems.

Older persons may also want to contact the state or local office on aging, local housing and community development office, and social service organizations. They should request a list of local assisted living facilities and any firsthand information available on particular facilities. The more information that can be gathered, the more confident one will be of reaching a wise decision.

How much do assisted living facilities cost?

Because there is such great variation in these facilities the monthly fees will also vary greatly. The services provided and location determine, in part, how much one pays for residence in an assisted living facility. Some facilities include services provided in the rent; others charge lower rent and have residents pay on a fee-for-services basis for other amenities. The owner/

operator determines the monthly fees, which can vary from $240 a month to $2,500 a month.

Supplemental Security Income (SSI) payments are made by some states to facility owners for some residents, who receive SSI payments to make up the difference between the monthly fee and their monthly income. SSI recipients should inquire whether their state provides this supplemental payment.

Prospective residents may also want to negotiate a lease with the facility. A month-to-month lease will give both the resident and the provider flexibility and protection should the resident choose to move out of the facility.

THINGS TO REMEMBER

Ask what services are included in the monthly fee and what services cost extra. Ask for a listing of charges for all services so you know how much you'll be paying if you need these services.

Attempt to find a facility convenient to public transportation, shopping, and places of worship. Ask if the facility has rooms for guests.

The facility should offer both sufficient privacy and security. Rooms should have locks. Residents should be able to bring their own furniture.

CONSUMER CHECKLIST

Do the facility rules suit your life style?

____ Are bedrooms and bathrooms shared?

____ Will there be enough privacy? Enough socializing? Enough space for all these activities?

____ Are there restrictions about the use of alcohol and tobacco?

____ Can residents bring their own furnishings?

____ What about pets?

____ Are guests welcome? Is there a space for private get-togethers? What about telephone use?

Where is the facility located?

____ What is the neighborhood like?

____ Does it seem safe in this neighborhood during the day? At night?

____ Are there friends who live nearby?

____ Is the facility near shopping? Near places of worship? If not, is safe and reliable transportation available?

____ Is public transportation easily accessible?

____ Is there a park or recreational facility nearby?

Is the facility licensed?

____ Are all necessary licenses up to date?

____ If the facility is not licensed, is it because a license is not required or is it because the facility is operating illegally?

____ Has any license ever been revoked or suspended? If so, for what reason(s)?

Does the facility appear to be safe?

____ Is there a sprinkler system?

____ Are there smoke detectors? Fire extinguishers? Alarms? Do they ring at the fire station?

____ Are there fire drills?

____ Are the exits accessible, not blocked by furniture?

____ Are the main rooms of the facility or the stairway insulated by a heavy door that is kept closed?

____ How many staff are on duty at night?

____ How would residents get out of their bedrooms in case of fire?

____ Is the staff trained to respond to an emergency?

____ Are stairs and railings in good repair? Is the rest of the facility well-maintained and clean?

____ Is garbage properly disposed? Are there rodents or bugs?

____ Are bathtubs equipped with hand rails?

____ Is a manger on duty 24 hours a day? Is there an emergency call service?

____ Are the manager and staff trained to respond to emergencies such as fire or sudden illness?

____ Are there loose carpets or other obvious hazards?

How is the food service?

____ What meals are provided? On what schedule?

____ Are the meals nutritious and appetizing?

____ Can special dietary needs be met?

____ Can residents keep snacks in their rooms?

____ Are kitchen privileges extended to residents?

Can the facility provide the services you need?

____ Does the facility provide a written service plan for each resident?

____ Are residents consulted regarding a service plan for meals?

____ Is the plan in writing? Is it specific?

____ How often is the plan reviewed?

____ Who else will be involved in preparing a resident's service plan and providing the services? A doctor? A social worker? Family? Anyone else?

____ What outside agencies does the home have arrangements with or access to?

How long has the facility been in business and is it likely to stay in business?

____ Are any financial records available for review?

____ Does the operator of the facility seem to enjoy running it?

____ How recently have improvements been made in the structure or in the provision of services or activities for the residents?

What are the facility's discharge policies?

____ Must residents leave the facility if they need more services, or will the facility contract for them?

____ Will the manager help a resident find a new assisted living facility, or a nursing home, if it is necessary to move?

____ Who makes the decision about whether a resident leaves or stays?

____ If a resident has a prolonged hospital or nursing home stay, will that resident have to continue to pay for his or her room while he or she is away? How long will a room be held for a resident?

Is the facility's manager bonded?

____ If the manager is to handle a resident's money, is she or he trustworthy?

____ Are financial records kept in order and current? How often are residents permitted to review them?

____ Can someone else handle a resident's money, such as a child or a friend?

____ Does the manager of the facility manage the finances of others? Are these people satisfied?

What do the current residents think of the facility?

____ How long have they lived there?

____ What do they find to be satisfying about the facility?

____ Do they have complaints about the facility or the manager? The staff?

SOURCE: Adapted from *A Home Away from Home: Consumer Information on Board and Care Homes,* 1986, with permission from the American Association of Retired Persons.

Continuing Care Retirement Communities (CCRCs)

Continuing care retirement communities (CCRCs) are designed to provide services, personal care, and health care, as needed, as an older person moves along the continuum of care from complete independence to greater dependence to, perhaps, a requirement for skilled nursing care. CCRCs combine all the elements of retirement villages, congregate housing, and assisted living facilities in one campus-like setting. Those concerned about future health needs and medical expenses often seek the security of continuing care retirement communities.

In addition to the 700 CCRCs nationwide, there are also several hundred retirement communities that offer the continuum of care in one location. These communities have a combination of independent housing, convenience services, personal care, and/or health care, but do not have one or both of the distinguishing features of a CCRC: a resident contract and an entrance fee requirement.

Key Data

- There are approximately 700 continuing care retirement communities nationwide.

- CCRCs are found across the country but are most heavily concentrated in California, Florida, Pennsylvania, Ohio, and Illinois.

- Continuing care retirement communities provide the full continuum of housing and long-term care from independent living through nursing home care.

- Almost 95 percent of all continuing care retirement communities are sponsored by non-profit organizations.

What is a continuing care retirement community?

A continuing care retirement community (also known as a life care community) is a retirement community that offers a contract based on an entrance fee. In the contract, the CCRC agrees to provide facilities for independent living and various health care services to an older person who is eligible to remain in the CCRC for the balance of his or her life. The two distinguishing features of a CCRC are the resident contract and the entrance fee. Continuing care contracts are usually grouped into the following three categories:

Extensive. Entrance fee and monthly fees cover the costs of shelter, residential services, and amenities. Also offers long-term nursing care for little or no increase in monthly payments, except for normal operating costs and inflation adjustments.

Modified. Entrance fee and monthly fees cover the costs of shelter, residential services, and amenities, however, only a specified amount of long-term nursing care (usually 15–30 days per year) is provided for little or no increase in monthly payments. After the specified amount of nursing care is used, residents pay either a discounted rate or the full per diem rate for nursing care required.

Fee-for-service. Entrance fee and monthly fees cover the costs of shelter, residential services, amenities, and emergency and infirmary nursing care. Access to long-term nursing care is guaranteed, as it may be required, at full per diem rates.

Each of the above contract types is offered by roughly one-third of the total CCRCs in the country.

The extensive plan is often more expensive, but it is also the most comprehensive. Residents know what they are getting and know the future cost. A fee-for-service plan is less expensive initially, but future costs are unpredictable and will depend upon the amount of care required. The modified plan is in between: The cost of living in the independent unit is predictable, but the cost of long-term nursing care will depend upon the amount needed.

The other distinguishing feature of a CCRC is the entrance fee or endowment fee. Entrance fees usually vary by the size and location of the housing unit. The entrance fee is not for the purchase of a housing unit; a prospective resident is not buying anything tangible like a condominium. Instead, the resident is purchasing a contract for care, and the entrance fee assures him or her of future nursing and medical care. Although CCRC residents may not be purchasing physical housing units with their entrance fees, they are purchasing something that gives them tremendous security. That security is the knowledge that if and when it is needed, long-term care will be available. A CCRC resident knows that a continuum of resources will be applied to a continuum of needs.

Some plans allow for a percentage of the entrance fee to be refunded. CCRC policies differ, but facilities generally choose one of three options:

Nonrefundable. The entrance fee immediately becomes an asset of the CCRC upon payment.

Refundable. A large portion if not all of the entrance fee is refunded to one's estate. Usually these fees are 35–50 percent higher than other entrance fees because the provider receives only the interest income that accumulates while the contract is valid.

Amortized. The CCRC "earns" the entrance fee over a period of five to eight years. The longer a resident lives in a community, the smaller the refund, and, after a specified number of years, no refund is made.

Continuing care is not a new phenomenon. The average age of CCRCs is 19 years, and most communities are generally well established. The original CCRCs evolved from the need to provide a modest but secure retirement for aged ministers, missionaries, and/or single or widowed women. By pooling available resources and raising additional funds from contributors, the sponsoring organizations sought to provide a continuity of care for the balance of residents' lifetimes in community settings, usually old church campgrounds, large private homes, and outdated school and hospital buildings.

CCRCs can be located in urban high-rise buildings, in suburban garden apartments, in small rural facilities, and in every combination thereof. Generally, a CCRC consists of approximately 100–250 apartment units; a central facility that includes a resident dining room and recreational areas; and a health center that contains a combination of personal care, intermediate care, and skilled nursing facilities. In addition, most CCRCs contain an outpatient clinic that provides for the routine health needs of residents.

The large majority of CCRCs today are sponsored by not-for-profit religious or fraternal organizations. A relatively small number of for-profit developers, investors, and corporations are entering the continuing care industry and building and operating CCRCs in which they hold equity interests.

Today, approximately 700 CCRCs market continuing care contracts to older persons and the number is expected to grow in response to the dramatically increasing number of people living and enjoying good health beyond age 75.

Regulation and Accreditation

Thirty-one states have enacted legislation to regulate CCRCs. These laws usually focus on consumer protection and the requirement that communities disclose information about their operations, sponsors, and financial arrangements. In addition, the more comprehensive state laws regulate financial disclosure, contract specifications, reserve funds and escrow requirements, and advertising. There is no uniformity from one state to another as to which state agencies have responsibility to administer these regulations. Federal legislation regulating CCRCs or continuing care contracts has not been enacted.

In addition to legislative safeguards, current and prospective residents can be protected through private accreditation of continuing care retirement communities. Helping consumers find retirement communities that focus on both quality of life and quality of care is a primary goal of the Continuing Care Accreditation Commission (CCAC), the nation's only system for accrediting continuing care retirement communities. Accreditation means that a CCRC has been scrutinized by experts and has been found to meet national standards for quality of care.

The accreditation process is a rigorous one. It involves extensive self-study by the CCRC's staff, board of directors, and residents, all of whom measure the facility against its stated mission and against the established standards of excellence of the continuing care industry. It involves an onsite evaluation by trained continuing care professionals, who analyze and verify the self-study, and cumulates in the review by a national commission based in Washington, D.C. Accreditation provides a seal of approval for continuing care retirement communities able to meet exacting requirements and provides consumers with a standard of comparison for evaluating different CCRCs. The accreditation process is fairly new, however, and many communities have not had the opportunity to be evaluated. Prospective residents should ask if the CCRC they are considering is accredited and, if not, if it intends to apply for accreditation.

When is a CCRC appropriate?

Generally, older people who are still active, capable of getting around on their own, and able to contribute to and enjoy the benefits of community life are good candidates for CCRCs. Older people looking for both a continuing range of services and a level of security about long-term care needs are most likely to be attracted to this type of living arrangement. The typical person moving into a CCRC is 78 years old, is a single or widowed woman in fairly good health, and has been a homeowner. Often an older person will sell his or her home and use the equity as the basis of paying the entrance fee.

How does one find a CCRC?

Older people interested in finding a continuing care retirement community should begin by contacting their state association of homes for the aging, the department of health or insurance, or the state office on aging for more information about CCRCs in their state (see Chapter 5). For details about fees, special features, and services provided by individual communities, consult the *National Continuing Care Directory* (listed in Chapter 6).

How much does a CCRC cost?

Minimum financial requirements are imposed by most CCRCs. When applying to the community, prospective residents must show financial resources sufficient to meet the entrance fee and anticipated monthly fee increases. Complete financial disclosure is not usually necessary. Exact requirements to be met vary depending on the type of services and housing offered, the type of contract and the fees charged for the living unit chosen.

The most common type of continuing care arrangement requires the resident to pay a one-time entrance fee upon entering the facility and to make monthly payments thereafter. These fees vary from place to place depending on the type of contract and services provided. In 1988 an average entrance fee for a one-bedroom unit was $47,500, and the average monthly fee was $830. In addition, the majority of all CCRCs require prospective residents to make a deposit in order to reserve a place in the community. These range from $25 to $5,000, with the average being $1,000. Some continuing care retirement communities require that residents have both Part A and Part B Medicare coverage as well as private insurance. Extensive continuing care contracts cover much of the cost, most significantly the cost of long-term nursing care, not paid by these insurance plans.

THINGS TO REMEMBER

Each continuing care retirement community is unique. You may want to begin your search by looking through the appropriate directories and sending for a full information packet including application for admission, the current fee schedule, and the resident contract from each community that interests you.

Visit as many CCRCs as possible to learn what is available and how they compare. Some CCRCs are large; others are small. Some are well established with solid reputations; others are just beginning. Look for the combination that suits your own needs, preferences, activities, and life style.

When visiting a community, dine with several of the residents. Also talk with members of the staff and read the resident handbook. Assess the management's philosophy and relationship with residents and the sense of community among the residents. Many CCRCs have guest suites where you can spend a night or two to get a better sense of community.

Many communities have waiting lists. If you are particularly interested in a CCRC ask how priority is assigned, whether a deposit is required, and, if so, how it is secured. Get an estimate of how long you would have to wait to move in.

Although accreditation is relatively new to this industry, it is a good way for consumers to compare whether or not a community is committed to excellence. If the community is not accredited, ask management if and when it intends to apply for accreditation. Communities that are just starting and have less than a 90 percent occupancy are not eligible for accreditation.

Find out about the board of directors and who is currently serving on the board. Ask whether or not residents have the opportunity to discuss concerns at board meetings on a regular basis. Learn who currently manages the CCRC. Is there a management company under contract, or does the board hire an administrator? What is the administrator's background? What is the attitude toward the residents?

Inquire how residents are kept informed of the CCRC's financial condition.

Review the applicable state law, if any, that regulates the CCRC contracts and providers in the state where you plan to live. Learn which state department or agency is responsible for enforcing regulations.

CONSUMER CHECKLIST

—— Check with several continuing care retirement communities in your area offering similar services and contracts to determine if the fees are competitive.

—— Find out how you will be expected to pay for the care you receive.

—— Find out under what circumstances, if any, the monthly charges will be raised or lowered.

—— Know what the community's policy is concerning residents who become unable to pay the monthly charges.

—— Make sure any refundable deposit you are required to make in order to reserve accommodations for the future is adequately protected.

—— Receive assurance in writing that any large payment you are making prior to occupancy to reserve accommodations will be returned in full in the event you decide not to enter the community.

—— Learn what insurance coverage is required upon entering the community.

—— Make sure the contract spells out the terms for refunding any fees paid in the event of terminating the contract.

____ Find out what adjustment, if any, will be made in the monthly fee in the event you are transferred to other accommodations within the community, such as the nursing care facility.

____ Find out how long your living unit would be maintained if you were temporarily transferred to other accommodations within the community.

____ Find out what refunds will be made in the event you decide to leave the community voluntarily.

____ Find out whether or not an entrance fee refund is available in the event of your death.

____ Find out the circumstances under which a contract can be terminated by the community.

____ Find out the circumstances under which you can be transferred within the community, and learn how the decision is made.

Community Sponsorship

____ Learn who sponsors or owns the community.

____ Determine the sponsor's financial and other relationships to the community.

____ Find out who is on the board of directors and determine their responsibilities to the community.

Community Management

____ Meet the administrator.

____ Review a copy of the rules and regulations and determine the role residents have in establishing them.

____ Ask for, and make sure you receive, a copy of the most recent government inspection report for any nursing unit the community maintains.

____ Determine whether the community is properly licensed and certified, if required by law.

____ Visit with residents of the community to find out if they are satisfied.

____ Discuss the community with its volunteers and staff.

____ Ask about the admission policies and requirements.

The Community's Financial Condition

____ Discuss with your financial advisor the community's audited annual report, or discuss projected financial statements with appropriate facility personnel.

____ Determine the community's financial condition with your banker, accountant, or another qualified financial advisor.

____ Ask for, and obtain, a copy of a report on the community's most recent financial or actuarial audit.

____ Determine what kinds of reserves are being held by the community and how they are presented on the annual financial audit.

About Shelter, Services, and Care

____ Find out what shelter, services, and care are covered by the terms of the contract.

____ Find out what shelter, services, and care are available only for additional fees.

____ Determine how often each service will be available and be sure this information is stated in the contract.

____ Determine for how long each service will be provided, as stated in the contract.

____ Tour the nursing or health care facilities and meet the medical director and other staff members.

About Signing the Contract

____ Review the contract with your legal representative.

____ Review the contract with the community's administrator or other paid staff member in authority.

SOURCE: Reprinted from *The Continuing Care Retirement Community: A Guidebook for Consumers,* 1984, with permission from the American Association of Homes for the Aging.

Nursing Facilities

Facilities in which older people receive or have available to them 24-hour nursing care are generally referred to as nursing facilities. While these facilities provide many of the elements of shelter, food services, and health care that are present in some retirement communities, nursing facilities are essentially health care facilities that are based on a medical model. Nursing facilities are most appropriate for those persons who require constant health care attention.

Key Data

- More than two million older Americans resided in nursing facilities in 1988.

- Around 19,000 nursing facilities provided care to about 5 percent of the older population of the United States.

- Nursing facility care is the most comprehensive and most expensive long-term care service.

- Medicaid pays a large portion of the cost of nursing facility care for nearly one-half of nursing facility residents in the United States.

- The average length of stay in a nursing facility is 2.5 years.

- In 1986, the average cost per year in a nursing facility was $22,000.

- Almost 50 percent of nursing facility costs are paid for directly by individuals.

What are nursing facilities?

Nursing facilities offer comprehensive long-term care services. Skilled nursing facilities (SNFs) deliver skilled care. Registered or licensed nurses provide 24-hour nursing services that must be prescribed by a physician. Emphasis is on medical care with physical and occupational therapy. Many nursing facilities also offer additional personal care services, such as help with meals, bathing, and grooming, and some regular supervision. Some also have counseling services, religious services, and recreational activities. Older people who need intensive care but do not require hospitalization may be prescribed an SNF by their physicians. These facilities are licensed by the state. Oversight is also provided by the federal government for those facilities that participate in the Medicare and Medicaid programs.

In addition to providing skilled care, some, but not all, nursing facilities may offer intermediate and custodial care. Intermediate care is less extensive than skilled care and is provided by registered and practical nurses on staff. Intermediate care provides basic medical procedures such as those needed by some stroke victims or Alzheimer's patients. Custodial care is nonmedical care such as assistance with dressing, personal hygiene, and grooming.

Facility Ownership

Nursing facilities fall under three categories of ownership:

Profit. Operated specifically to earn a profit for investors (also referred to as proprietary or for-profit nursing facilities). These represent a majority of the industry.

Nonprofit. Operated by religious, fraternal, community, or charitable groups in accordance with nonprofit corporation statutes. These facilities reinvest any cash surpluses they may have to improve operations or buy new equipment.

Government/public nonprofit. Operated by state and local governments and classified as public nonprofit facilities because they are funded through the collection of taxes or the sales of municipal bonds. They are often referred to as county homes, and admissions are often restricted to local residents.

Regulation and Licensing

Local, federal, and state governments regulate nursing care facilities. States inspect nursing facilities at least once a year to determine their compliance with federal and state standards and their qualifications to receive Medicare and Medicaid reimbursement. Inspections ensure that minimum standards for such things as fire protection, maintenance, housekeeping, and direct resident care have been met. Some nursing facilities also choose to participate in an additional quality assurance program through the Joint Commission on Accreditation of Healthcare Organizations (JCAHO).

Although a facility may be licensed, that does not necessarily mean it is delivering high-quality care. It only means that the facility met certain minimum standards on a particular day. Although all facilities must be licensed in order to operate, licenses are not seals of quality care.

Nursing Facility Reform

The Nursing Home Quality Reform Provisions, passed as part of the Omnibus Budget Reconciliation Act of 1987 (OBRA), effected the most sweeping changes for nursing facilities since the implementation of Medicare and Medicaid in 1965. The new law's major provisions, some of which are effective in 1990, include how nursing facilities operate and how they are to be regulated. These provisions will establish a new focus on residents' rights and quality of life and will require interdisciplinary teams of medical providers to do comprehensive patient assessments to guide care in facilities. They will also eliminate the distinction between skilled nursing facilities and intermediate care facilities.

Other major provisions of OBRA include:

As of January 1, 1989, states must establish a registry of nurses' aides who have successfully completed a training and competency evaluation program. The registry must also document findings of abuse, neglect, and misappropriation of residents' property by any nursing facility staff.

After January 1, 1989, states must have pre-admission screening programs for mentally ill or mentally retarded persons seeking admission to a facility. Beginning April 1, 1990, states must conduct annual reviews of each mentally ill or mentally retarded resident.

Beginning July 1, 1989, nursing facilities must provide a training and competency evaluation program for all nurses' aides. All nurses' aides must receive a minimum of 75 hours of training.

By October 1, 1989, OBRA required states to establish intermediate sanctions for facilities that do not meet standards. These sanctions include assessment of fines, denial of payment, monitoring, and appointment of a temporary manager until there is compliance with all requirements.

By October 1, 1990, all facilities must have licensed nurses (registered nurses or licensed practical nurses) present 24 hours a day and a registered nurse on duty at least 8 consecutive hours a day, 7 days a week.

Beginning October 1, 1990, facilities must conduct an assessment of the medical, nursing, and psychosocial needs, and changes in condition of each resident. These assessments are to be reviewed quarterly and upon any significant change in a resident's condition.

Although all facilities are currently inspected periodically, beginning October 1, 1990, state survey agencies will conduct unannounced inspections of nursing facilities at least every 15 months and, on the average, every 12 months. The focus of these surveys will be on residents' care, directly targeting the actual care provided to residents, rather than on paper compliance. Each facility that does not meet federal requirements under a standard survey will be subjected to an extended survey that includes an expanded review of the facility's policies and procedures.

When is a nursing facility appropriate?

Making the decision that nursing facility care is necessary is a difficult one for everybody involved. When disabilities or chronic health problems interfere with an older person's ability to live independently, some decision about the type and setting of care he or she will need must be made. If 24-hour care and supervision are required, the best option may be a nursing facility.

Older people should begin the decision process by talking with their doctors and family members. If a nursing facility appears to be the only solution, family members should seek to find a facility that combines medical efficiency and a reasonable degree of comfort with sensitivity and compassion on the part of the staff. The search for a nursing facility can be nerve-racking because there are too few beds available; waiting lists may be long.

How much do nursing facilities cost?

Nursing facility care is expensive. The cost of a nursing facility stay averages approximately $24,000–$50,000 per year. Financing nursing facility care is an important factor to be considered when planning for a nursing facility stay of any length.

Medicare and Medicaid

Medicare and Medicaid are the two governmental programs that help older persons pay for nursing care expenses. Medicare is the federal government program intended to pay for acute medical care for people 65 years or older. Medicaid is the state-funded program designed to assist people of all ages who are unable to pay health care expenses. Contrary to what many people believe, Medicare does not pay for nursing care over an extended period of time either in a nursing facility or at home. Medicare pays for *limited skilled nursing care under specified conditions.*

The Medicare program has two parts: Part A, Hospital Insurance (HI), provides basic protection against the costs of hospital and some related post-hospital care, home health services, and hospice care; Part B, Supplemental Medical Insurance (SMI), is a voluntary program for which enrollees in Part A pay 80 percent of reasonable charges for medical and related health services.

The requirements for Medicare coverage in a nursing facility are

The person must be in a Medicare-certified facility.

The person must be transferred to the nursing facility and start receiving skilled care within 30 days of being discharged from the hospital.

A claim must be filed by the nursing facility.

A doctor must certify that daily skilled care is needed.

The person must need to be in a nursing facility in order to receive care.

The person must be receiving skilled care for a condition treated in the hospital or that arose while receiving care in the nursing facility for a condition treated in the hospital.

If these strict criteria are met, one can anticipate reimbursement under Medicare. Medicare pays for 100 percent of the covered services for the first 20 days in the nursing facility. From the 21st through the 100th day, the beneficiary is responsible for a co-payment equal to 120 percent of the hospital inpatient deductible. This deductible was $74 in 1990. After Medicare Part A stops paying because of the time limit, Medicare Part B will pay for specialized services such as speech therapy, audiology, physical therapy, and occupational therapy delivered within a skilled nursing facility.

Although many older people have a supplemental Medicare health insurance policy or Medigap policy to help pay for Medicare co-pays and deductibles, these policies do not pay for long-term care either in the home or in a nursing facility unless Medicare pays for some portion. If Medicare does not cover a service, a Medigap policy will not cover it either. Before choosing a nursing facility, older people should read their Medigap policies carefully and be certain of what is and is not covered.

The only significant financial help for long-term nursing facility care comes from Medicaid. The Medicaid program is administered and financed by individual states with matching funds from the federal government. Today, Medicaid pays for almost 50 percent of nursing facility care in the United States. An older person must meet certain income and resource limits as well as medical eligibility criteria in order to qualify for Medicaid. Each state regulates eligibility, application procedures, and services covered. To learn about the state's specific regulations, interested persons can call the local area agency on aging or the county social service department.

Although Medicaid pays for a substantial portion of nursing care costs, the program is limited to those in severe financial need. If a stay in a nursing facility is for a long time and the older person has spent most of his or her assets, Medicaid coverage may be available. Getting to the point where an older person is eligible for Medicaid can be both emotionally and financially difficult. In practical terms, a person must exhaust nearly all of his or her assets before becoming eligible for assistance. Although financial criteria for eligibility differ for each state's program, all programs require income and asset limits. If a couple applying for assistance lives together, their combined nonexempted income and assets are considered when determining Medicaid eligibility.

In cases where one spouse resides in the family home and the other is already in a nursing facility, income is separated, so the house is excluded as an asset when determining Medicaid eligibility for the nursing facility resident. Federal law requires state Medicaid plans to allow spouses of nursing facility patients who have qualified for Medicaid to retain about $790 a month in income and $12,000 in liquid assets.

Assets limitations and tests leave older people with two options. First, if they foresee the potential need for Medicaid well in advance of applying, they can transfer assets to their heirs. Or, they must spend virtually all their life savings except the equity in their homes on medical needs before being eligible for Medicaid.

It is possible to legally transfer assets. With any transfers occuring on or after July 1, 1988, states are required to determine, at the time of application for Medicaid benefits, whether an applicant has disposed of assets for less than fair market value within the past 30 months. If such a disposal occurred, states will delay eligibility for Medicaid benefits according to a mathematical formula.

In addition, there are legal ways an older person can bypass regulations. Some of these are

Establish a joint tenancy ownership of assets.

Deed a home, car, and other assets to heirs

Purchase income-producing property to shelter liquid assets

Obtain divorce for the communal spouse

An attorney can help evaluate and discuss an older person's options. Remember, steps taken to protect assets must be done

30 months before a person applies for Medicaid. There are other government programs to help with nursing facility care. U.S. veterans are entitled to Veterans Administration (VA) benefits. The VA provides hospital and outpatient care for all service-related medical conditions. More about these benefits and eligibility can be learned by contacting the local VA office.

The Older Americans Act

Another (nonfinancial) government program intended to provide assistance to nursing facility residents is the Older Americans Act (OAA). Under the Older Americans Act, local Area Agencies on Aging (AAAs) are required to reach out to community residents in nursing facilities. An ombudsman program encourages volunteers to regularly visit nursing facility residents. In every state an ombudsman program provides supervised volunteers to encourage constructive liaisons between residents and nursing facility staff. Volunteers funnel complaints from residents to the nursing facility administration. Many improvements in resident comfort and services are accomplished with the help of this program. The local Area Agency on Aging has more information about the ombudsman program. The telephone number is in the telephone book under local government listings.

Long-Term Care Insurance

Finally, private long-term care (LTC) insurance may become an increasingly popular option for paying for nursing facility care. Virtually unknown a decade ago, LTC insurance is growing faster than any other insurance in the country. The number of insurers offering LTC policies has grown from fewer than a dozen in 1982 to nearly 100 today. Long-term care insurance policies pay a set amount of money for each day in a nursing facility. These are known as indemnity benefits and are based on such factors as age, the number of days or years for which the benefits are to be made, and the point at which benefits will be paid (after 20 days, after 100 days, etc.). There are often restrictions on LTC insurance policies, such as prior hospitalizations and the level of care received. Some policies pay only for skilled care, not for intermediate or custodial care.

Premiums for LTC policies vary widely, depending on the terms and the age of the policyholder at purchase. A typical policy that offers $50-a-day benefits, makes adjustments for inflation, does not require hospitalization as a condition of payment for long-term care, and has a 20-day deductible period will cost $610 a year if bought at age 55, $733 at age 65, $1,357 at age 70, and $2,515 at age 75.

As with other forms of insurance, personal, financial, and family circumstances will dictate LTC insurance needs. Experts recommend thinking of LTC insurance mostly in terms of protecting one's assets. In general, an LTC policy may be appropriate if a single person's income is above $15,000 a year and his or her assets total $30,000 or more. One should shop carefully for an LTC policy. Careful evaluation may buy valuable protection against a future financial catastrophe. But if people make careless or hasty choices, they could end up draining their incomes for policies that won't provide the coverage they need.

How does one find a nursing facility?

For those older people who think they will need a nursing facility at some time in the foreseeable future, it pays to plan ahead. Many of the good nursing facilities have very long waiting lists, so it is a good idea to get on a waiting list well in advance of the time when one may actually need a room. Doing a thorough search well ahead of time will also help an older person get mentally adjusted to the idea of making such a move.

One should start by making a list of nursing facilities in the area and asking for opinions of these facilities from relatives or friends who might be familiar with them. A personal physician might be another good source of information. Once a list has been gathered, one should visit as many facilities as possible. Visiting and talking with residents of these nursing facilities about their experiences will also prove helpful. Request a copy of the facility's most recent survey and plan of correction and review it carefully.

Someone seeking a nursing facility can also contact the local nursing facility ombudsman for a list of facilities that he or she might recommend. One can also ask the Better Business Bureau and the local Area Agency on Aging for their lists of facilities. The local state health department might be another source for a list.

THINGS TO REMEMBER

> Discuss the matter with close friends and relatives as well as your physician. Let them know how you feel about the facilities in your area.
>
> When visiting a facility, pay attention to how the staff interacts with the residents. Get a sense of how pleasant the surroundings are and what activities are available for the residents. If you have a special need or hobby, ask if it is available.
>
> Once you have found a facility you are comfortable with, ask about costs and services. With this information you may be able to adjust your own financial resources to suit your future needs. If you choose a facility that is more expensive than you can afford, you have time to consider a different facility or to arrange additional financing.

CONSUMER CHECKLIST

General Questions

____ Do you have special diet or rehabilitation needs? If so, does the facility satisfy them?

____ Is the facility certified by Medicare and/or Medicaid? Is the facility licensed by the state?

____ Does the administrator have a current license? Is he or she helpful and courteous?

____ What is the general atmosphere of the facility? Is it a cheerful, pleasant place? Do the staff members seem warm, caring, and interested in the residents?

____ Do the residents appear to be well cared for and happy? Is there a place for residents to visit with family and friends? Can residents bring some of their own belongings with them to decorate their rooms?

____ Do residents speak favorably about the facility?

____ Is there a patients' rights statement? How is the statement implemented?

____ Does the facility provide care that is "customized" for a resident's particular situation and needs?

____ Does the facility provide interdisciplinary training for all staff on the care, needs, and expectations of older people?

____ What is the facility's policy regarding the use of physical and chemical restraints? Does the facility make the environment as safe as possible in order to allow all residents the freedom to move about?

Nursing/Medical Services

____ Is there at least one registered nurse (RN) or licensed practical nurse (LPN) on duty 24 hours a day?

____ Does an RN serve as director of nursing services? Is an RN on duty 7 days a week?

____ Does each patient have an emergency call button or cord in reach of the bed and in the bathroom?

____ Is there a full-time physical therapy program available? Are occupational and speech therapy available?

____ Is a physician available 24 hours a day for emergencies? Does the facility have an agreement with a nearby hospital to transfer residents quickly in an emergency? Is emergency transportation readily available?

____ Does the facility provide access to dental services?

____ Does a qualified pharmacist maintain and monitor each resident's drug therapy record? Is there a separate, secured room for storing and preparing drugs?

Safety

____ Is the facility free of obstacles to residents? Are wheelchair ramps provided? Are doors unobstructed and unlocked from inside?

____ Is an emergency evacuation plan prominently posted in key areas? Are exits clearly marked and illuminated?

____ Are there smoke detectors, an automatic sprinkler system, and automatic emergency lighting?

____ Are there grab bars in bathing and toilet facilities and hand rails on both sides of the hallways? Do bathtubs and showers have nonslip surfaces?

____ Are certain areas posted with nonsmoking signs? Do staff, residents, and visitors observe them?

Nutrition

____ Ask to see the meal schedule. Are at least 3 meals a day served? Are the meals served at normal hours with plenty of time for leisurely eating? Are nutritious snacks available?

____ Ask to sample a meal. Is the food tasty and appetizing? Is the dining room pleasant and comfortable?

____ Ask for a tour of the kitchen. Is it clean? Is food in its proper place and waste disposed of appropriately?

Social and Recreational Activities

____ Ask to see an activities schedule. Are there activities offered each day? Do they seem interesting to you? Is there a suitable space for activities? Are materials made available?

____ Is there an activities director on staff? Is there a varied program of cultural and recreational activities available?

____ Are residents who are relatively inactive encouraged to participate in activities?

____ Do residents have the opportunity to attend religious services and speak with clergy inside and outside the facility?

____ Are visiting hours flexible and convenient?

____ Is there a public telephone available for residents to use?

Resident's Environment

____ Is the facility located near friends and family?

____ Does the facility appear to be clean and orderly? Is it free of unpleasant odors?

____ Are the bathing and toilet facilities accessible to handicapped residents?

____ Is the facility well-lighted? Are the rooms ventilated?

____ Do all the rooms have access to the hallways? Does each room have a window to the outside?

____ Is there adequate privacy for each resident? Does each room have comfortable chairs, reading lights, and storage space for personal belongings?

____ Is there a lounge where residents can relax, play games, or watch television?

____ Is there an outdoor area where residents can get fresh air and sunshine?

Financial and Related Matters

____ Compare costs (including monthly and other charges) with other facilities in the area.

____ Are appropriate financial statements available to current and prospective residents?

____ Are refunds made for unused days paid for in advance?

____ Review all contracts and financial materials with a trusted advisor.

PART
TWO

Resources

Chapter 5

Directory of Organizations

National Organizations

Administration on Aging (AoA)
Commissioner: Joyce Berry
330 Independence Avenue, SW, Room 4146
Washington, DC 20201
(202) 245-0724

> Established in 1965, AoA is the principal federal agency responsible for programs authorized under the Older Americans Act of 1965. It is the focal point for the aging network, which includes, in addition to AoA, the Federal Council on the Aging, the State Units on Aging (SUAs), and the Area Agencies on Aging (AAAs). AoA advises federal departments and agencies on the characteristics and needs of older people and develops programs designed to promote their welfare; advocates for the needs of the elderly in program planning and policy development; provides advice, funding, and assistance to promote the development of state-administered, community-based systems of comprehensive social services for older people; and conducts training programs.

Alzheimer's Association
President: Edward Truschke
70 East Lake Street
Chicago, IL 60601
(800) 621-0379

A national membership organization founded in 1979, the association's objectives are to support research into the causes of and cures for Alzheimer's disease, to aid in organizing family support groups, to sponsor educational forums on the disease for lay people and professionals, to advise federal and local government agencies on the needs of afflicted families, and to promote national research on the disease. The Alzheimer's Association has chapters throughout the United States.

American Association of Homes for the Aging (AAHA)
President: Sheldon L. Goldberg
1129 20th Street, NW, Suite 400
Washington, DC 20036
(202) 296-5960

Founded in 1961, AAHA is a national, nonprofit organization representing community-based, nonprofit nursing homes; independent housing; continuing care retirement communities; and community service programs for the aging. AAHA works with its members to enhance their ability to meet the social and health needs of the individuals they serve. Also offers publications on housing options and community services and publishes *Industry in Action: The National Continuing Care Data Base.* (See the listing of state offices later in this chapter.)

American Association of Retired Persons (AARP)
Executive Director: Horace B. Deets
1909 K Street, NW
Washington, DC 20049
(202) 872-4880

AARP is a nonprofit, nonpartisan organization dedicated to helping older Americans achieve lives of independence, dignity, and purpose. Founded in 1958, AARP is open to anyone age 50 or older, whether working or retired. The association offers a wide range of membership services, legislative representation at federal and state levels, and educational and community service programs carried out through a national network of volunteers and local chapters. The organization's consumer affairs division provides information on housing options and offers a wide range of publications on housing options and community services. Members receive *Modern Maturity,* a bimonthly magazine, and a monthly newsletter, *AARP News Bulletin*. The National Retired Teachers Association (NRTA) is a division of AARP.

American Health Care Association (AHCA)
Executive Vice President: Paul Willging
1200 15th Street, NW
Washington, DC 20005
(202) 833-2050

> Founded in 1949, AHCA and its affiliated state associations represent licensed nursing homes and allied long-term care facilities in the United States, the majority of which are proprietary. It focuses on issues that directly impact the availability, quality, consistency, and affordability of long-term health care and represents its members' concerns before federal agencies and the Congress.

American Mobilehome Association (AMA)
President: Richard White
12929 West 26th Avenue
Golden, CO 80401
(303) 232-6336

> This association of manufactured housing homeowners keeps members informed of legislation that affects them, provides group discounts, and attempts to influence legislation and zoning for the betterment of manufactured home owners.

American Society of Home Inspectors (ASHI)
Executive Director: Bob Dolivoris
655 15th Street, Suite 320
Washington, DC 20005
(202) 842-3096

> ASHI is a national organization of home inspectors. The group refers consumers to engineers that will inspect homes, especially condos and co-ops, and provide prospective buyers with an objective report of the home's condition.

American Society on Aging (ASA)
Executive Director: Gloria Cavanaugh
833 Market Street, Suite 512
San Francisco, CA 94103
(415) 543-2617

ASA represents housing, health care and social service professionals, educators, researchers, students, and older people. Works to enhance the well-being of older individuals and to foster unity among those working with and for the elderly.

Children of Aging Parents (CAPS)
Executive Director: Mirca Liberti
2761 Trenton Road
Levittown, PA 19056
(215) 945-6900

Children of Aging Parents (CAPS) is a national organization founded in 1980 dedicated to educating the community about aging and the issues of caregiving. It serves as a national clearinghouse for caregivers, provides information and referral services, provides individual counseling, and distributes manuals to assist caregivers in identifying resources in their communities. CAPS publishes a *Case Management Services Directory* and a bimonthly *Advice for Adults with Aging Parents or a Dependent Spouse*.

Commission on Legal Problems of the Elderly (CLPE)
Staff Director: Nancy Coleman
American Bar Association
1800 M Street, NW
Washington, DC 20036
(202) 331-2297

The American Bar Association established this 15-member interdisciplinary commission in 1978 to analyze and respond to the legal needs of older people in the United States. The commission's work focuses on Social Security, housing, long-term care, age discrimination, and improving the availability of legal services to the elderly. The commission makes available a number of publications including its quarterly newsletter, *Bifocal*.

Community Associations Institute (CAI)
Executive Vice President: C. J. Dowden
1423 Powhatan Street, Suite 7
Alexandria, VA 22314
(703) 548-8600

Founded in 1973 to assist in the establishment and ongoing management of homeowners' associations run by owners of condominiums, co-ops, or other types of housing units, the Community Associations Institute provides information services, educational conferences, workshops, seminars, and professional development programs for managers, board members, and others involved in community associations. Members of CAI include over 7,000 managers, homeowners, and associations, as well as supporting professionals in real estate, insurance, lending, developing, law, government, accounting, and service and supply companies.

Continuing Care Accreditation Commission (CCAC)
Director: Ann Gillespie
1129 20th Street, NW, Suite 400
Washington, DC 20036
(202) 828-9439

> The Continuing Care Accreditation Commission is an independent accrediting commission that oversees and directs a national accreditation process for continuing care retirement communities (CCRCs). The purposes of this national accreditation program are to assure consumers that accredited CCRCs are effectively pursuing their missions and meeting CCAC standards, and to promote the continuation of high quality administration and services in accredited communities. The commission's listing of accredited facilities is published and available free of charge.

Cooperative Housing Foundation (CHF)
Executive Director: Jim Upchurch
1010 Wayne Avenue, Suite 240
Silver Spring, MD 20910
(301) 587-4700

> The work of the foundation is dedicated to the development of better housing and related community services for low- and moderate-income families. The foundation emphasizes social aspects of housing programs, both in the United States and abroad. CHF's assistance to cooperatives includes research and information services, training and technical assistance, and other information and advisory services.

Department of Health and Human Services (HHS)
Director: Dr. Louis Sullivan

330 Independence Avenue, SW
Washington, DC 20201
(202) 245-0724

> HHS is the Cabinet-level department of the federal executive
> branch primarily responsible for the health and welfare concerns
> of the nation's people. It was created in 1953 and until 1979 was
> called the Department of Health, Education, and Welfare. The
> HHS secretary advises the president on the health, welfare and
> income security plans, policies, and programs of the federal gov-
> ernment.

Foundation for Hospice and Homecare (FHHC)
Chief Executive Officer: William Halamandaris
519 C Street, NE
Stanton Park
Washington, DC 20002
(202) 547-6586; (800) 232-FHHC

> The foundation has two divisions. One is the National Home-
> Caring Council, which accredits homemaker/home health aide
> services, conducts research, and provides technical assistance.
> They are also establishing a certification program for home-
> maker/home health aides. The council promotes understanding
> of the values of homemaker/home health services, conducts a
> consumer education and protection program, provides a central
> source of information and agency referral with a toll-free num-
> ber, promotes development of standards, and administers an
> agency accreditation and approval program. The other division,
> the Caring Institute, is devoted to research. The organization
> maintains a lending library of materials and visual aids of inter-
> est to communities and agencies. Also publishes books, pam-
> phlets, and audiovisual aids.

Gerontological Research Institute (GRI)
Director: Dr. Powell Lawton
5301 Old York Road
Philadelphia, PA 19141
(215) 456-2900

> This academic organization, affiliated with the Philadelphia
> Geriatric Center, conducts research on the social, psychological,

and biological aspects of aging and services to the aging. Emphasis is on evaluating programs for older people, especially housing and social services.

Gray Panthers (GP)
Director: Cheryl Clearwater
311 South Juniper Street, Suite 601
Philadelphia, PA 19107
(215) 545-6555

The Gray Panthers is a membership organization of people of all ages, founded in 1970 by Maggie Kuhn. Working through local chapters and at the national level, the organization carries out programs of consciousness-raising and education, petition drives, lawsuits, congressional testimony, and media monitoring on a variety of aging issues.

Joint Commission on Accreditation of Healthcare Organizations (JCAHO)
President: Dennis O'Leary, M.D.
875 North Michigan Avenue, Suite 2201
Chicago, IL 60611
(312) 642-6061

JCAHO is a private organization that offers voluntary accreditation programs for hospitals, nursing homes, and other health care organizations. JCAHO is dedicated to improving the quality of health care delivery through consultation, evaluation, and education.

Lampert Tours–National Retirement Concepts (LTNRC)
Executive Director: Janet Lampert
1454 North Wieland Court
Chicago, IL 60610
(800) 888-2312; (312) 951-2866 in Illinois

This travel agency conducts group tours to retirement communities in many southern and western states. Tour members go to one or two communities each day, visiting model homes and asking the developer and local residents questions. Each traveler receives a checklist of items—such as taxes, social events, health care facilities, and housing options—for each location. The cost is about $700 (plus air fare) for an eight-day tour.

Low Income Housing Information Service (LIHIS)
Executive Director: Barry Zigas
1012 14th Street, Suite 1006
Washington, DC 20005
(202) 662-1530

>The Low Income Housing Information Service, established in 1975, is a national nonprofit organization providing information and technical assistance to meet low-income housing needs. The organization's purpose is to provide low-income people, housing organizations, advocates, and activists with the necessary tools to obtain or provide decent, affordable housing. LIHIS's primary emphasis is on national housing programs and policies, which establish the framework and provide support for local efforts.

Manufactured Housing Institute (MHI)
V.P.–Public Affairs: Bruce Butterfield
1745 Jefferson Davis Highway, Suite 511
Arlington, VA 22202
(703) 979-6620

>A trade association founded in 1936, MHI represents and promotes its members' interests before federal government lawmakers and officials. The institute's liaison, research, educational, information, and public relations activities are concerned with equitable financing, construction standards, building technologies, zoning issues, and the increased use of manufactured homes to meet the national demand for affordable housing. Suppliers to manufactured housing and builders are represented by MHI's Supplier Division.

National Alliance of Senior Citizens (NASC)
Executive Director: Curt Clinkscales
2525 Wilson Boulevard
Arlington, VA 22201
(703) 528-4380

>Group informs its membership of the needs of older people and of the programs and policies being carried out by the government and other groups. Represents the views of its members before Congress and state legislatures. Issues include housing, nursing homes, nutrition, and retirement communities.

National Association of Area Agencies on Aging (N4A)
Executive Director: John Linkous
600 Maryland Avenue, SW, Suite West 208
Washington, DC 20024
(202) 484-7520

> N4A is a national association of Area Agencies on Aging (AAA),
> founded in 1965. It promotes cooperation and communication
> within the national aging network and with the federal govern-
> ment and other interested persons and organizations. It provides
> technical and administrative assistance to AAAs.

National Association of Housing Cooperatives (NAHC)
Executive Director: Herbert Levy
1614 King Street
Alexandria, VA 22314
(703) 549-5201

> Promoting the concept of cooperative housing and providing
> support for existing cooperative housing communities are the
> primary functions of the National Association of Housing Coop-
> eratives, founded in 1950 as a nonprofit national federation.
> Members include state and regional associations of housing coop-
> eratives; individual housing cooperatives; and other organiza-
> tions, firms, government agencies, professionals, and individuals
> with an interest in cooperative housing. NAHC promotes the
> philosophy and practice of cooperative housing through research
> and information services, conferences and seminars, technical
> assistance, consulting and training activities, member liaison, and
> a service network. Government relations programs and a legisla-
> tive hotline provide lobbying and government-related informa-
> tion services.

National Association of Meal Programs (NAMP)
Administrative Director: Michael Giuffrida
204 E Street, NE
Washington, DC 20002
(202) 547-6157

> The NAMP includes over 800 individual, organization, and
> cooperative members active in delivery of meals to older persons,
> both in the home and in group settings. NAMP provides technical
> assistance, information exchange, and leadership in legislative

action. The association also maintains a resource center on nutrition education and offers assistance with establishing and operating meal programs.

National Association of Nutrition and Aging Services Programs (NANASP)
Executive Director: Connie Benton Wolfe
2675 44th Street, S.W., Suite 305
Grand Rapids, MI 49509
(800) 999-6262

> This group's members include directors and staff of congregate and home-delivered nutrition services programs for older people. Its objectives are to promote professional growth; raise the standards of the profession; and encourage communication among aging services programs, federal agencies, and governmental bodies.

The National Association of Private Geriatric Care Managers (NAPGCM)
Director: Vernon Lowe
1315 Talbott Towers
Dayton, OH 45042
(513) 222-2621

> An association of private practitioners who seek to develop and promote humane and dignified social and psychological health care for the elderly and their families through counseling, treatment, and the delivery of concrete services by qualified, certified providers. NAPGCM publishes a directory listing all approved members.

National Association of Residential Care Facilities (NARCF)
Executive Director: Barbara Jameson
1205 West Main Street, Room 209
Richmond, VA 23220
(804) 355-3265

> Incorporated in 1984, NARCF is a nonprofit association representing the owners and operators of homes providing shelter, meals, and personal care services to older people and to the mentally and physically disabled. The purposes of NARCF are to provide information and training to enhance the quality of care for residents and to promote efficient management practices.

National Association of Senior Living Industries (NASLI)
Executive Director: Darryl Callahan
184 Duke of Gloucester Street
Annapolis, MD 21401
(301) 858-5001

> NASLI is a membership organization of developers, architects, and owners of housing facilities for older persons; financial institutions involved in funding retirement housing construction; product suppliers; and geriatric research institutes. Disseminates cassette tapes on marketing, housing, and advertising.

National Association of State Units on Aging (NASUA)
Executive Director: Daniel Quirk
2033 K Street, NW, Suite 304
Washington, DC 20006
(202) 785-0707

> NASUA, founded in 1964, is a membership association of the State Units on Aging for the 50 states, the District of Columbia, and the U.S. territories. They monitor legislation, serve as a voice at the national level for the state perspective on aging issues, and provide training and assistance. (See the listing of State Units on Aging at the end of this chapter.)

National Caucus and Center on Black Aged, Inc. (NCBA)
President: Samuel Simmons
1424 K Street, NW, Suite 500
Washington, DC 20005
(202) 637-8400

> NCBA is an inter-racial membership organization founded in 1970. It focuses its efforts on improving the economic status and quality of life for lower income and minority elderly through a comprehensive program of advocacy and services in the areas of housing, employment, and professional training.

National Center for Home Equity Conversion (NCHEC)
Executive Director: Ken Scholen
1210 E. College Drive
Room 300
Marshall, MN 56258
(507) 532-3230

A nonprofit organization dedicated to promoting the more wide-spread availability of home equity conversion. The center tracks legislative and programmatic developments and publishes periodic updates on home equity conversion activity.

National Citizens' Coalition for Nursing Home Reform (NCCNHR)
Executive Director: Elma Holder
1424 16th Street, NW, Suite L2
Washington, DC 20036
(202) 797-0657

Founded in 1975, NCCNHR is a national nonprofit organization of local and state nursing home advocacy groups and individuals. Its purpose is to improve long-term care services and the quality of life for nursing home and assisted living facility residents. Publications include a bimonthly newsletter, *Quality Care Advocate*.

National Council of Senior Citizens (NCSC)
Executive Director: Lawrence T. Smedley
925 15th Street, NW
Washington, DC 20005
(202) 347-8800

NCSC is a national membership organization that works for state and federal legislation to benefit the elderly. The council was founded in 1961 to work for the passage of Medicare. It is a nonprofit, nonpartisan organization, but it does not consider itself apolitical. NCSC administers numerous programs for the low-income elderly, is one of the nation's largest builders of senior citizen housing, and offers its members a variety of benefits and services. It publishes *Senior Citizen News* and maintains a library of books and other materials on Medicare and other programs.

National Council on Aging (NCOA)
Executive Director: Dr. David Thursz
600 Maryland Avenue, SW, West Wing 100
Washington, DC 20024
(202) 479-1200; (800) 424-9046

Founded in 1950, the National Council on Aging is an association of professionals who work with older Americans to improve the quality of life of the nation's elderly. In addition to its information services and annual conference, NCOA sponsors more than 20 major demonstration projects, programs, national centers, and institutes. NCOA also encompasses six specialized affiliate organizations: the National Institute of Adult Daycare, the National Center on Rural Aging, the National Institute of Senior Housing, the National Institute on Community-Based Long-Term Care, the National Association of Older Worker Employment Services, and the National Voluntary Organization for Independent Living for the Aging. NCOA individual members include professionals from senior centers, health care facilities, and other service organizations. Member organizations are day care and senior centers, senior housing facilities, and many other organizations and companies serving older people.

National Low Income Housing Coalition (NLIHC)
President: Barry Zigas
1012 14th Street, NW, Suite 1500
Washington, DC 20005
(202) 662-1530

> Group represents individuals and organizations concerned with improving and expanding low-income housing programs. Carries out a program of education, organization, and advocacy designed to provide decent housing, suitable environments, adequate neighborhoods, and housing choices for low-income people.

National Manufactured Housing Federation, Inc. (NMHF)
Executive Director: Daniel Gilligan
1015 15th Street, Suite 1240
Washington, DC 20005
(202) 789-8690

> The purpose of the National Manufactured Housing Federation, founded in 1977, is to serve as the national representative of its membership, which consists of state and regional manufactured housing associations. These associations represent approximately 30,000 manufactured housing manufacturers, retailers, and park operators and developers. The federation provides its members with a means of expressing their views and making suggestions at the federal level on proposed legislation and federal regulatory actions. The federation also informs members about government activities that affect the manufactured housing industry.

National Shared Housing Resource Center (NSHRC)
Executive Director: Joyce Mantell
6344 Greene Street
Philadelphia, PA 19144
(215) 848-1220

> Founded in 1981, the National Shared Housing Resource Center advocates the shared housing concept as an alternative form of affordable housing, especially for older people and intergenerational groups. The center uses grants for national shared housing development work and sponsors two local projects in Philadelphia. Activities currently underway at NSHRC include the development of a low-interest loan fund for shared housing projects; research and local advocacy aimed at removing barriers to shared housing; and information services, educational workshops, and technical assistance.

Older Women's League (OWL)
Executive Director: Joan A. Kuriansky
730 11th Street, NW, Suite 300
Washington, DC 20001
(202) 783-6686

> OWL is a national membership organization formed to provide mutual support for its members, who are midlife and older women, and family caregivers. The league's area of activities include information dissemination, public policy formation, and support for members. Publications include the monthly *Field Advocate* and the bimonthly *Owl Observer*.

Scripps Foundation—Miami University
Director: Dr. Robert Atchley
327 Hoyt Library
Oxford, OH 45056
(513) 529-2914

> This research center focuses its activities in the area of social, psychological, and economic aspects of population growth, with emphasis on demography and social gerontology. The foundation provides information and consulting services for organizations concerned with programs serving the aging, including nursing homes and retirement communities.

Select Committee on Aging

Chairman: Representative Edward Roybal (D-CA)
U.S. Congress, House of Representatives
Room 712, House Office Building
Annex 1
300 New Jersey Avenue, SE
Washington, DC 20515
(202) 226-3375

The Select Committee on Aging, established in 1974, is primarily a fact-finding body and has no legislative responsibility. It has four subcommittees: Retirement Income and Employment, Health and Long-Term Care, Housing and Consumer Interests, and Human Services. The committee informs the House of Representatives of problems of older Americans, advises House committees with legislative jurisdiction over issues that affect the elderly, and oversees the executive branch to ensure that laws applicable to the elderly are properly executed.

Special Committee on Aging

Chairman: Senator David Pryor (D-AR)
U.S. Congress, Senate
G-41 Dirksen Building
Washington, DC 20510-6400
(202) 224-5364

The Special Committee on Aging was established in 1961. The committee is responsible for studying all issues affecting older people. It conducts studies and investigations into issues such as Medicare, Social Security, health, retirement income, employment, housing, energy assistance, and crime. The committee's housing team focuses on both federal and private housing options. Its findings and recommendations are submitted to other Senate committees for legislative action. The committee also conducts oversight of federal agencies and programs designed to assist older people.

Third Age Center (TAC)

Director: Msgr. Charles Fahey
Fordham University
113 West 60th Street
New York, NY 10023
(212) 814-5347

The Third Age Center concentrates on the intellectual, emotional, economic, spiritual, and cultural opportunities that confront older people. Programs include studies on the interface of informal and formal support systems, long-term care and service delivery, alternative forms of housing, and older persons in families.

State Organizations

American Association of Homes for the Aging (AAHA) State Offices

Alabama Association of Homes for the
Aging
Mr. Wray Tomlin, President
c/o Methodist Homes for Aging
1424 Montclair Road
Birmingham, AL 35210
(205) 956-4150

Arizona Association of Homes for the
Aging
Ms. Randi Weiss, Executive Director
204 Abacus Tower
3030 North Third Street
Phoenix, AZ 85012
(602) 264-1984

California Association of Homes for
the Aging
Mr. Dean R. Shetler, President
7311 Greenhaven Drive, Suite 175
Sacramento, CA 95831
(916) 392-5111

Colorado Association of Homes &
Services for the Aging
Mr. John Torres, Executive Director
2140 South Holly Street
Denver, CO 80222
(303) 759-8688

Connecticut Association of Non-Profit
Facilities for the Aged
Ms. Rosalind Berman, President
110 Barnes Road
P.O. Box 90
Wallingford, CT 06492
(203) 269-7443

Florida Association of Homes for the
Aging
Ms. Karen Torgesen, Executive Director
1018 Thomasville Road, Suite 200Y
Tallahassee, FL 32303-6236
(904) 222-3562

Georgia Association of Homes &
Services for the Aging
Ms. Vickie Moody-Beasley, President
2719 Buford Highway, Suite 213
Atlanta, GA 30324
(404) 728-0223

Illinois Association of Homes for the
Aging
Mr. Dennis R. Bozzi, Executive
Director
911 North Elm Street, Suite 228
Hinsdale, IL 60521
(708) 325-6170
FAX (708) 325-0749

Indiana Association of Homes for the
Aging
Mr. George F. Heighway, Executive
Director
1265 West 86th Street
Indianapolis, IN 46260
(317) 257-1115

Iowa Association of Homes for the
Aging
Ms. Judi Pierick, Executive Director
4685 Merle Hay Road, Suite 101
Des Moines, IA 50322
(515) 270-1198

Kansas Association of Homes for the
Aging
Mr. John Grace, President
641 S.W. Harrison Street
Topeka, KS 66603
(913) 233-7443

Kentucky Association of Homes for the
Aging
Ms. Louise Schroader, Executive Director
1244 South Fourth Street
Louisville, KY 40203
(502) 635-6468

Louisiana Association of Homes &
Services for the Aging
Ms. Allison Gremillon, Executive
Director
2431 South Acadian Thruway, Suite 280
Baton Rouge, LA 70808
(504) 928-6894

Maryland Association of Nonprofit
Homes for the Aging
Ms. Ann M. MacKay, President
6263 Bright Plume
Columbia, MD 21044-3749
(301) 740-4585
FAX (301) 290-5285 (cover sheet must
include Ann's name and phone
number)

National Capital Area Assn. of Homes
for the Aging
Mr. David Zwald, President Pro Tem
c/o Ginger Cove
4000 River Crescent Drive
Annapolis, MD 21401
(301) 266-7300

Association of Massachusetts Homes
for the Aging
Mr. Merlin Southwick, Executive
Director
45 Bromfield Street
Boston, MA 02108
(617) 423-0718

Michigan Nonprofit Homes Association,
Inc.
Mr. Donald J. Bentsen, Executive
Director
1615 East Kalamazoo Street
Lansing, MI 48912
(517) 372-7540

Minnesota Association of Homes for
the Aging
Ms. Gayle Kvenvold, President & CEO
2221 University Avenue, S.E., Suite 425
Minneapolis, MN 55414
(612) 331-5571

Missouri Association of Homes for the
Aging
Mr. James Nagel, President
6925 Hampton Avenue
St. Louis, MO 63109-3902
(314) 353-9050
FAX (314) 353-4771

Montana Association of Homes for the
Aging
Ms. Jean Johnson, Executive Director
34 West Sixth Street, 2E
P.O. Box 5774
Helena, MT 59601
(406) 443-1185

Nebraska Association of Homes for the
Aging
Mr. Ron Jensen, Executive Director
1320 Lincoln Mall, Suite 9
Lincoln, NE 68508
(402) 477-7015

Northern New England Association of
Homes and Services for the Aging
Ms. Christine C. Hallock, President
c/o Hunt Community
10 Allds Street
Nashua, NH 03060
(603) 882-6511

New Jersey Association of Nonprofit
    Homes for Aging
Ms. Karen J. Uebele, Executive Director
760 Alexander Road, CN #1
Princeton, NJ 08540
(609) 452-1161
FAX (609) 452-2907

New York Association of Homes &
    Services for the Aging
Mr. Carl Young, President
194 Washington Avenue, 4th Floor
Albany, NY 12210
(518) 449-2707
FAX (518) 455-8908

Rochester Area Association of Homes
    & Services for the Aging
Ms. Nancy Newton, Executive Director
259 Monroe Avenue
Rochester, NY 14607
(716) 454-7300

North Carolina Association of Nonprofit
    Homes for the Aging
Ms. Sarah R. Shaber, Executive
    Director
1717 Park Drive
Raleigh, NC 27605
(919) 821-0803

North Dakota Nursing Home
    Association
Mr. Robert Howe, Senior Vice
    President
Kirkwood Office Tower
919 Arbor Avenue
Bismarck, ND 58501
(701) 224-9440

Association of Ohio Philanthropic
    Homes and Housing for the Aging
Mr. Clark R. Law, Executive Director
36 West Gay Street
Columbus, OH 43215
(614) 221-2882
FAX (614) 221-4490

Oregon Association of Homes for the
    Aging
Ms. Sally P. Goodwin, Executive
    Director
7150 South West Hampton Street,
    Suite 206
Tigard, OR 97223
(503) 684-3788

Pennsylvania Association of Nonprofit
    Homes for the Aging
Rev. David J. Keller, Executive Director
P.O. Box 698
3425 Simpson Ferry Road
Camp Hill, PA 17011
(717) 763-5724
FAX (717) 763-1057

Rhode Island Association of Facilities
    for the Aged
Ms. Sheila Sousa, President
St. Antoine Residence
400 Menden Road
North Smithfield, RI 02895
(401) 767-3500

South Carolina Association of
    Nonprofit Homes for the Aging
Ms. Joan V. Young, President
c/o Presbyterian Home of South
    Carolina
Highway 56 North
Clinton, SC 29325
(803) 833-5190

South Dakota Association of Homes
for the Aging
Ms. Betsy Reck, Executive Director
330 North Main Avenue, Suite 201
P.O. Box 639
Sioux Falls, SD 57101
(605) 338-6621
FAX (605) 338-0770

Tennessee Association of Homes for the
Aging
Ms. Jennifer Humphreys, Executive
Director
1305 Rolling Meadow Court
Mt. Juliet, TN 37122
(615) 758-7440

Texas Association of Homes for the
Aging
Ms. Sandy Derrow, President
720 Brazos Street, Suite 1104
Austin, TX 78701
(512) 477-6994

Virginia Association of Nonprofit
Homes for the Aging
Ms. Ann McGee, President
4900 Augusta Avenue, Suite 104
Richmond, VA 23230
(804) 353-8141

Washington Association of Homes for
the Aging
Ms. Karen L. Tynes, Executive Director
444 N.E. Ravenna Boulevard, Suite
109
Seattle, WA 98115
(206) 526-8450

Wisconsin Association of Homes &
Services for the Aging
Mr. John Sauer, Executive Director
6400 Gisholt Drive, Suite 203
Madison, WI 53713
(608) 222-5086

AAHA Regional Directors

Ms. Leslie A. Knight
Director, Midwest Region
American Association of Homes for the
Aging
911 North Elm Street, Suite 228
Hinsdale, IL 60521
(708) 323-6755
FAX (708) 325-0749

Ms. Mary M. Reilly
Director, Western Region
American Association of Homes for the
Aging
5010 Aspen Drive
Littleton, CO 80123
(303) 795-5465

Ms. Anne Brooks
Executive Director, Northeast Region
American Association of Homes for the
Aging
2001 Jefferson Court
Ambler, PA 19002
(215) 628-2232

Canadian Associations

Ontario Association of Non-Profit
Homes and Services for Seniors
Mr. Michael J. Klejman, Executive
Director
7 Director Court, Suite 102
Woodbridge, Ontario, Canada L4L 4Z5
(416) 851-8821

Association des Centres D'Accuiel du
Quebec
Mr. Michel Clair, Director General
1001 de Maisonneuve Est #1100
Montreal, Quebec, Canada H2L 4P9
(514) 597-1007

Saskatchewan Association of Special
Care Homes
Mr. Bun Wasiuta, Executive Director
2-1540 Albert/Regina
Saskatchewan, Canada S4P 2S4
(306) 565-0744

National Association of State Units on Aging (NASUA)

Alabama
Commission on Aging
Second Floor
136 Catoma Street
Montgomery, AL 36130
(205) 261-5743

Alaska
Older Alaskans Commission
Department of Administration
Pouch C-Mail Station 0209
Juneau, AK 99811-0209
(907) 465-3250

Arizona
Aging and Adult Administration
Department of Economic Security
1400 West Washington Street
Phoenix, AZ 85007
(602) 255-4446

Arkansas
Division of Aging and Adult Servs.
Arkansas Department of Human
  Services
1417 Donaghey Plaza South
7th and Main Streets
Little Rock, AR 72201
(501) 682-2441

California
Department of Aging
1600 K Street
Sacramento, CA 95814
(916) 322-5290

Colorado
Aging and Adult Services
Department of Social Services
1575 Sherman Street, 10th Floor
Denver, CO 80203-1714
(303) 866-5931

Connecticut
Department on Aging
175 Main Street
Hartford, CT 06106
(203) 566-3238

Delaware
Division on Aging
Department of Health and Social
  Services
1901 North DuPont Highway
New Castle, DE 19720
(302) 421-6791

District of Columbia
Office on Aging
1424 K Street, NW, 2nd Floor
Washington, DC 20005
(202) 724-5626

Florida
Program Office of Aging and Adult
  Services
Department of Health and
  Rehabilitative Services
1317 Winewood Boulevard
Tallahassee, FL 32301
(904) 488-8922

Georgia
Office of Aging
878 Peachtree Street, N.E., Room 632
Atlanta, GA 30309
(404) 894-5333

Guam
Division of Senior Citizens
Department of Public Health & Social
  Services
Government of Guam
P.O. Box 2816
Agana, Guam 96910

Hawaii
Executive Office on Aging
Office of the Governor
335 Merchant Street, Room 241
Honolulu, HI 96813
(808) 548-2593

Idaho
Office on Aging
Room 114—Statehouse
Boise, ID 83720
(208) 334-3833

Illinois
Department on Aging
421 East Capitol Avenue
Springfield, IL 62701
(217) 785-2870

Indiana
Division of Aging Services
Department of Human Services
251 North Illinois Street
P.O. Box 7083
Indianapolis, IN 46207-7083
(317) 232-7020

Iowa
Department of Elder Affairs
Suite 236, Jewett Building
914 Grand Avenue
Des Moines, IA 50319
(515) 281-5187

Kansas
Department on Aging
Docking State Office Building, 122-S
915 S.W. Harrison
Topeka, KS 66612-1500
(913) 296-4986

Kentucky
Division of Aging Services
Cabinet for Human Resources
CHR Building—6th West
275 East Main Street
Frankfort, KY 40621
(502) 564-6930

Louisiana
Office of Elderly Affairs
P.O. Box 80374
Baton Rouge, LA 70898
(504) 925-1700

Maine
Bureau of Maine's Elderly
Department of Human Services
State House—Station 11
Augusta, ME 04333
(207) 289-2561

Maryland
Office on Aging
State Office Building
301 West Preston Street, Room 1004
Baltimore, MD 21201
(301) 225-1100

Massachusetts
Executive Office of Elder Affairs
38 Chauncy Street
Boston, MA 02111
(617) 727-7750

Michigan
Office of Services to the Aging
P.O. Box 30026
Lansing, MI 48909
(517) 373-8230

Minnesota
Board on Aging
4th Floor, Human Services Building
444 Lafayette Road
St. Paul, MN 55155-3843
(612) 296-2770

Mississippi
Council on Aging
301 West Pearl Street
Jackson, MS 39203-3092
(601) 949-2070

Missouri
Division on Aging
Department of Social Services
P.O. Box 1337
2701 West Main Street
Jefferson City, MO 65102
(314) 751-3082

Montana
Department of Family Services
48 North Last Chance Gulch
P.O. Box 8005
Helena, MT 59604
(406) 444-5900

Nebraska
Department on Aging
P.O. Box 95044
301 Centennial Mall—South
Lincoln, NE 68509
(402) 471-2306

Nevada
Division for Aging Services
Department of Human Resources
340 North 11th Street
Las Vegas, NV 89101
(702) 486-3545

New Hampshire
Div. of Elderly and Adult Servs.
6 Hazen Drive
Concord, NH 03301-6501
(603) 271-4680

New Jersey
Division on Aging
Department of Community Affairs,
 CN807
South Broad and Front Streets
Trenton, NJ 08625-0807
(609) 292-4833

New Mexico
State Agency on Aging
224 East Palace Avenue—4th Floor
La Villa Rivera Building
Santa Fe, NM 87501
(505) 827-7640

New York
Office for the Aging
New York State Plaza
Agency Building 2
Albany, NY 12223
(518) 474-4425

North Carolina
Division of Aging
1985 Umstead Drive, Kirby Bldg.
Raleigh, NC 27603
(919) 733-3983

North Dakota
Aging Services
Department of Human Services
State Capitol Building
Bismarck, ND 58505
(701) 224-2577

Northern Mariana Islands
Office of Aging
Department of Community and Cultural
 Affairs
Civic Center—Susupe
Saipan, Northern Mariana Islands
96950
Tel. Nos. 9411 or 9732

Ohio
Department of Aging
50 West Broad Street—9th Floor
Columbus, OH 43266-0501
(614) 466-5500

Oklahoma
Aging Services Division
Department of Human Services
P.O. Box 25352
Oklahoma City, OK 73125
(405) 521-2281

Oregon
Senior Services Division
313 Public Service Building
Salem, OR 97310
(503) 378-4728

Pennsylvania
Department of Aging
231 State Street
Harrisburg, PA 17101-1195
(717) 783-1550

Puerto Rico
Gericulture Commission
Department of Social Services
Apartado 11398
Santurce, PR 00910
(809) 721-4010

Rhode Island
Department of Elderly Affairs
79 Washington Street
Providence, RI 02903
(401) 277-2858

(American) Samoa
Territorial Administration on Aging
Office of the Governor
Pago Pago, American Samoa 96799
011 (684) 633-1252

South Carolina
Commission on Aging
400 Arbor Lake Drive, Suite B-500
Columbia, SC 29223
(803) 735-0210

South Dakota
Office of Adult Services and Aging
700 North Illinois Street
Kneip Building
Pierre, SD 57501
(605) 773-3656

Tennessee
Commission on Aging
706 Church Street, Suite 201
Nashville, TN 37219-5573
(615) 741-2056

Texas
Department on Aging
P.O. Box 12786, Capitol Station
1949 IH 35, South
Austin, TX 78741-3702
(512) 444-2727

Trust Territory of the Pacific
Office of Elderly Programs
Community Development Division
Government of TTPI
Saipan, Mariana Islands 96950
Tel. Nos. 9335 or 9336

Utah
Division of Aging and Adult Services
Department of Social Services
120 North—200 West
Box 45500
Salt Lake City, UT 84145-0500
(801) 538-3910

Vermont
Office on Aging
103 South Main Street
Waterbury, VT 05676
(802) 241-2400

Virgin Islands
Department of Human Services
6F Havensight Mall—Charlotte Amalie
St. Thomas, Virgin Islands 00801
(809) 774-5884

Virginia
Department for the Aging
700 Centre, 10th Floor
700 East Franklin Street
Richmond, VA 23219-2327
(804) 225-2271

Washington
Aging and Adult Services
Administration
Department of Social and Health
Services
OB-44A
Olympia, WA 98504
(206) 586-3768

West Virginia
Commission on Aging
Holly Grove—State Capitol
Charleston, WV 25305
(304) 348-3317

Wisconsin
Bureau of Aging
Division of Community Services
One West Wilson Street, Room 480
Madison, WI 53702
(608) 266-2536

Wyoming
Commission on Aging
Hathaway Building—Room 139
Cheyenne, WY 82002-0710
(307) 777-7986

Chapter 6

Reference Materials

General

Administration on Aging. *Where To Turn for Help for Older Persons.*
Washington, DC: U.S. Government Printing Office, 1988. 14p. No
charge. Pub. no. 100-660.

> A booklet prepared by the Administration on Aging for the U.S.
> House of Representatives Select Committee on Aging, designed to
> help someone find assistance when he or she is faced with an
> urgent situation regarding an older person. The first section con-
> tains the most frequently asked questions and the second section
> includes telephone numbers of the state offices on aging.

American Association of Homes for the Aging. *Directory of Members.*
Washington, DC: American Association of Homes for the Aging. 1988.
247p. $20. ISBN 0-943-77438-1.

> A state by state listing of nursing homes, personal care facilities,
> and independent living units that include congregate and shel-
> tered housing. Each entry is coded for type, sponsorship, and
> outreach services. Also listed are multi-facility sponsors, state and
> local organizations, business firms, and suppliers.

American Association of International Aging. *U.S. Directory and
Source Book on Aging.* Silver Spring, MD: Business Publishers, Inc.,
1989. 374p.

> The *U.S. Directory and Source Book* is a complete, interdisci-
> plinary guide to the U.S.-based aging community. It includes

private voluntary organizations, academic institutions, mass membership organizations, public interest groups, for-profit firms, foundations, corporations, and publishers of works of interest to members of the aging community. Most profiles include information on principal areas of activities, special services, and resources. Includes index.

American Association of Retired Persons. *A Profile of Older Americans.* Washington, DC: American Association of Retired Persons, 1988. 8p. No charge. Stock no. D996.

A brochure providing a statistical overview of the nation's population age 65 or over. It provides facts on marital status, living arrangements, geographic distribution, income, and other factors.

American Association of Retired Persons. *Guide to Local Housing Resources for Older Persons.* Washington, DC: American Association of Retired Persons, 1986. 32p. No charge. Stock no. D12785.

This guide, or workbook, to local housing resources for older persons briefly describes programs and services that help meet housing needs. Space is available for the reader to insert names of facilities or services, addresses, phone numbers, and eligibility requirements and costs, where applicable.

American Association of Retired Persons. *Housing Options for Older Americans.* Washington, DC: American Association of Retired Persons, 1984. 42p. No charge. Stock no. D12063.

This booklet is designed for older persons who are considering a change in their living arrangements. Included are options for remaining in one's home as well as for making a move. A list of additional resources is provided.

American Association of Retired Persons. *Making Wise Decisions for Long Term Care.* Washington, DC: American Association of Retired Persons, 1989. 27p. No charge. Stock no. D12435.

A comprehensive consumer guide to long-term care services. Publicly and privately funded and sponsored services are briefly described.

American Association of Retired Persons. *Medicare: What It Covers, What It Doesn't.* Washington, DC: American Association of Retired Persons, 1989. 11p. No charge. Stock no. D13133.

This descriptive brochure is a helpful tool in discerning the benefits and limitations of the Medicare insurance program. Included are basic facts about the Medicare law, Medicaid, supplemental insurance, and the Medicare appeals process.

American Association of Retired Persons. *Your Home, Your Choice: A Workbook for Older Persons and Their Families.* Washington, DC: American Association of Retired Persons, 1985. 32p. No charge. Stock no. D12143.

> This workbook is designed to encourage older Americans who may be considering a change in living arrangements to take an active role in decision making. Sections on various alternatives include questions that should lead to the best decision for each person.

Boyer, Richard. *Retirement Places Rated,* 2nd ed. Chicago, IL: Rand McNally, 1987. 219p. $12.95 (paper). ISBN 0-528-88081-0.

> This guide ranks and discusses climate, money matters, personal safety, services, housing, and leisure living in 131 towns or communities.

Carlin, Vivian F., and Ruth Mansberg. *Where Can Mom Live? A Family Guide to Living Arrangements for Elderly Parents.* Lexington, MA: Lexington Books, 1987. 206p. $12.95 (paper). ISBN 0-669-13666-2.

> Written primarily for adult children, this book describes how some families have found housing solutions for aging relatives. Carlin and Mansberg describe a variety of options, from group shared homes to congregate housing to staying put, in the words and experiences of real people. Includes index.

Dickinson, Peter A. *Retirement Edens Outside the Sunbelt,* updated and expanded edition. Washington, DC: American Association of Retired Persons; Glenview, IL: Scott, Foresman, 1987. 400p. $10.95 (paper). ISBN 0-673-24836-4.

> This book describes over 800 towns in states in the northern United States, including information on cost of living, taxes, health care facilities, and climate. It also looks at cultural and recreational activities and housing.

Dickinson, Peter A. *Sunbelt Retirement,* updated and expanded edition. Washington, DC: American Association of Retired Persons; Glenview, IL: Scott, Foresman, 1986. 367p. $11.95 (paper). ISBN 0-673-24832-1.

> A guide to places to retire in the sunbelt states of the South and West. It describes the benefits of retiring to the sunbelt and provides descriptions of some towns and cities in each state. Information is provided on cost of living, taxes, health care services, climate, cultural and recreational activities, and housing.

Enders, Alexandra, ed. *Technology for Independent Living Sourcebook.* Washington, DC: Rehabilitation Engineering Society of America, 1984. 155p. $25. ISSN 0738-2316.

> This helpful guide lists sources from medical supply stores to self-help organizations. It includes sections on hearing, sight, and mobility impairments. Unfortunately, the print is small.

Gelfand, Donald E., ed. *The Aging Network: Programs and Services,* 3rd ed. New York: Springer Publishing Company, 1988. 340p. $19.95. ISBN 0-8261-3054-2.

> A guide to existing programs and services for older persons, focusing on programs emanating from the Older Americans Act and related programs resulting from various federal and state legislation. Gelfand describes the present status of older Americans, income maintenance programs, and details on major programs in aging. Donald E. Gelfand, PhD, is a sociologist and professor at the School of Social Work and Community Planning at the University of Maryland at Baltimore.

Gold, Margaret. *The Older American's Guide to Housing and Living Arrangements.* Mt. Vernon, NY: Institute for Consumer Policy Research, 1984. 115p. No charge. ISBN 1159-5693.

> This guide is a good source of information on housing options, describing a range of alternatives including accessory apartments, small group residences, retirement communities, and senior apartments. Along with descriptive information, Dr. Gold has included questions to ask, guidelines on when to ask them, and suggestions on how to organize the information received. Health and financial checklists are included in the appendices.

Manser, Nancy. *Older People Have Choices: Information for Decisions about Health, Home and Money.* Minneapolis, MN: Augsburg, 1984. 32p. No charge.

> This helpful booklet reviews some of the options available to help older persons live independently and outlines factors to use in assessing one's ability to live independently. Financial issues are discussed, including health insurance, and the special needs of older persons with dementia are addressed. The appendix includes possible solutions to specific needs and lists organizations that may be useful resources.

Myers, Phyllis. *Aging in Place: Strategies To Help the Elderly Stay in Revitalizing Neighborhoods.* Washington, DC: The Conservation Foundation, 1982. 106p. $7.50 (paper). ISBN 0-89164-075-4.

> Myers has compiled a summary of local strategies designed to improve city neighborhoods and respond to the special housing needs of older persons, particularly their preference to stay in familiar places. Among these strategies are accessory apartments and shared housing.

Sumichrast, Michael, et al. *Planning Your Retirement Housing.* Washington, DC: American Association of Retired Persons, 1984. 270p. $8.95. ISBN 0-673-24810-0.

> This is an overview of housing options including a discussion of considerations in decision making. Issues such as housing costs, climate, design, and regulations are addressed. Charts are out of date but text is useful.

United Seniors Health Cooperative. *Long Term Care: A Dollar and Sense Guide.* Washington, DC: United Seniors Health Cooperative, 1988. 64p. $6.95. ISBN 0-944847-03-X.

> This manual presents various options regarding financial support for long-term care. It discusses how older persons or their adult children can pay for these services. The pros and cons of each option are discussed.

Wilson, Albert J. E., III. *Social Services for Older Persons.* Boston: Little, Brown and Company, 1984. 270p. $18.95. ISBN 0-316-94409-2.

> Wilson describes trends in gerontology and service delivery policy, including alternatives to institutional care, access services,

income maintenance and employment services, health-related services, housing, and supportive services.

Home Health Care and Homemaker Services

American Association of Retired Persons. *A Handbook about Care in the Home*. Washington, DC: American Association of Retired Persons, 1986. 24p. No charge. Stock no. D995.

> A guidebook designed to help older persons and their families understand the concept of home care, the types of services available, and the agencies that provide them. It also provides guidance on evaluating the cost and quality of care.

American Association of Retired Persons. *Information on Medicare and Health Insurance for Older People*. Washington, DC: American Association of Retired Persons, 1987. 32p. No charge. Stock no. C38, ML2654.

> This booklet, organized in a question-and-answer format, explains what Medicare does and does not cover. The booklet describes the merits, shortcomings, and relative availability of various kinds of private health insurance.

Friedman, Jo-Ann. *Home Health Care: A Complete Guide for Patients and Their Families*. New York: W. W. Norton and Company, 1986. 567p. $22.50. ISBN 0-393-01889-X.

> A comprehensive guide to home health care covering everything from post-surgical recuperation to recovery from stroke to daily living with a chronic illness. A champion of home health care over nursing home care, Friedman describes how to determine what public and private insurance will cover and how to find home care products. The resource directory includes names, addresses, and phone numbers of organizations in every state that can provide help for a variety of home care needs.

Nassif, Janet Zhun. *The Home Health Care Solution: A Complete Consumer Guide*. New York: Harper and Row, 1985. 433p. $17.95. ISBN 0-06-015471-3.

> A comprehensive guide to home health care featuring tips on how to get the best care and the financial side of home care.

Nassif devotes considerable discussion to building consumer savvy in selecting an agency and home care services and do-it-yourself home care. Ms. Nassif is a consultant to organizations involved in home care. She is the author of *Medicine's New Technology* and *Handbook of Health Careers,* and co-author of *Modern Health,* the leading high school health text. Includes index.

Taber, Merlin A., Mary Ann Anichini, Steve Anderson, and Robert A. Weagant. *A Handbook of Practical Care for the Frail Elderly.* Phoenix, AZ: The Oryx Press, 1986. 99p. $32.50 (paper). ISBN 0-89774-289-3.

This manual, prepared to train workers in public programs, is equally applicable for any adult caring for another, whether in a home or nursing home. The handbook explains how to meet personal care, health care, and housekeeping requirements for the frail elderly. Among the topics discussed are meal planning, emotional needs, personal care, and community resources.

Upham's Corner Health Committee, Inc. *Home Health Care Handbook: A Guide for the Family of the Homebound Patient Who Is Chronically or Terminally Ill.* Owings Mills, MD: National Health Publishing, 1987. 150p. $17. ISBN 0-932500-75-7.

This is a convenient reference for persons who are new to their role as caregiver. The handbook includes nutritional tables and offers solutions to the problem of improving nutrition. It reviews eligibility for benefits and services and provides helpful ideas for obtaining assistance, including suggestions for speeding up the application process.

Adult Day Care

National Institute on Adult Day Care. *Standards for Adult Day Care.* Washington, DC: National Council on the Aging, 1984. 52p. No charge.

A set of standards for the operation and maintenance of adult day care centers, with useful information about how such centers are organized. By reading the standards, the reader can glean important questions to ask when considering an adult day care center.

O'Brien, Carol L. *Adult Day Care: A Practical Guide*. Boston, MA: Jones and Bartlett, 1982. 429p. $35. ISBN 0-8185-0506-0.

> A reference handbook that provides detailed information on establishing and operating adult day care programs. Included are a history of adult day care and discussion of program development, staffing, funding, needs assessment, and evaluation. The appendices include examples of functional assessment tools and a community needs survey.

Care Management

American Association of Retired Persons. *Miles Away and Still Caring: A Guide for Long-Distance Caregivers*. Washington, DC: American Association of Retired Persons, 1986. 17p. No charge. Stock no. D12748.

> This is a guide for individuals who are responsible for coordinating and monitoring the care of an aging relative from a distance. It provides a care management worksheet that lists 20 possible care concerns and suggests the types of services that may be helpful in dealing with each. Appropriate readings and resources are listed, including suggestions for locating community resources. It emphasizes the importance of recognizing the strain of long-distance caregiving and of taking care of oneself.

National Institute on Community-Based Long Term Care. *Care Management Standards: Guidelines for Practice*. Washington, DC: The National Council on the Aging, 1988. 23p. $8. ISBN 0-910883-44-0.

> A set of basic, generic, national care management standards, particularly applying to older persons. The standards include definitions, philosophy and clients' rights, target population, goals, roles of the care manager, and other functions supportive of the care management process.

Personal Emergency Response Systems (PERSs)

American Association of Retired Persons. *Meeting the Need for Security and Independence with Personal Emergency Response Systems*. Washington, DC: American Association of Retired Persons, 1987. 8p. No charge. Stock no. D12905.

Developed by AARP's Consumer Affairs Section, this booklet provides helpful consumer information on how PERSs (personal emergency response systems) work and features that are available. It also includes a chart describing the key elements of various nationally available systems. Units are not rated.

Home Repair and Maintenance

Berko, Robert L. *Small Home Repairs Made Easy*. South Orange, NJ: Consumer Education Research Center, 1987. 72p. $6. ISBN 0-93487-3097.

>A manual that lists step by step directions on how to do household repairs, such as unstopping a toilet, fixing a doorbell, and repairing a garage door. There are hundreds of illustrations and helpful hints.

Spiegel, Monroe, and Robert L. Berko. *Consumer's Guide to Home Repair Grants and Subsidized Loans*. South Orange, NJ: Consumer Education Research Center, 1986. 178p. $6. ISBN 0-934873-070-0.

>This easy-to-read guide provides a compendium of programs and agencies designed to help with home repair, maintenance, and weatherization needs. Information on how programs work as well as sources for financial help are included. Spiegel and Berko also provide useful tips on selecting a home repair contractor, assessing loan costs, and determining repair needs.

U.S. Consumer Product Safety Commission. *Safety for Older Consumers*. Washington, DC: U.S. Government Printing Office, 1986. 29p. No charge. Pub. no. D-491-120(52706).

>A highly illustrative guide to identifying and correcting safety hazards in the home. The checklist is organized by areas in the home, with potential hazards that may be in more than one area of the home highlighted. This guide is very readable and widely distributed.

Home Adaptations

Adaptive Environments Center. *A Consumer's Guide to Home Adaptation*. Boston, MA: Adaptive Environments Center, 1989. 52p. $8.50.

A readable, heavily illustrated guide designed to help individuals make their homes more comfortable and safer. Included are a discussion on evaluating needs, a planning worksheet, and construction guidelines. A useful resource section includes references for products and equipment, as well as books and catalogues.

Agosta, John M., Mary-Ann Allard, John Ashbaugh, Valerie J. Bradley, and Ann Rugg. *Assessing Housing Needs for Persons with Disabilities: A Guide and Resource Book*. Washington, DC: Office of Policy Development and Research, U.S. Department of Housing and Urban Development, 1984. 269p. $18. Pub. no. HUD-004030.

This is a general guide for conducting a needs assessment of the housing needs of persons with disabilities. While written for decision makers, the assessment information is useful. Included in the resource section are several assessment instruments that address such issues as primary disability, functional limitations, housing-related limitations, and housing design needs.

Bostrom, James A., Ronald L. Mace, and Maria Long. *Adaptable Housing: A Technical Manual for Implementing Adaptable Unit Specifications*. Washington, DC: Office of Policy Development and Research, U.S. Department of Housing and Urban Development, 1987. 80p. $5. Doc. no. HUD 1124-PDR.

Both technical and general information are included in this book about adaptable housing. The development of adaptable design is reviewed and methods for providing adaptable features are explained; illustrations support the explanations. Products that enhance adaptable design are discussed and examples of useful products are provided. Appendices include information on national and federal standards, addresses of product manufacturers, and additional sources of information.

Hopf, Peter S., and John A. Raeber. *Access for the Handicapped: The Barrier-Free Regulations for Design and Construction in all Fifty States*. New York: Van Nostrand Reinhold, 1984. 701p. $62.95. ISBN 0-442-23545-3.

This manual provides detailed descriptions of all 50 states' laws and regulations related to the design and construction of buildings providing barrier-free access to handicapped individuals. Diagrams and graphical summaries are included.

Minnesota Housing Finance Agency. *Cost of Accessibility in New Single Family Homes.* Minneapolis, MN: The Minnesota Documents Center, 1985. 31p. No charge.

> A theoretical analysis of specification changes required in modifications in newly constructed single-family homes to make them accessible to the disabled, this report is unique in its inclusion of cost estimates (based on 1984 dollars in the Minneapolis area). Cost estimates vary depending on the nature of the handicap.

Raschko, Bettyann B. *Housing Interiors for the Disabled and Elderly.* Florence, KY: Van Nostrand Reinhold, 1982. 368p. $43.95. ISBN 0-442-22001.

> In this multidisciplinary approach to functional and accessible design, Raschko has incorporated sections on applied research, information on disabilities and assistive devices, as well as a walk through the rooms of a home. Included are the entry, living room, kitchen, dining room, bathroom, bedroom, storage, mechanical systems, and design considerations for the blind. The appendices include a large bibliography, lists of organizations, and information on fire codes and flammability tests. Ms. Raschko has been involved in design for over 30 years, focusing on interiors and furniture, both nationally and abroad.

Salmen, John P. S. *The Do Able Renewable Home: Making Your Home Fit Your Needs.* Washington, DC: American Association of Retired Persons, 1986. 36p. No charge. Stock no. D12470.

> This book identifies and explains the design concepts, products, and resources that can help make an existing home more comfortable for its older occupants who may experience physical limitations. While not a comprehensive study, it is a good introduction. Includes index.

Accessory Apartments

American Association of Retired Persons. *A Consumer's Guide to Accessory Apartments.* Washington, DC: American Association of Retired Persons, 1987. 20p. No charge. Stock no. D12775.

A brief guide describing key consumer issues involved in creating accessory apartments. Among these issues are financing, impact of rental income, zoning, and apartment design. A model accessory apartment ordinance and sample lease agreement are included.

Hare, Patrick H., and Jolene N. Ostler. *Creating an Accessory Apartment,* illus. ed. New York: McGraw-Hill, 1987. 256p. $16.95. ISBN 0-07-026087-2.

This is a complete resource guide for homeowners who wish to install an accessory apartment. It covers each step of the process: determining feasibility, estimating costs and income, financing, handling taxes, zoning and building codes, working with architects and contractors, finding a tenant, and negotiating a lease. Checklists, pro forma calculations, and typical floor plans are included. Hare and Ostler are land-use planners.

Hodges, Samuel J., III, and Ellis G. Goldman. *Allowing Accessory Apartments: Key Issues for Local Officials.* Washington, DC: Office of Policy Development and Research, U.S. Department of Housing and Urban Development, 1983. 23p. $3. Pub. no. HUD-003029.

This report describes, in a straightforward way, why accessory apartments can be beneficial, a response to community concerns, building public support, and designing regulations. One town's experience is described as a case study.

Shared Housing

American Association of Retired Persons. *A Consumer's Guide to Homesharing.* Washington, DC: American Association of Retired Persons, 1987. 8p. No charge. Stock no. D12774.

A brief review of key consumer issues in shared housing, including a discussion of different types of homesharing arrangements, suggestions for determining if homesharing is appropriate, and what it takes to make homesharing work. The booklet features guidelines for a lease in a homesharing arrangement.

Horne, Jo, and Leo Baldwin. *Homesharing and Other Lifestyle Options.* Washington, DC: American Association of Retired Persons, 1988. 259p. $12.95. ISBN 0-673-24886-0.

This is an overview of housing options that involve living with or in close proximity to unrelated persons. Particular emphasis is placed on shared housing and group residences. Practical information about assessing yourself and your potential homesharer, checking references, and understanding a sample contract is included. The primary author, Jo Horne, is an administrator of an adult day care center in Milwaukee, Wisconsin. She has also published *Caregiving: Helping an Aged Love One*.

National Shared Housing Resource Center. *A Guide for Finding a Housemate: Supplemental Materials*. Philadelphia, PA: National Shared Housing Resource Center, 1983. 17p. $3.

This is a booklet containing tips on advertising and interviewing, a checklist for homesharing issues, and a model homesharing lease agreement.

Utility Assistance

American Association of Retired Persons. *At Home with Energy*. Washington, DC: American Association of Retired Persons, 1986. 20p. No charge. Stock no. 0722.

A guide to help individuals check the energy efficiency of their homes. It includes considerable information about temperature control in the home, including some important safety tips.

American Association of Retired Persons. *The AARP Guide to State Energy Assistance Offices*. Washington, DC: American Association of Retired Persons, 1986. 103p. No charge. Stock no. D1204.

This guide lists state offices for energy assistance for low-income persons, weatherization assistance, offices on aging, state energy offices, and state energy conservation programs. Updated periodically.

National Consumer Law Center. *Energy and the Poor—The Forgotten Crisis*. Washington, DC: National Consumer Law Center, May 1989. 59p. $20.

This report provides a state-by-state analysis of the energy situation facing the nation's poor, including the elderly, the unemployed, and households with children. Average residential energy costs for low-income households in each state are analyzed. Included are a number of useful tables.

Property Tax Relief

American Association of Retired Persons. *Relocation Tax Guide: State Tax Information for Relocation Decisions.* Washington, DC: American Association of Retired Persons, 1988. 8p. No charge. Stock no. D13400.

> This handy guide lists each state and designates which of the three major types of property tax relief programs are available. Included also are a glossary of terms and basic information about personal income tax. Addresses and phone numbers of state departments of revenue are included.

Home Equity Conversion

Scholen, Ken. *A Financial Guide to Reverse Mortgages.* Madison, WI: National Center for Home Equity Conversion, 1989. 60p. $35.

> A comprehensive guide to reverse mortgages describing in detail how they work and what costs are associated with them. Features of various products on the market are described and costs are analyzed. Charts and tables enhance the text.

Scholen, Ken. *Home Made Money: Consumer Guide to Home Equity Conversion.* Washington, DC: American Association of Retired Persons, 1987. 44p. No charge. Stock no. D12894.

> A readable guide for consumers to home equity conversion, explaining clearly the advantages and disadvantages. Loan and sale plans are described.

Condominiums and Cooperatives

Bush, Vanessa A. *Condominiums and Cooperatives: Everything You Need to Know.* Chicago: Contemporary Books, 1986. 96p. $5.95. ISBN 0-8092-4835-2.

A guide to help prospective buyers understand how condos and cooperatives work. Included are discussions about buying and financing, owners' rights and responsibilities, maintenance, management, resale, and rental considerations.

Kennedy, David W. *The Condominium and Cooperative Apartment Buyer's and Seller's Guide,* 2nd ed. New York: John Wiley & Sons, 1987. 312p. $16.95. ISBN 0-471-62732-1.

A guide for those in the market to buy or sell a condominium or cooperative. It answers questions on price, closing costs, and other key features of a sale or purchase. The second edition includes changes in real estate law to reflect the Tax Reform Act of 1986. It takes the consumer step by step through both the buying and selling process.

Ludy, Andrew. *Condominium Ownership: A Buyer's Guide.* Landing, NJ: Landing Press, 1982. 128p. $7.95. ISBN 0-943912-00-8.

This is a consumer's guide, providing a good overview of a variety of topics including the condo concept, legal documents, homeowners' associations, and a step-by-step financing guide.

Metropolitan Washington Planning and Housing Association. *From Rental to Cooperative: A Technical Process.* Washington, DC: Metropolitan Washington Planning and Housing Association, 1981. 310p. $100.

A detailed manual designed to serve as a tool for teaching and a catalyst for new ideas in the field of tenant-initiated purchase and conversion. It provides information that is specific to the District of Columbia, but that would be valuable to tenant leaders and members of tenant associations in other jurisdictions as well.

National Association of Home Builders. *A Condominium Buyer's Guide.* Washington, DC: National Association of Home Builders, 1980. 31p. $3. Stock no. 016-1.

A resource guide for prospective buyers, emphasizing management and buyer financing.

Manufactured Homes

Council of Better Business Bureaus, Inc. *Tips on Buying a Mobile/ Manufactured Home.* Arlington, VA: Council of Better Business Bureaus, Inc., 1983. 14p. No charge. Pub. no. 311-03227.

A thorough review, in a short brochure, of the major issues involved in purchasing, selling, and locating a manufactured home.

Manufactured Housing Institute with the Federal Trade Commission. *How To Buy a Manufactured Home,* rev. ed. Arlington, VA: Manufactured Housing Institute, 1989. 24p. $0.50.

This useful consumer's manual for those considering a manufactured home focuses on selection, placement, and warranties.

Retirement Communities

National Directory of Retirement Facilities, 2nd ed. Phoenix, AZ: The Oryx Press, 1988. 888p. $175. ISBN 0897744500.

This directory provides a listing of over 18,000 residential alternatives, including personal care, congregate care, independent living, and continuing care. There are separate state by state and alphabetical listings of facilities.

Congregate Housing

Carlin, Vivian F., and Ruth Mansberg. *If I Live To Be One Hundred: Congregate Housing for Later Life.* West Nyack, NY: Parker, 1984. 216p. $8.95 (paper). ISBN 0-13-450379-1.

This informative volume focuses on a middle-income, congregate high-rise apartment in a semi-urban northeastern community, in which a relatively homogeneous group of 200 residents engages in both independent living and cooperative activity. It also discusses other communal housing choices and the importance of planning ahead.

Thompson, Marie McGuire, and Wilma T. Donahue. *Planning and Implementing Management of Congregate Housing for Older People.* Washington, DC: International Center for Social Gerontology, 1980. 102p. No charge.

This manual presents the concept, legislative basis, social goal, and composition of residents as a background to assist sponsors, boards, and managers in planning and operating these facilities.

Assisted Living

American Association of Retired Persons. *A Home Away from Home: Consumer Information on Board and Care Homes.* Washington, DC: American Association of Retired Persons, 1986. 63p. No charge. Stock no. D12446.

> A consumer's guide to selecting and evaluating board and care/ assisted living facilities, including information on key legislative and regulatory issues.

Continuing Care Retirement Communities (CCRCs)

American Association of Homes for the Aging. *Continuing Care Retirement Communities: An Industry in Action: Analysis and Developing Trends.* Washington DC: American Association of Homes for the Aging. 1989. 72p. $95. ISBN 0-943774-34-9.

> A report describing the results of a national survey of continuing care retirement communities. Similarities and differences across the industry are described, including, in particular, payment plans and contract provisions.

American Association of Homes for the Aging. *The Continuing Care Retirement Community: A Guidebook for Consumers,* rev. ed. Washington, DC: American Association of Homes for the Aging, 1984. 13p. $4. ISBN 0-943-774-16-0.

> This popular guidebook examines the complex contractual arrangements offered by continuing care retirement communities. Included is information about payment plans, checking out the financial condition of the facility, style of shelter, services, refunds, and fees. The booklet includes a checklist of facts a consumer should know before signing a continuing care contract.

American Association of Homes for the Aging. *Current Status of State Regulation of Continuing Care Retirement Communities.* Washington, DC: American Association of Homes for the Aging, 1987. 36p. $30. ISBN 0-943774-36-5.

> A state by state summary of laws and regulations affecting continuing care retirement communities. Statutes are referenced,

regulating agency is listed, and key features of the regulations are discussed. Updated periodically.

Continuing Care Accreditation Commission. *CCAC Consumer Brochure.* Washington, DC: Continuing Care Accreditation Commission, American Association of Homes for the Aging, 1989. 6p. No charge.

> This brochure outlines the standards and process associated with the only national accreditation program for continuing care retirement communities. Included is a list of accredited facilities. Updated periodically.

Raper, Ann Trueblood. *National Continuing Care Directory: Retirement Communities with Nursing Care,* rev. ed. Washington, DC: American Association of Retired Persons, 1988. 448p. $19.95. ISBN 0-673-24837-2.

> A national directory, by state, listing many of the continuing care retirement communities. Descriptive information on each facility is provided, including fees, services, amenities, sponsorship, and management.

Winklevoss, Howard E., and Alwyn V. Powell. *Continuing Care Retirement Communities: An Empirical, Financial and Legal Analysis.* Homewood, IL: Richard D. Irwin, Inc., 1984. 347p. $25.95. ISBN 0-256-03125-8.

> A detailed and technical analysis of the actuarial, financial, and legal issues involved in keeping existing continuing care retirement communities financially sound, and providing for the formation of new communities, in ways that protect the rights of residents while assuring the perpetuation of the community.

Nursing Facilities

American Association of Retired Persons. *Before You Buy: A Guide to Long Term Care Insurance.* Washington, DC: American Association of Retired Persons, 1987. 24p. No charge. Stock no. D12893.

> This consumer guide provides information to use in evaluating long-term care insurance as an option to help plan for financial

costs associated with long-term care services. It offers tips on evaluating different long-term care insurance policies.

American Association of Retired Persons. *The Nursing Home Handbook: A Guide for Families.* Des Plaines, IL: AARP Books, 1989. 172p. $9.95 postage and handling. ISBN 0-673-24924-7.

> A guide filled with practical advice to help families make informed and successful nursing home choices. Offers thoughtful guidance to help a family find a nursing home that best suits its needs.

Burger, Sarah Greene, and Martha D'Erasmo. *Living in a Nursing Home: A Complete Guide for Residents, Their Families and Friends.* New York: Ballantine Books, 1989. 178p. $2.50 (paper). ISBN 0-345-28198-5.

> This guide, written by two registered nurses, covers a range of nursing home–related topics including how to evaluate homes, legal rights of residents, and common mistakes made by well-meaning families. The emphasis is on family decision making.

Directory of Nursing Homes, 3rd ed. Phoenix, AZ: The Oryx Press, 1988. 1,280p. $195. ISBN 0-89774-414-4.

> This directory contains information, arranged alphabetically by state, including name, address, telephone, number of beds, level of care provided, and Medicaid/Medicare certification. Also included is an Affiliations Index, which lists facilities sponsored by religious or fraternal organizations.

Fox, Nancy. *You, Your Parent and the Nursing Home.* Buffalo, NY: Prometheus Books, 1986. 175p. $10.95 (paper). ISBN 0-87975-317-X.

> This book is written for those involved with an older person who is considering nursing home care. Readers are guided toward the crucial role they play in the well-being of the older individual. It includes checklists and additional resources.

Inlander, Charles B., et al. *How To Evaluate and Select a Nursing Home.* New York: Addison-Wesley, 1988. 96p. $7.95. ISBN 0-2-1-07263-7.

> A comprehensive guide to selecting a nursing home and making certain a resident gets the most out of the facility and its staff. The authors provide detailed lists of features to look for and questions to ask administrators, staff, and residents.

Jones, Clyde C. *Caring for the Aged: An Appraisal of Nursing Home Alternatives,* text ed. Chicago, IL: Nelson Hall, 1982. 181p. $18.95. ISBN 0-88229-709-0.

> This review of the literature on nursing homes highlights imaginative and innovative approaches to resident care. All points along the continuum of care are examined, from supportive services for people living in their own residences to skilled nursing homes. It includes an annotated bibliography of books, periodical articles, and government documents.

Manning, Doug. *The Nursing Home Dilemma: How To Make One of Love's Toughest Decisions.* San Francisco, CA: Harper and Row, 1986. 128p. $12.95. ISBN 0-06-0654-25-2.

> A compassionate book to help families understand the needs of elderly residents and make positive decisions about nursing homes. The author uses a conversational style and guides the reader through the process of choosing the best option, communicating with the older person, and establishing an ongoing, caring partnership with the nursing home.

Mongeau, Sam, ed. *Directory of Nursing Homes: A State-by-State Listing of Facilities and Services,* 2nd ed. Phoenix, AZ: The Oryx Press, 1984. 1,301p. $145 (paper). ISBN 0-89779-145-5.

> This directory lists state-licensed long-term care facilities throughout the United States. Citations include level of care provided, ownership type (profit, nonprofit, public), admission requirements, special activities, and services. Also listed are multi-facility sponsors. An alphabetical listing of all facilities is provided.

Pieper, Hanns. *The Nursing Home Primer: A Comprehensive Guide to Nursing Homes and Other Long-Term Care Options.* Crozet, AZ: Betterway Publications, 1989. 136p. $7.95. ISBN 1-55870-115-X.

> Drawing on material from lectures he has given to families and caregivers, the author discusses key things to look for when visiting a nursing home and how to help the older person adjust to nursing home life. An overview of other long-term care options is provided.

Richards, Marty, et al. *Nursing Home Placement: A Guidebook for Families*. Seattle, WA: University of Washington Press, 1985. 110p. $7.95. ISBN 0-29596221.

> A helpful guide for those faced with the necessity of deciding whether to place a family member in a nursing home.

Chapter 7

Nonprint Materials

Audiovisual Materials

Assisted Residential Living, A Form of Congregate Housing
Type: Film or video
Length: 20 min.
Source: North Texas State University
           Media Library
           P.O. Box 13438 NT Station
           Denton, TX 76203
Date: 1979

> Describes what congregate housing is. Demonstrates the importance of such housing and shows with facts and figures that nursing homes are more expensive than congregate housing.

At Home with Energy
Type: Slide/tape
Length: 20 min.
Cost: Purchase $26.50, available for loan at no charge
Source: AARP A/V Programs
           Resource Promotion Section/BV
           1909 K Street, NW
           Washington, DC 20049

> Includes presenter guide, script, poster, and handouts. Low-cost, easy ways to substantially reduce energy bills.

At Home with Home Care

Type: Video
Length: 14 ten-min. programs
Source: Billy Bud Films
F.D.R. Station, P.O. Box 6194
New York, NY 10150
(212) 755-3968
Date: 1985

Series stresses the importance of patient independence, encouraging the patient to do as much as possible for himself or herself.

A Family Decision

Type: Video
Length: 25 min.
Source: Terra Nova Films
9848 South Winchester Avenue
Chicago, IL 60643
Date: 1985

Program focuses on the emotional difficulties of placing a family member in a nursing home. Family members openly discuss the experiences and feelings that made up their own decision-making process.

Living in Housing with Care and Services

Type: Slide/tape
Length: 15 min.
Cost: Purchase $23.50, available for loan at no charge
Source: AARP Program Scheduling Office
1909 K Street, NW
Washington, DC 20049

Presentation on supportive housing. Included are discussions of board and care homes, congregate housing, continuing care retirement communities, and nursing homes.

Major Barriers

Type: Video
Length: 34 min.
Cost: Rental $15

Source: Barriers Free Design Center
2075 Bayview
Toronto, Ontario
Canada M4N-3M5

A humorous look at barriers, physical and psychological, that exist for people with disabilities.

Making Life a Little Easier: Self Help Tools for the Home
Type: Slide/tape
Length: 10 min.
Source: AARP Program Scheduling Office
1909 K Street, NW
Washington, DC 20049

Explores creative ways older people can use inexpensive tools to promote independent functioning in safe living arrangements.

Making Wise Decisions: Long-Term Care and You
Type: Slide/tape
Length: 16 min.
Cost: Purchase $21, available for loan at no charge
Source: AARP A/V Programs
Resource Promotion Section/BV
1909 K Street, NW
Washington, DC 20049

Long-term care does not necessarily require a nursing home. Explores the housing alternatives, service options, and what they cost.

No Place Like Home
Type: Video
Length: 55 min.
Source: Filmmakers Library, Inc.
133 East 58th Street
New York, NY 10022
(213) 355-6545

According to this documentary, providing home care rather than institutionalized care is often less costly to the public and more desirable for the older person.

Nutrition in the Later Years

Type: Film or video
Length: 24 min.
Source: Churchill Films
          662 North Robertson Blvd.
          Los Angeles, CA 90069-9990
          (800) 334-7830
Date: 1982

Gives an understanding of the special nutritional requirements of older people, as well as the changes and discomforts of too much or too little. Motivation and tips on how to change.

100 Years to Live

Type: Film or video
Length: 29 min.
Source: Edward Feil Productions
          4614 Prospect Avenue
          Cleveland, OH 44102
          (216) 771-0655
Date: 1980

Film features a 100-year old mother and her 80-year-old daughter over a two-year period as they try to adjust to the trauma of moving from a shared home to a care facility.

Opening Doors: Independent Living in Your Home

Type: Slide/tape
Length: 15 min.
Cost: Purchase $23.50, available for loan at no charge
Source: AARP Program Scheduling Office
          1909 K Street, NW
          Washington, DC 20049

Addresses services that help people remain in their homes, as well as ways to make changes in one's home.

Remodeling for Accessibility

Type: Video
Length: 15 min.
Cost: Purchase $39.95

Source: Housing Resource Center
          1820 West 48th Street
          Cleveland, OH 44102

          Remodeling for accessibility, people, and profit as seen through
          the eyes of contractors, builders, and consumers.

Where Should I Go When I Can't Go Home?
Type: Video
Length: 30 min.
Source: Lansing Community College
          Center for Aging Education
          419 North Capitol Avenue
          Box 40010
          Lansing, MI 48901-7211
Date: 1980

          Through narration and interviews with resource experts and
          older persons, housing options available to older adults are dis-
          cussed and illustrated.

Computer-Based Information

Abledata
National Rehabilitation Information Center
8400 Colesville Road, Suite 935
Silver Spring, MD 20910
(800) 346-2742

          Abledata is a service of the National Rehabilitation Information
          Center (NARIC). It is a comprehensive database on products
          available nationwide, listing over 10,000 products. It is updated
          regularly. Each listing provides brand name, manufacturer, cost,
          description, and any evaluation that may be available. NARIC
          will conduct a modest search for $10. The following categories
          are used to describe products: personal care, vocational/educa-
          tional, seating, communication, ambulation, orthotics/prosthet-
          ics, home management, mobility, transportation, recreation,
          therapeutic aids, and sensory aids.

Ageline
National Gerontology Resource Center
1909 K Street, NW
Washington, DC 20049
(202) 728-4895

> Ageline, the database of the American Association of Retired Persons (AARP), contains citations to the literature on sociological and psychological aspects of aging and middle age. The database is of interest to aging-related organizations, academic institutions, government agencies, and the general public.

Benefits Eligibility Check-Up
United Seniors Health Cooperative
1334 G Street, NW, Suite 500
Washington, DC 20005
(202) 393-6222

> Benefits Eligibility Check-Up is a software package developed to help social service workers quickly determine which benefits—ranging from property tax relief to utilities discounts—are available to any applicant. Users simply tell the computer the applicant's vital statistics, such as his or her financial and medical condition. The package works on IBM PCs, lists available benefits, and provides instructions on how to obtain them. The cost is $15,000.

HUD USER Database
P.O. Box 280
Germantown, MD 20874
(800) 245-2691; (301) 251-5154 in Maryland and the Washington, D.C., metropolitan area

> HUD USER database provides access to a comprehensive collection of reports produced by HUD's Office of Policy Development and Research. Other divisions within HUD as well as other federal and state agencies and a small number of commercial publishers are also represented in the file. Subjects covered include HUD programs, affordable housing, community development, building technology, assisted housing, fair housing, elderly and handicapped housing, housing finance, infrastructure, and public/private partnerships.

RETIRE
Martlet, Inc.
P.O. Box 37
Herndon, VA 22070

RETIRE is a computer software program designed to help older people choose potential cities in which to retire. Through a series of menus, a person indicates what his or her interests are. The program then compares these preferences against its database of cities and responds with a list of up to 30 possibilities. A limitation is that it appears to be geared to the sunbelt and to people with middle to upper incomes. Cost is $39 for individuals, $79 for multiple users.

Glossary

accredited   Recognized by a professional organization to meet basic standards of quality. National accrediting programs are available to nursing homes, home health care agencies, and continuing care retirement communities.

activities of daily living   Include personal care activities such as bathing, dressing, grooming, toileting, eating, getting in and out of bed and chairs, walking, and going outside.

adult day care   A program provided under health leadership in an ambulatory care setting for adults who do not require 24-hour institutional care and yet, due to physical and/or mental impairment, are not capable of full-time independent living.

ANSI A117.1 standards   In 1980, the American National Standard Institute developed "specifications for making buildings and facilities accessible to and usable by physically handicapped people." These standards have been adopted by building codes, making public buildings accessible.

Area Agency on Aging (AAA)   AAAs were established by the 1973 amendments to the Older Americans Act. They are public or private organizations or units of local government responsible for developing and administering a comprehensive and coordinated system of services to meet the needs of older people in a specific geographic area. AAAs along with the State Units on Aging, the federal-level Administration on Aging, and the Federal Council on the Aging comprise the aging network.

assisted living facility   A living arrangement that integrates shelter and services for frail older persons who are not independent and need 24-hour supervision.

care management   Care management is a process that involves looking at and assessing a person's needs and resources, linking the person with appropriate services, and monitoring the care provided over an extended period of time.

care plan   A detailed description of the services a client is to receive, the treatment goals, and the equipment and supplies that will be necessary.

case managers   Case managers are usually social workers who assess the needs of individuals, help them negotiate the services they need, and pull together a comprehensive personalized care plan that is carefully monitored.

certified   Approved by the state health department to receive payment for Medicare or Medicaid services.

chore services   Chore services offer help in and around the home and can include minor repairs, heavy housecleaning, and yard work.

circuit breaker   A property tax relief measure that directly reduces the amount of property taxes paid in excess of a percentage of household income.

condominium (condo)   A particular type of real estate ownership. A condo owner has full title to his or her individual living unit, plus a share in the grounds, recreational facilities, and other common elements in the complex.

congregate housing   A living arrangement that integrates shelter and services for older persons who are frail, chronically ill, or socially isolated but do not need 24-hour supervision.

continuing care retirement community (CCRC)   A CCRC is a type of retirement community that, through a contract, guarantees a resident housing, health care, and meals for the remainder of the resident's life. It may also provide additional services and activities such as transportation and recreation facilities. Typically, a CCRC requires an entrance fee as well as monthly charges. It may ask potential residents to meet certain age, health, and financial requirements. A CCRC is sometimes called a life care community.

cooperative (co-op)   Nonprofit corporations that own and operate living facilities for the benefit of the occupants. Cooperatives are often viewed as the middle ground between homeownership and renting.

copayment   The fixed dollar amount that one must pay for specific services under a health insurance plan, while the insurer pays the remaining costs. The copayment amount is set periodically and usually does not vary with the cost of the service.

declaration   A document that contains conditions, covenants, and restrictions governing the sale, ownership, use, and disposition of a property within the framework of applicable state condominium laws.

deductible   The total initial amount that one must pay for services covered under an insurance plan before benefits are paid by the insurer.

deed   The legal instrument that embodies ownership of property and passes title from the seller to the purchaser.

Department of Housing and Urban Development (HUD)   Established in 1965, HUD is the principal federal Cabinet-level agency responsible for programs concerned with housing needs, fair housing opportunities, and improving and developing the nation's communities.

Disability Insurance (DI)   See Social Security Act of 1935, Title II.

discharge planner   A professional staff member at a hospital or nursing home who develops a plan of future care for a patient prior to discharge.

equity   The interest of value that an owner has in real estate over and above the mortgage against it.

Fair Housing Act   Federal law that prohibits discrimination because of race, religion, sex, age, handicap, familial status, or national origin in housing and related facilities owned, operated, or funded by the federal government, including mortgage insurance and guarantee programs and lending institutions that provide loans on government insured or guaranteed property.

fair market rents (FMR)   Geographic benchmarks determined by the Department of Housing and Urban Development (HUD) to establish rents permitted under federally subsidized programs.

fee simple   Outright ownership of land in the highest degree. The only limitations on this type of ownership are governmental limitations.

FHA/Veterans Administration/FMHA loans   Federally insured home loan programs for the public and eligible veterans who want to purchase approved residential property.

group residence   A home occupied by a group of unrelated people, who share in meal preparation, housekeeping, household maintenance, and financial activities.

guardianship   A protective service for elderly persons who are thought to be unable to manage their personal or financial affairs in their own best interests.

Health Care Financing Administration (HCFA)   Created in 1977, HCFA has oversight of the Medicare and Medicaid programs (see Social Security Act of 1935, Titles XVIII and XIX) and related federal medical care quality control staffs. It is part of the U.S. Department of Health and Human Services.

health maintenance organization (HMO)   An organization that provides a wide range of health care services for a fixed advance payment.

home health aide   A trained professional who works under the supervision of a registered nurse.

homestead exemption   A fixed percentage reduction in the assessed valuation of the primary residence (homestead) of the eligible taxpayer.

independent nurse practitioner   A highly trained nurse who is able to diagnose and treat illnesses and prescribe medications without a physician's supervision.

information and referral   A service providing information about the availability of services and how to make use of them, designed to link older persons with opportunities, services, and resources to help meet particular needs.

instrumental activities of daily living   Include home management activities such as preparing meals, shopping for personal items, managing money, using the telephone, and doing light and heavy housework.

Keys Amendment   The Keys Amendment to the Social Security Act was passed in 1976 in response to public outcry resulting from tragic fires in board and care homes (assisted living facilities). The amendment requires states to establish, maintain, and ensure the enforcement of standards for residences where a significant number of SSI recipients reside or are likely to reside. It also requires the federal government to reduce a recipient's SSI payment by the amount of any state supplement for medical or remedial care if the recipient resides in a facility that has not been approved by the appropriate state or local authorities as meeting the standards established by the state.

licensed   Having a permit to operate or practice issued by an appropriate state or local agency.

licensed practical nurse (LPN)   A trained nurse who is licensed by the state. An LPN works under the supervision of a registered nurse.

long-term care   The health, social, and support services available to older people and others on a long-term basis to help them live independently. There are services for the active and the confined, the chronically ill, the disabled, and the mentally handicapped. An older person may receive these services in his or her home or by changing his or her living arrangement.

long-term care ombudsman   A program under the Older Americans Act that requires each state to have a statewide watchdog, or ombudsman, over nursing homes and other long-term care facilities. The state ombudsman investigates and resolves complaints by residents and provides information to the state agency responsible for licensing the facilities.

manufactured home   A house that is produced in a factory rather than at the actual home site. Also referred to as mobile homes. Manufactured homes require installation and connection to appropriate services and facilities at the site.

Medicaid   See Social Security Act of 1935, Title XIX.

Medicare   See Social Security Act of 1935, Title XVIII.

nursing home   A living arrangement that integrates shelter with medical, nursing, psychological, and rehabilitative services for persons who require 24-hour nursing supervision.

Older Americans Act of 1965 (OAA)   OAA is directed to provide to older Americans opportunities for full participation in the benefits of our society. The 10 original objectives, under Title I, recognized the rights of older persons to an adequate income; the best possible physical and mental health; suitable housing; full restorative services; employment without age discrimination; retirement in health, honor, and dignity; participation in civic, cultural, and recreational activities; community service; immediate benefit from research; and freedom and independence. The act has been amended 12 times, most recently in 1987. The 1987 amendments authorized the commissioner on aging to report directly to the secretary of health and human services rather than the office of the secretary and instituted measures to improve minority participation in systems for the aged, disabled, and low-income persons.

personal care   Assistance given to people who need help with dressing, bathing, personal hygiene, grooming, and eating.

property tax deferral   A program that allows an eligible older person to defer payment of property taxes, or a portion of property taxes, until the home is sold or the homeowner dies.

property tax freeze   A total program that excuses eligible older persons from all future tax increases on the home, fixing the tax rate at the rate that existed when the homeowner reached a certain age.

registered nurse (RN)   Completes between two and four years of education and training before being permitted to take a state licensure examination. A registered nurse is required to perform patient assessment, establish a plan of care, and carry out skilled nursing functions.

retirement community   A large or small housing complex that provides some services, usually recreational, to its residents.

skilled nursing facility (SNF)   A nursing facility that delivers skilled, intermediate, and custodial care. Registered nurses provide 24-hour nursing services that must be prescribed by a physician. These facilities are licensed by each state.

Social Security Act of 1935

Title II—Federal Old-Age, Survivors, and Disability Insurance Benefits (OASDI)   Enacted in 1935, Social Security replaces a portion of earned income lost as a result of a person's retirement, disability, or death. Monthly benefits are paid as a matter of earned right to workers who gain insured status and to their eligible spouses, children, and survivors. Retirement benefits can begin at age 62 and are payable for life. Disability benefits are payable to those insured workers who meet the act's definition of disability.

Title XVI—Supplemental Security Income for the Aged, Blind, and Disabled (SSI)   The SSI program was enacted as part of the 1971 Social Security amendments. It replaced the federal-state public assistance programs to the aged, blind, and disabled, which the states had administered. The program is now federally administered and provides a supplemental public assistance payment to those who are eligible. States have the option of increasing the amount of the supplement at their expense. In many cases, SSI recipients are automatically eligible for other forms of assistance such as Medicaid, food stamps, and social services.

Title XVIII—Health Insurance for the Aged and Disabled (Medicare)   The Medicare program was enacted in 1965. It provides health insurance coverage for persons age 65 or older, some disabled persons under age 65, and persons who have end-stage renal disease. The program consists of two parts: Part A, Hospital Insurance (HI) and Part B, Supplemental Medical Insurance (SMI). The program is administered by the Health Care Financing Administration (HCFA). The HI program provides basic protection against the costs of hospital and related post-hospital care, home health services, and hospice care. The SMI program is a voluntary program for which enrollees in Part A must pay 80 percent of reasonable charges for medical and related health services and supplies furnished by physicians (or others in connection with physicians' services). Generally, it does not pay for out-of-hospital prescription drugs, glasses, hearing aids, or immunizations.

Title XIX—Medical Assistance Program (Medicaid)   This program became law in 1965. It provides medical assistance for certain low-income individuals and families. It is financed jointly by state and federal funds and administered by the individual states within broad federal guidelines. Generally, all who qualify for public assistance under federally funded categories (aged, blind, disabled, and families with dependent children) are eligible for Medicaid. Others may qualify at a state's option. For the low-income elderly, Medicaid provides a particularly important provision, payment of nursing home care. All states except Arizona currently have Medicaid programs. Programs vary from state to state.

Title XX—Block Grants to States for Social Services   This title provides social services such as adult day care, protective services, health support services, and homemaker services. The federal government provides money to the states and the states determine which services they will fund. Regulations passed in 1981 eliminated some restrictions placed on the states by the federal government, including several eligibility restrictions and the requirement that states provide matching funds.

State Units on Aging (SUA)   Established by the Older Americans Act of 1965, the State Units on Aging are agencies of state governments designated by the governor and the state legislature as the focal point for all matters relating to the needs of older persons within the state. The 57 SUAs are responsible for planning, coordinating, funding, and evaluating programs for older persons authorized by both state and federal governments. The goal of SUAs is to improve the quality of life for older Americans by advocating on their behalf and by promoting the development of a comprehensive and coordinated system of social and health services.

Supplemental Security Income (SSI)   See Social Security Act of 1935, Title XVI.

Veterans Administration (VA)   Established in 1903 to administer laws authorizing benefits for former members of the armed forces and their dependents. Examples of these benefits include compensation payments for disabilities or death related to military services; home loan and home improvement mortgages; and a comprehensive medical program involving a system of nursing homes, clinics, and medical centers.

Index